Enhancing the Effectiveness of Innovation

Enhancing the Effectiveness of Innovation

New Roles for Key Players

Edited by

Willem Molle

Professor of International Economics, Erasmus University Rotterdam and Senior Adviser of ECORYS Research and Consulting, Rotterdam, the Netherlands

Julia Djarova

Vice Chair of ECORYS International

Edward Elgar
Cheltenham, UK • Northampton, MA, USA

Published by
Edward Elgar Publishing Limited
The Lypiatts
15 Lansdown Road
Cheltenham
Glos GL50 2JA
UK

Edward Elgar Publishing, Inc.
William Pratt House
9 Dewey Court
Northampton
Massachusetts 01060
USA

A catalogue record for this book
is available from the British Library

Library of Congress Control Number: 2009921834

Mixed Sources
Product group from well-managed
forests and other controlled sources
www.fsc.org Cert no. SA-COC-1565
© 1996 Forest Stewardship Council

FSC

ISBN 978 1 84844 257 3

Printed and bound by MPG Books Group, UK

Contents

Contributors

Valentijn Bilsen (PhD) is a senior expert at IDEA Consult (Brussels, Belgium). He focuses on projects related to entrepreneurship, small and medium-sized enterprises (SMEs), sectoral studies, EU enlargement, Eastern Europe, environment, tourism, as well as on economic impact studies. Bilsen developed several decision support tools for strategy and policy purposes in the areas of innovation, measuring additionality, information and communication technology (ICT) and business cycle analysis. He has published on entrepreneurship, corporate restructuring, foreign direct investment, regional economics, additionality and tourism.

Jacob Dencik (PhD) is a senior economist. He was associated to ECORYS Rotterdam at the time the study on which his chapter is based was carried out. Before that he worked as a tutor and lecturer at the University of Bath (UK) and as a researcher at the Institute for Public Policy Research (UK) and Industri Kapital (Sweden). His main interest is in the various dimensions of the new knowledge economy, e.g. service innovation, ICT development, human investment and organisational innovation.

Julia Djarova (PhD) is a managing partner of ECORYS Netherlands and vice chairman of ECORYS International. She joined the Netherlands Economic Institute (NEI), one of the predecessors of ECORYS, in 1996. For many years Dr Djarova has combined an academic and a consultancy career that has driven her applied research and her affinity to policy analysis and consultancy. Djarova has been managing a number of projects in the field of innovation, R&D and ICT carried out by ECORYS. Some of these resulted in advice to the Polish government on governance models for innovation, in national innovation strategy and in establishing an innovation fund in Bulgaria, in advising the SME (small and medium-sized enterprise) agency in Slovakia on policy measures to boost innovation in SMEs, among others.

Dr Djarova is an evaluator of the FP7 programme for research of the European Commission.

Dr Djarova has taught at Erasmus University Rotterdam, Sofia University 'St Kliment Ohridski' and the Higher School of Economics in Moscow. She has published three monographs and five edited books, as well as numerous articles.

Paulina Fabrowska is a lead consultant in the ECORYS Polska economic research team. Her main fields of interest are innovation policies and institutions supporting innovation and technology transfer. She is an author in publications on regional innovation strategies in Poland.

Adrian Healy (BA, MSc) is a director of ECOTEC Research and Consulting and an honorary research fellow at Cardiff University. His research interests cover regional innovation, the European Structural Funds and spatial development. He has worked extensively with local, regional and national authorities in the UK as well as with the European Commission and other member states. His experience includes working as an adviser on the regional dimension to research and innovation for the European Commission's Directorate General Research and as an expert adviser to the Office of the Deputy Prime Minister House of Commons Select Committee Inquiry into Regional Disparities in Prosperity in the UK. Healy is currently completing doctoral research, examining the regional dimension to EU R&D policies, at Cardiff University.

Elissavet Lykogianni (PhD) works as a consultant at IDEA Consult (Brussels, Belgium). She holds a PhD in applied economics from the KU Leuven in Belgium focusing on internationalisation of R&D and technology transfers in the context of multinational enterprises. Lykogianni is working in the area of science, technology and innovation (STI). Within STI she specialises in evaluation studies and surveys, STI policy analysis, econometric data analysis and internationalisation of R&D.

Marta Mackiewicz (PhD) is a senior consultant and head of the Innovation and Competitiveness Section at ECORYS Polska. She has been adviser to ministries and governmental agencies as well as author and co-author of numerous publications. Before joining ECORYS she worked as deputy head of the Public Finance Section at the Gdańsk Institute for Market Economics, a non-governmental research institution dealing with the economy and government policy. Her main interest is in the practical implementation on innovation strategies. She cooperates with the World Economy Research Institute of the Warsaw School of Economics.

Veerle Minne works as a senior expert at IDEA Consult (Brussels, Belgium). She holds a degree in applied economics and has more than ten years of research experience. Minne gained a broad experience with several research methods and has specific expertise in the field of spatial-economic studies and economic and financial impact analyses.

Willem Molle (PhD, Professor in Economics) combines two part-time affiliations. After graduation in economics and a graduate traineeship with the

European Commission in Brussels, he joined the Netherlands Economic Institute (NEI) in Rotterdam as a junior researcher. After having held several posts of responsibility he became chairman of the management board. Since its creation in 1999 until the end of 2004 Molle was chairman of the board of management of ECORYS, the organisation in which the operations of the NEI have been integrated. He is now associate partner/senior adviser for ECORYS.

Molle teaches 'Economics of integration' at the Faculty of Economics of Erasmus University Rotterdam. He has guest-lectured at many universities in Europe (e.g. Paris, Padua, Madrid) and in China (e.g. Shanghai, Suzhou, Macao).

Professor Molle's research and publications mostly concern the economic aspects of the European and worldwide integration processes. He has written well-received textbooks for each subject. His work focuses on problems of cohesion; on this subject he has recently published a textbook and in the course of his career he has written several specialist books and numerous articles. Some of these deal with questions of innovation and regional competitiveness.

Robert Pollock was senior director of Scottish Enterprise, the national economic development agency for Scotland. He has worked in a range of strategic and operational areas relating to economic and regional development including clusters, innovation, internationalisation and SME development. Pollock has worked with various international organisations including the EC, the OECD, the UN and the Competitiveness Institute. He participated as an associate of ECORYS Rotterdam in the study on which his part of Chapter 9 is based.

Geert Steurs (PhD) is a manager at IDEA Consult (Brussels, Belgium) in charge of the business area of 'competitiveness, regulatory management and innovation'. In 1994, he obtained a PhD on 'Spillovers and cooperation in R&D'. Given his background in industrial economics, he is especially interested in market, sector and cluster studies, and in innovation-related topics. He has worked on projects for national and international clients, and has authored and co-authored several contributions to peer-reviewed scientific journals and books.

Arnold Verbeek is a manager at IDEA Consult (Brussels, Belgium) in charge of the business area of 'competitiveness, regulatory management and innovation'. Besides his managerial tasks and responsibilities, he is a senior expert in innovation systems and governance, monitoring and evaluation, impact assessment, indicator development and foresight. He has advised various national and international clients such as the European

Commission, the OECD, the Flemish IWT, the Flemish Ministry for Economy, Science and Innovation, the Belgian Federal Science Policy Office, the Icelandic Centre for Research and several sector federations and companies. He is a member of various international networks of innovations experts and has authored and co-authored several contributions to peer-reviewed scientific journals and books.

Hans Wissema (PhD) is a management consultant to universities and professional services firms. He is Emeritus Professor of Innovation and Entrepreneurship at the University of Technology in Delft, the Netherlands, and managing director of J.G. Wissema Associates bv in the Netherlands and Wissema Consulting EOOD in Bulgaria. Professor Wissema has published numerous articles and 16 books on management issues, some of which have been widely reprinted and translated. The contribution to this volume is based on his book, *Towards the Third Generation University: Managing the University in Transition*, published in January 2009 by Edward Elgar Publishing. (Previous versions of this book were published in 2006 in Polish, Bulgarian and Macedonian.)

Walter Zegveld (Professor) has an engineering background. He has more than 40 years' experience in science and technology policy, innovation in SMEs, innovation policy research, governance of R&D and venture capital operations. Until his retirement he was managing director of the Policy Research Division of the Netherlands Organisation for Applied Scientific Research as well as chairman of the Netherlands Organisation for Technology Assessment. He has been an adviser to the governments of the Netherlands, Germany, Sweden and Finland, and to the OECD and the EU.

At present Walter Zegveld is chairman of the Netherlands Advisory Committee ICES-KIS, which aims to strengthen knowledge infrastructure.

Professor Zegveld has some 20 years' experience in university lecturing at the Inter-University Institute for Business Administration at Delft and at the Economics Faculty of the Free University in Amsterdam. He has published some 15 books and many papers on innovation and technology policy.

1. Introduction

Willem Molle and Julia Djarova

OBJECTIVES, STRUCTURE[1]

Objective, Structure and Specificity of the Book

The EU has embraced the Lisbon Strategy and translated the strategic objectives into programmes with concrete action by the European Commission,[2] by the member countries and by their constituent regions. These actions involve considerable efforts to increase the level of R&D, knowledge and innovation, and to improve the effectiveness of investments in these fields. This should lead to greater productivity, competitiveness and hence welfare.

In the past, much work has been done to come to a better understanding of the anatomy of the problem ('Where does this lack of innovativeness come from?') and the effectiveness of the therapy ('Which instruments work under what conditions?'). Very helpful in this respect has been the introduction of the concept of the innovation system. Notwithstanding this progress, our understanding of the innovation system and the role of its various actors is still far from perfect.

The objective of the present book is to shed more light on a number of points that can improve the effectiveness of innovation efforts in the EU. We thereby focus on the interplay of the various actors involved. We do this with the help of a number of case studies of the main segments of the innovation system: public sector (governments), industry (firms) and R&D providers (research institutions and universities).

Innovation systems play a central role in enabling processes of innovation. Introduced by Freeman (1987), the national innovation system[3] (NIS) refers to the network of institutions in the public and private sectors whose activities and interactions initiate, import, modify and diffuse new technologies and useful knowledge. An important element of this is the incentive structure to improve the effectiveness of the system. Accordingly, the innovation system can be illustrated as in Figure 1.1.

For an innovation system to function effectively, all players in the system must utilise their innovative competencies as well as their capacity to collaborate. The various interrelations between the actors are indicated

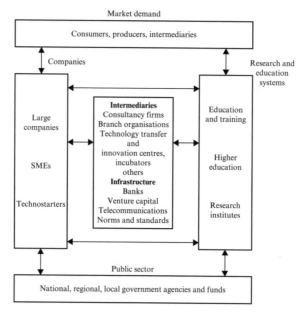

Source: Adapted from Freeman (1987).

Figure 1.1   National innovation system

in Figure 1.1. Research and educational organisations interact with companies in order to develop and transfer know-how. Intermediaries play an important role in facilitating this transfer, as do the constituents of the knowledge infrastructure. The role of the public sector is to develop an environment conducive to innovation and offer interventions where the high risk involved in innovation cannot be covered by private initiatives. Market demand acts as the driving force for companies and defines much of the dynamics of the entire system. If elements and links are missing or are weak, the innovation system lacks efficiency and speed of adaptation to new developments in the outside world.

   While it has been argued that these systems are primarily national (Lundvall, 1988), it is interesting to note that very little is known about how national borders affect the flow of technological information and capabilities (Nelson, 1988). More recent work has also highlighted the importance of the regional dimension in shaping innovation, and much analysis of innovation is now focused on the regional innovation system (Cooke and Morgan, 1998; Cooke, 2004). The constitution of players as well as their role stays the same as in the NIS. It should also be noted that the systems

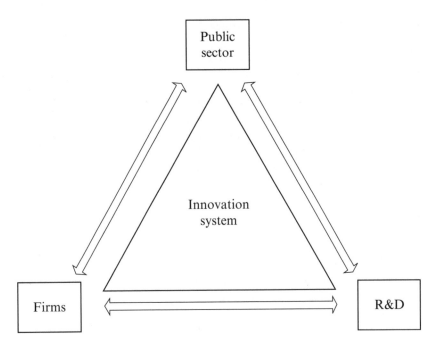

Figure 1.2   The three actors in the innovation system

of innovation are adapting themselves to technological developments. Accordingly, the institutional setting should by no means be seen as fixed, but rather as being in a continuous process of evolution.

The structure of the book follows the logic of the innovation system, where three main groups of actors and the links between them play an essential role in effective innovation. More specifically, the book is concerned with knowledge organisations, notably universities and private and public research units; firms from the private sector; and the public sector – European, national and local. In the first part of the book, we take the R&D sector as our point of departure; in the second part the business sector; and in the third part the public sector (see Figure 1.2).

The contributions to this book are all based on sound empirical analysis. They have been written by experts who have considerable experience in both the analytical and the operational aspects of the functioning of the innovation system. Moreover, some contributions are of particular interest in that they describe operational methodological improvements. All chapters are set in the framework of a thorough review of the existing literature on the subject.

Objective and Structure of this Introductory Chapter

The objective we pursue in this chapter is to present a synopsis of the main results of the various contributions to this book and to draw some general policy conclusions from them.

We structure this chapter as follows: first, we provide a brief introduction to the main characteristics and trends of the innovation system; second, we detail the changed role of the various actors in the system. Subsequently we take the standpoints of the three main groups of actors: the R&D sector; the business sector; and the public sector. For each we highlight the value added of this book by setting the results of the contributions to this book against the background of the main insights from the literature.

THE INNOVATION SYSTEM: THREE LAYERS AND THREE PLAYERS (GROUPS OF ACTORS)

Innovation

Innovation accounts for the overwhelming majority of productivity gains in most of the world's leading economies. In turn, productivity increments are the key to enhanced competitiveness. In short, innovation is the driver of competitiveness at the international, national and regional economic levels. Hence understanding the role of innovation in promoting economic development is essential to policy makers.[4]

This calls for a definition of innovation. In certain policy circles the term innovation has become misleadingly synonymous with science, R&D and industry. But there is more to it than mere technical change. Hence a broader definition is needed. This has been acknowledged by the UK's National Endowment for Science, Technology and Arts (NESTA, 2007), which warned that 'Science ≠ Innovation'. Indeed, an overly narrow technical definition of innovation has become inappropriate as national and regional wealth is increasingly generated via services and business model innovation. Rubalcaba (2007) notes that services constitute 70% of advanced economies, so their innovation process will be essential for (determining) growth. Yet the majority of studies regarding innovation have used the industrial sector as a reference, putting the tertiary sector to one side. In summary, it is best to adopt a broad definition of innovation. This is not a novelty. Classical writers have already indicated the way. For instance, Schumpeter (1934) interpreted innovation as changes to products, processes and organisations that create or increase value. A more recent broad definition of innovation is simply: 'new products, business processes and organic changes that create wealth'.

Three-player Innovation System

Innovations do not come about in isolation. They are engendered by a complex interplay of actors in specific institutional and regulatory environments. This has been termed 'systems of innovation'.

As discussed earlier, systems of innovation include actors such as firms, R&D establishments, universities and other higher education institutions (HEIs), providers of consultancy and technical services, state authorities and regulatory bodies, development agencies and other supporting and intermediary institutions (e.g. Chang and Chen, 2004). They are generally grouped into three: the knowledge infrastructure (R&D, HEI etc.), the corporate sector (both multinationals and small and medium-sized enterprises – SMEs); and government. The driver of the system is the firm that responds to market demands.

However, innovation and knowledge creation depend on a series of factors such as quality of staff, incentive structure, resources available etc. The ability of firms to successfully produce and implement innovations in a commercial way depends very much on the environment they have to work in: competitors, customers, human capital, knowledge infrastructure, institutions that facilitate diffusion, regulation and legislation, untraded interdependencies and a host of other factors (OECD, 1997a). For both knowledge providers and knowledge appliers, external links to the national and global economy are increasingly important. System means that there is interaction: this happens through both formal and informal networks.

Three-layer System of Innovation

In the past the main level of operation has been the national level. Several forces have been driving major changes to this picture:

- *Globalisation* has led to the internationalisation of markets and the possibility of splitting certain functions such as R&D and locate them in different places around the globe. Globalisation poses an increased challenge to all actors to become more competitive.
- *Europeanisation* has led to the centralisation of key R&D tasks and the adoption of common standards for products. The various enlargements of the EU have led to a wide diversity of situations. Europeanisation poses the challenge of realising a policy system capable of addressing this diversity in problems and goals.

● *Regionalisation* has led to stronger roles for regional clusters of innovative capacity. It poses the challenge to increase the capacity of regional authorities to strengthen competitive advantages.

Together these driving forces lead to a three-level system of innovation: European, national and regional.

Changing Interplay of the Three Key Actors of the Innovation System

The relationships between the three actors in the innovation system have changed over time. In many countries, each of these actors existed very much on its own terms, with little relation to the others. Firms did their own R&D in private R&D centres. They tried to shelter their results as much as possible from the competition. Governments supported public R&D, the results of which were considered as public goods. Moreover, governments tried to foster in general the conditions for a healthy corporate sector. This made for very simple innovation systems.

The relations between the main actors in the innovation system have changed in recent decades (see the evidence in the other chapters of this book). As a consequence, innovation systems are now much more diversified and complex. A few such changes are as follows:

● The locus of private sector innovation has shifted away from large private (firm-specific) R&D units towards scientific research sourced from universities and public-funded research centres. In the past decades, the central R&D laboratories of large international firms have been reduced in scale and number to save costs.
● Research institutes have become more involved in private sector innovation by stimulating spin-offs and by securing extra resources from the commercialisation of knowledge.
● Governments have become much more involved by setting up varieties of structures that facilitate the flows of knowledge.

Together these tendencies have blurred the precise borders that used to separate the domains of each of the three actors. This has led to interactive systems in which government, knowledge providers and industry operate in a synchronised way (the 'Three-Helix' system as discussed in Etzkowitz and Leydesdorff, 1997). Such three-way relationships were pioneered in the innovation systems of Finland and Sweden, and are now well embedded in the systems of the EU, member countries and regions.

FOCUS: R&D

Institutions

Innovations should lead to marketable products. This does not, however, mean that firms are the actors best equipped to take the necessary in-house steps to come to innovation. Many carry out only part of their innovative work internally. Most (including SMEs) perform development activities in house (the D segment of R&D). Many multinationals also carry out a significant part of their research (the R part of R&D) in specialised company centres. However, many more R&D activities are outsourced to knowledge institutions.

The contracted R&D is only a part of the total effort on R&D. Indeed, most research is not industry (demand) driven. It is done by specialised organisations such as universities and R&D centres, some of which are associated to higher education institutions (HEI). Most of these institutions in the EU depend on public money. Their research is science driven. The members of the staff of such knowledge institutes are motivated by the enhancement of science and the possibility of publishing the scientific results. They are less oriented towards the practical use of their work. In this way, much of the commercial potential of the research risks staying unused. There is a gap between the world of science and that of industry (for further illustration see Box 1.1) that influences economic growth negatively.[5] Hence any effort to bridge this gap contributes to economic growth.

BOX 1.1   THE 'GAP' BETWEEN THE WORLD OF BUSINESS AND THAT OF SCIENCE

World of business	World of science
● Seeks profit and market shares	● Seeks academic eminence
● R&D for private use	● R&D for moving frontiers
● Short-term orientation	● Long-term orientation
● Information is for commercialisation	● Information is for disclosure
● Interprets information versus opportunities	● Interprets information in the context of advancing science
● Communicates via prices/ brands	● Communicates via publications

---

For instance, OECD (2001) has shown that the interaction between universities, private firms and public R&D institutes had a positive influence on growth. This justifies government intervention to stimulate the quality of such institutions. In recent years, many efforts have been made to improve the quality of this interaction and thereby increase the growth and innovation effects of any investments made. Many financial and non-financial incentives are directed to universities and public R&D institutes. They aim to encourage entrepreneurship and, as a consequence, the number of high-technology start-up companies and technology transfer centres. Others aim to stimulate the industry to partner with universities and R&D public institutes in applied science development and its commercialisation.

The problem of the interaction between science and industry is the focus of some of the contributors to this book. Therefore we shall now go into more detail on the issues of R&D spin-offs and transfer mechanisms.

R&D (University) Spin-offs

One way to realise a better commercial use of R&D results from public institutes is to involve the inventors in academia and similar institutions in the commercialisation process.[6] The main incentive for them to do this while staying within the academic institute is to generate extra resources (financial and human) that permit them to make further progress in their scientific work. In some cases, however, there is also the motive to enter into business with possibilities for remuneration exceeding that provided by the R&D institute. The way in which this process takes place is by the transfer of knowledge from the university (or R&D institute) to a new venture in which the (group of) inventor(s) participate(s) actively.[7]

The attitude of universities towards commercialisation has changed over time. More and more universities are now aware of the importance of active involvement in stimulating entrepreneurial activities that commercialise knowledge (Etzkowitz, 1998). The change from a passive or even negative attitude towards a stimulating one is not always easy. It takes the creation of the right organisational context, the systematic identification of commercially interesting developments and of persons with entrepreneurial spirit, the setting up of an incentive structure etc. (see, e.g., O'Shea et al., 2004).

The process by which university spin-offs (USOs) are successfully created and developed has been studied intensively. Wright et al. (2007) distinguish between several types of spin-off. They detail the different institutional environments for successful incubation. They describe the pitfalls a new venture has to avoid to develop successfully, stressing the need for building teams of people with different competencies and for ensuring access to finance. Indeed, the success of USOs is crucially dependent on the speed with which the new venture can overcome a number of problems such as lack of credibility with clients, financiers etc.[8]

A number of universities have used their technology transfer offices as incubators of USOs. They provide them with facilities in the matter of offices and mediate to find the elements often lacking among academic entrepreneurs, such as management skills, (venture) capital and so on. Sometimes they themselves act as key investors as they use the rewards of earlier ventures to stimulate new ones. To that end they have sometimes set up staff that can support the entire start-up phase and bring the investment to the market as soon as it has reached some stage of maturity. However, many other universities still shy away from such involvement. This attitude limits the number of USOs and thus the possibilities for dynamic innovative ventures.

In his contribution to this volume (Chapter 2) Hans Wissema addresses the problem faced by universities in creating structures that facilitate such spin-offs. He focuses on technostarters – spin-offs from technical universities. Such technostarters are particularly interesting as a subject, as they make an indispensable contribution to the economy by creating new employment at a higher professional level. Wissema uses the example of Cambridge (UK), where a lucky constellation of factors has created a cluster of knowledge institutes and new innovative firms, some of which were offsprings of the university. The university has acknowledged the importance of technostarters and now deliberately fosters their development, supported by government grants. This support takes the form of facilities such as a science park, an innovation centre etc. Another role model is Leuven University (Belgium), which has also done much for starters, focusing more on specialised research centres (such as micro-electronics).[9] Wissema argues that universities that assume such extended responsibilities for support to the regional environment (in supporting technostarters) do not neglect their prime task of research but can actually see this enhanced by the stronger 'infrastructure' and financial base that it creates.[10]

This latter recommendation supports the one that was drawn from a study into a larger sample of practical experiences in different regions in the EU (Huntingford and Frosini, 2007, pp. 81–92). They divide the whole process of spin-offs and start-ups into five stages: awareness raising and entrepreneurial education; checking the feasibility of the spin-off; preparation for foundation of the company; actual creation of the company; support during the first five years. They see this as a role not only for the university, but point to the responsibility of other regional actors. In particular, the regional government needs to make sure that complementary support is provided where needed. These support activities should be specifically tailored to the needs of R&D-intensive starters; applying general measures to this category of starters does not lead to success (Storey and Tether, 1998).

Transfer Mechanisms

There is a second way to stimulate the commercial use of the results of publicly financed R&D. That is by taking away the barriers to the transfer to the market of scientific and technological know-how from R&D establishments. Indeed, the mere production of knowledge does not by itself lead to more competitiveness and hence growth. The knowledge needs to be channelled to firms that can actually use it in their production and production processes. However, information does not always flow easily and hence many of the results risk staying under- or even un-utilised. So it is important to increase the effectiveness of this link.

The deficiencies in the industry–science link (illustrated by Box 1.1 above) are well documented in the literature; they have been cynically stated to stem from academics being only interested in an extra source of finance, and industry only in testing at lower cost than consultants (Cooke et al., 2000). Much has been done to improve the relation between knowledge institutes and the corporate sector. Solutions to the problem often take the university as the starting point. The problem is then subdivided into more specific problems about the context, the structure and the processes that universities use to bring their knowledge to the market. A number of European research universities have experimented with different forms. From these experiments a few conclusions can be drawn as to important success factors (Debackere and Vleugelers, 2005):

- *Knowledge generation* The knowledge base needs to provide for excellence in certain areas. A good combination of basic and applied research is instrumental to the identification of commercially interesting uses of scientific knowledge.
- *Knowledge transfer capacities* The university needs to show that it is committed to commercial uses as part of its central mission, networking between university staff with industry at all levels.
- *Organizational structures* A decentralised model where research groups receive incentives that stimulate their direct and active involvement in the exploitation of their research.
- *Supporting services* Specialised central services offering intellectual property management.

Given its key importance for competitiveness and growth, the issue of increasing the effectiveness of the R&D–industry link has been high on the policy agenda. Efforts to improve the link have been intensified. However, it remains unclear to what extent these efforts bore the fruits expected from them. Methods to evaluate the impact of policy efforts in this domain are rather deficient. To improve on that situation, IDEA[11] has developed a new method (the multidimensional innovation impact assessment method; MI[2]A). This method distinguishes between the economic (e.g. induced value added), fiscal (returns to government due to taxes on income profits etc.), scientific (e.g. knowledge) and technological (e.g. patents) impacts.

Arnold Verbeek and his colleagues have applied that method to the case of the Flemish centres of excellence. They show (in Chapter 3) that these centres play a major role in strengthening the knowledge base in their specific areas (sectors) and in stimulating international competitiveness of Flemish companies. The positive fiscal effects they engender mean that the net cost to the government of their activities is much lower than originally budgeted.

The role of university knowledge transfer activity has received much attention from policy makers. This is based partly on the assumption that proximity to a university can offer advantages in terms of the quantity and quality of knowledge exchanged with local businesses, thus stimulating greater innovation in the business base and leading to economic benefits to their region. However, the importance of proximity for local development is highly debated. Some writers argue that, at present, technology effectively allows instant access to information and communication anywhere on the globe.[12] If this were true, the premise of a policy of stimulating local innovation would collapse. Others find that the proximity factor is very important, and that contacts between partners are subject to strong distance decay. For knowledge-intensive SMEs in particular, proximity of partners is a determining factor for their performance (Arndt and Sternberg, 2000). In the EU-25 context only the innovative efforts pursued within a 180-minute travel radius have a positive and significant impact on regional growth performance (Rodríguez-Pose and Crescenzi, 2006).

In order to explore the geography of university knowledge transfer activity in practice, Adrian Healy reports (in Chapter 4) on three regions in the UK: South East England, London and the East of England. In each case interviews were undertaken with a sample of universities, particular departments and key academics. The research found a complicated and uneven geography of knowledge transfer activity that owes as much to individual contacts and interests as to corporate strategy or spatial factors. The research also identified that distinct spatial patterns are discernible between different knowledge transfer programmes, providing important pointers to policy makers and regional strategists. The research suggests that in knowledge transfer activity, consideration should be given to notions of relational spaces next to traditional conceptions of geographical proximity.

FOCUS: FIRMS

The Drivers of Firm Innovation

A key role for driving innovation is the behaviour of the entrepreneur (Schumpeter, 1934). In the face of competition and declining profits, entrepreneurs are driven to make technical and financial innovations. The spurts of activity resulting from these innovations generate economic growth. Through a process of 'creative destruction' waves of innovation hit different industries at different points in time. Firms have an incentive to engage in innovative activities because of the expectation that new technologies will generate monopoly profits – at least until the new technology becomes public knowledge (Grossman and Helpman, 1991).[13]

However, this technical concept is not the only valid one. In line with the broad definition of innovation we adopted for this book, we also have to see what other factors may be of influence. One such factor is the capital of knowledge that is available in a certain area (Antonelli, 2006) that permits combinations of product and production process innovations. The internal organisation of a firm can also have a strong impact on its innovation performance. Organisational rigidities in innovation projects have a negative impact on productivity (Lööf and Heshmati, 2002). A survey of studies in the management literature on the determinants of organisational innovation identified three main determinants (Read, 2000):

- management support for an innovative culture;
- a customer/market focus;
- a high level of internal and external communication/networking.

Innovative ideas at company level come from many different sources.[14] Very important among them is the market: indeed, users provide many ideas for improvement. Next to this is internal and external R&D. Innovation is moreover stimulated by discussions with other companies. Finally, the acquisition of equipment, notably ICT, plays a significant role. ICT is a major motor for innovation and hence for growth in the knowledge-based economy. There are large differences in ICT adoption levels by firms over the EU space. This suggests a very unequal geographical pattern of ensuing innovation (Vicente and Lopez, 2006). Stimulating the performance in the low adoption areas by the enhancement of the use of ICT by firms requires a better understanding of the ICT diffusion process. Numerous studies have been made into the subject (see the review by Hollenstein, 2004).[15] Many limit themselves to the problem of diffusion. Yet a more detailed understanding is needed of the factors that determine the successful implementation of ICT by SMEs to design good policies that can stimulate innovation, notably by firms in countries that are catching up with the average EU living standard (see Chapter 7). This is all the more relevant as empirical studies show that the competitiveness of SMEs (in terms of export performance) in the countries of Central and Eastern Europe is strongly dependent on ICT, notably the judicious use of the Internet (Clarke, 2008).

This is exactly the approach that is followed in the chapter by Jacob Dencik and Julia Djarova (Chapter 5). They have made an investigation at the firm level into the dynamics of ICT adoption in a number of countries in Central and Eastern Europe. They found that ICT is one of the main factors determining the performance of firms, both through improved efficiency of the production process and the increased innovativeness of firms. A major finding of the study was that the regulatory environment strongly influences (facilitates or inhibits) the take-up and use of ICT among firms. The surveyed firms found that the most constraining elements were inadequate education and training, and inappropriate taxation. The authors define six policy areas where priority government action is needed in order to create an environment for firms that is conducive to further ICT use and hence for the innovative performance of firms.

The Key Role of Finance

Numerous empirical studies have demonstrated that one of the key determinants of innovation is access to funding (in the form of cash flow, bank loans, venture capital, stock exchange etc). Many innovative companies use a 'bootstrapping' model of finance, depending on their own resources, revenues and prioritisation. Others prefer 'smart money': funding that comes with advice via business experts, business angels, active investors etc.[16]

In many cases the money from private sources is not enough. Indeed, in quite a few cases the market is not performing well. Theoretical studies show that external financing is likely to stop short of the optimum (Bergemann and Hege, 2005), resulting in a loss of opportunities and waste of resources. Empirical studies show that the internal sources (cash flow) are often insufficient (see, e.g., Bond et al., 2003) and that external sources are rather expensive while the availability of funds is in many markets limited, due to information gaps and other market imperfections (Hall, 2005).

Investments in R&D are intangible and uncertainties are always attached to such investment. In addition, in the 'markets' for science and technology there are clear market imperfections. Linking demand and supply cannot be done by such market mechanisms as price, for instance. This is why national governments saw it for a long time as their task to invest in R&D. The justification for policies to promote company R&D is based on the same argument: for the sake of society as a whole, it may be justified to provide subsidies for corporate R&D in order to persuade individual firms to take more risk and work on longer time horizons than they would have done for company reasons only. Especially justifiable is the government intervention in the case of SMEs, where the regular sources of finance are often not available (EC, 2007). It is also the case for projects of large firms, where the risks are fairly large. Most governments have set up schemes to provide funds to firms to stimulate their innovative activities and especially their R&D.[17]

One of the other main instruments by which the government tries to stimulate R&D in business is by providing direct financial support. It assumes thereby that such support will enhance the size and the effectiveness of the efforts of the firm and thus enhance the competitiveness of the firm. The question is, however, whether the assumptions on which this action is based do indeed hold in practice and to what extent the financial resources spent lead to the expected result.

The evaluations of government-supported finance schemes (based on microdata) are generally positive; they tend to conclude that private R&D has increased by the same amount as the government stimulus. However, there are quite a few methodological problems to be resolved before this inference can be upheld with confidence (see, e.g., Klette et al., 2000; Hall and Van Reenen, 2000; Hall, 2005).

A group of researchers at IDEA has attacked this problem. Geert Steurs et al. show in their contribution to this book (Chapter 6) that the usual method of using input and output measures cannot give a good answer to the question at hand. What is needed is a measure of the change in the behaviour of the firm due to the subsidy. This extra effort (additional to the present one) can be called 'behavioural additionality'. It can be measured in terms of increases in the size of the R&D programmes, in the speed with which they are executed and the number of partners involved. Steurs et al. make their method operational in their analysis of the effects of subsidies by a government agency in Flanders. Their findings are clear: subsidies have a positive effect on the efforts of firms on all three scores (size, speed, partners). They are thus important drivers of firm performance.

FOCUS: PUBLIC SECTOR

Role of the Public Sector

Economic systems alone cannot always provide solutions to the problems they are confronted with. Governments have to intervene to correct such failures. In matters of innovation this is true as well. The literature gives abundant reasons for a strong role of the government (e.g. OECD, 1997b). In the previous sections of this chapter, we have given examples of cases where government intervention is essential in coming to a solution. As mentioned earlier, much research in government-sponsored R&D centres is science driven, and its application in commercial use does not come about without government policies that stimulate the relation between the R&D centre and the corporate sector. The same is true for innovation within the corporate sector, where government stimuli can help to overcome the barriers to development.

In discussing the role of government, it has been traditional to refer to that of national governments. However, this view is now completely inadequate for reasons indicated earlier in this chapter. Indeed, in Europe a three-layer structure of government has developed in which the main actors are the European Commission, the national governments and the regional governments. The distribution of responsibilities between the actors in this multi-layered government system has been changing over time (see, e.g., Jordan and Schout, 2006; Molle, 2006). Over the first three decades of the existence of the EU, changes in this distribution between the EU and national states have come about as answers to specific challenges. This has led to unbalanced situations. Since 1986 the principle of subsidiarity has governed this distribution: it says that the EU should do only what cannot be done efficiently at the national or regional level. The distribution between national governments and the regions has also changed. Partly under the impetus of the EU, many countries have empowered their regions to take responsibility for economic development matters.

European Policies and Systems

The EU policy on innovation has gradually evolved (EC, 2003a; Peterson and Sharp, 1998; Nauwelaers and Wintjes, 2008). An assessment of the various segments of innovation policy on the subsidiarity criteria shows that there are good reasons for involvement at the EU level (Horst et al., 2006). The 'economies of scale' argument applies notably to large R&D projects characterised by indivisibilities. In this way the 7th Framework Programme (FP7) funds such activities to pool and leverage resources, foster human capital and excellence. The EU also supports innovation in SMEs. Its involvement there is justified as it reduces the cost of regulation and promotes the policy learning between member states.

The European innovation system is limited in its ambitions with respect to R&D and firms to the elements just mentioned. Its main feature is its steering of the efforts of national and regional governments to improve the innovation systems on these levels. This involves a great deal of coordination in order to improve consistency of efforts. This coordination is ensured in two ways:

- a bottom-up process, in which the specificities of the regional and national layers are framed in a EU setting of priorities and rules; and
- a top-down process in which EU priorities are set, benchmarks defined and the performance of the national and regional layers constantly monitored against the objectives at the EU level.

In his contribution to this volume (Chapter 7) Willem Molle describes how the EU has set its innovation policy in the framework of the realisation of its overriding goal to improve its competitive position in the global knowledge economy. He indicates, however, that the EU has limited chances to realise this goal through the deployment of instruments available under the heading of innovation policy. Much has to be realised by coordinating national and regional efforts, and this coordination in itself is unlikely to be effective without adequate frameworks for coordination and without some financial stimuli. The EU systems for innovation policy are inadequate on both scores. However, in the framework of EU cohesion policy, highly sophisticated and effective coordination and implementation systems have been elaborated for which very considerable sums are available. The EU has put this system to the use of innovation. Molle concludes that this integration of part of the cohesion system with the European innovation system appears distorted in theory but is in practice quite effective. He makes a number of suggestions to further optimise the coordination mechanisms.

National Governments

The national innovation capacity can be defined as the ability of a country to produce and commercialise a flow of innovative technology over the long term. The internationalisation of R&D has changed profoundly the room for manoeuvre of national governments, in particular those of small countries (Spithoven and Teirlinck, 2005). The national innovative capacity depends to a large extent on the strength of a nation's common innovation infrastructure and environment for innovation, its industrial clusters and the strength of the linkages between the two (Furman et al., 2002). There is considerable debate about the contribution of each of these elements. Yet some factors stand out as important: first, the level of spending on R&D; and second the productivity of R&D outlays. R&D productivity is determined by factors that stimulate the effectiveness with which R&D is translated into usable products. These in turn are influenced by factors such as openness of universities to private sector funds and private sector commercialisation of innovations.

The factors cited above can be influenced by government measures in order to improve the performance of the system. To that end, an evaluation has to be made of the present situation and measures taken to improve the weak points.

In their contribution to this volume (Chapter 8) Julia Djarova and Walter Zegveld stress the importance of national innovation systems as essential building blocks of the multi-layer structure of innovation policy in the EU. However, they argue that the traditional NIS approach suffers from a number of inadequacies, related to a lack of effectiveness due to poor coordination of the efforts of the various actors involved. They stress the importance of an innovation policy mix consisting of a set of interrelated policy measures that responds to specific combinations of challenges. The policy mix needs to govern all stages of the policy cycle: design, implementation and evaluation. Policy mixes fall into the area of responsibilities of different government departments and can thus only be effective when they are well coordinated. The authors argue that this is best done at a very high level of authority.

Regional Governments

Regions are the building blocks of Europe's economy: it is at the level of the region that the factors of competitiveness and innovation can be identified,[18] and effective tools for sustainable, endogenous development applied. It is at the regional level that the notion of innovation system finds its most concrete application in the form of regional innovation systems (RIS). The task of the regional governments is essentially to assess the component factors of the regional innovation system and to improve them where possible.

The first component is formed by the regional R&D organisations. In principle, these are easy to identify. They constitute the backbone of the regional knowledge infrastructure. Other elements in that group are higher education institutions (HEIs), which provide the human capital most ready to enter into innovative activities of the region.[19] Regional governments can influence the innovative climate of the region by stimulating these institutes to take entrepreneurial attitudes (in line with those discussed by Wissema in Chapter 2 of this book).

The second component is formed by firms. The innovative capacity of regional firms is not always easy to identify, but on many occasions simple surveys permit taking stock. The important element in this respect is not the individual firm, but the quality and density of business network structures: entrepreneurs in knowledge-based firms, when compared with traditional firms, invest more time in networking and also build more focused networks.[20]

The innovative attitude of firms is determined by many external factors that support access to knowledge and diffusion of knowledge. One important element here is the quality of key personnel.[21]

The role of the regional government is important, as it is the main actor capable of developing, in a systematic way, the RIS. This role consists first in the building of effective linkages that transfer knowledge and innovation within and beyond the regional economy, especially involving technology-based industries and businesses.[22] However, this is not sufficient. The development of the RIS should also address factors such as social capacity, networks and institutional thickness, and assist the functioning of untraded interdependencies.[23] Indeed, experience has shown that the success factors for an RIS are to a large extent organisational and cultural (Cooke et al., 1997): culture of cooperation, associative governance, ability and experience to carry out institutional change; coordination and public–private consensus and existing interface mechanisms located in scientific, technological productive and financial fields. The policy makers themselves need to give proof of entrepreneurship; experiments with new approaches should be adopted and lessons drawn from them (the learning region – Morgan, 1997). Finally, the regional government needs to address the improvement of the regional business climate in general.[24]

In those regions where the factors that determine innovation are weak (in particular most new member states), the role of the government is more pronounced (see, e.g., Morgan and Nauwelaers, 2003). Depending on the specific situation in a region, the role of the government may indeed be more facilitating or dirigiste (Braczyk, et al., 1998).[25]

The policy lessons that result from the previous survey of the literature are not easy to put into practice. Many difficulties need to be overcome. The first is the mere assessment of the actual situation. If it is a question of only one region, a qualitative description of the many components seems certainly possible. However, when it comes to benchmarking, a comparison with other regions or with average values will be necessary. This supposes the quantification of a number of variables. This seems fairly easy as far as the basic components (such as R&D activity) are concerned, but almost impossible as far as the cultural components (such as untraded interdependencies) are concerned. Various typologies of RIS have been constructed (see Chapter 7) on the basis of the available information. Their capacity to guide policy making in the whole EU is limited, however, due to lack of data (particularly for the new member states).

In order to improve on that state of affairs, Marta Makiewicz, Robert Pollock and Paulina Fabrowska analyse (in Chapter 9) the situation in the largest of the new member states: Poland. Notwithstanding the important improvements realised over the past decades, the country and all its regions rank low on the EU innovation monitor. There are serious deficiencies in the quasi-totality of the RIS of the country. The authors set out to get to grips with the situation. They first define four types of regions with their specific models of innovation and policy intervention. They next assemble new data for all the Polish regions on the basic components of the RIS and construct an index that produces a ranking of the regions in terms of innovativeness. This shows that the country has effectively only one region with an innovative potential that compares to the rest of the EU: the capital city Warsaw. All the other RISs are rather weak. The authors conclude that the country needs to make a very great effort to improve the situation in all its regions. The authors argue that these efforts should be carefully designed so as to fit the particular situation of each region. Finally they plead for a more in-depth study of each of these regions to determine quickly the policy packages that will best suit their particular problems and ambitions.

SOME CONCLUSIONS AND KEY MESSAGES

Recall of Key Features of this Book

This book is based on the view that innovation systems (e.g. European, national, regional) have become increasingly complex and that their dynamics are dependent on a multitude of interrelated factors. Thus what is essential are not the individual components, but the systemic factors. Hence it is important to study the relationships between the actors in an innovation system. We consider the innovation system as a three-player (R&D, firms and the public sector) and three-layer system (regional, national and European). Our view is that the solution to the problems is not only in the R&D sector, nor in the industry sector, nor in the public sector. It is in fact at the same time in all of the 3×3 elements of the system and in the interrelations between them.

In line with this view, we clustered the individual contributions according to this 'three-player, three-layer concept'. We asked each contributor to pay due attention to the interrelations between the actors (players) and levels (layers).

Finally, we can now list the main conclusions and the main messages that can be drawn from our work.

Conclusions

The results of the cooperative effort of the contributors to this book consist first of a set of interesting new insights into important problems that confront the major actors in the innovation system and their relationship. These can be listed by main group of actors as follows:

- *R&D institutes* The introduction of more entrepreneurial activities into these institutes should improve both their academic output and the success of innovation of the private sector.
- *Firms* The improvement of the regulatory and institutional environment of firms enhances their efforts in matters of R&D and in networking, resulting in increased innovation and a better market position.
- *Public authorities* The streamlining of the present set-up and the better attribution of roles over the various authorities involved should reduce the cost of coordination (higher efficiency) and improve the results (higher effectiveness).

Key Messages

The various contributions to the book have an important aspect in common: all challenge the traditional (and sometimes simplistic) view of the problem at hand and develop the more modern (and often more complicated) approach to the issues. In this common vein the various authors all make suggestions for increasing the effectiveness of innovation policy. These can be specified by subject (chapter) as follows:

- The role of the universities and public R&D institutions has traditionally been limited to conducting research and teaching students. A more modern view of their role stresses the importance of adding economic value through enterprising. In view of the latest development of 'out-of-house' rather than 'in-house' research for many private companies, the team suggests forms of organisation of knowledge institutes and of government regulation concerning these institutes.

- Technology transfer has been seen for a long time as a one-way transaction. R&D organisations provided technology to some business directly or to business in general through patenting. Technology transfer nowadays is multidimensional and has brought to life new organisational forms such as centres of excellence, technology institutes etc., where the R&D–industry link is supported by policy instruments. The effects of traditional technology transfer have been studied quite extensively in the past. The study of the effects of the new forms of transfer needs a different approach, such as the multidimensional impact assessment method developed in Chapter 3.

- Geographical proximity used to be the prominent feature of knowledge transfer. This is no longer the case. Consideration should now be given to notions of relational density and intensity next to traditional conceptions of the cost of overcoming distance. The role of geographical proximity is also challenged by young graduates, choosing their research facilities over a wide area. The factors of choice here have moved up even higher than the national level.

- Entrepreneurship has traditionally been seen as a characteristic inherent in an individual person that can hardly be transferred let alone copied. In this perspective there is no role for government intervention on the subject. Today we argue that one can develop entrepreneurial capacities, and that these are essential for innovation. Consequently, public authorities at regional, national and European level support entrepreneurship. Financial support instruments are increasing in variety and in number. The issue, however, is: does the provision of financial stimuli lead to the expected results? Our team has argued that the usual method of using input and output measures cannot give a satisfactory answer. What is important is to measure the change in the behaviour of the firm that receives the subsidy. Only in such a way can one tackle the persistent problem of building up sufficient learning capacity in the system.

- Best practice has been promoted as a learning tool for many public authorities at different levels. Searching for best practice the contributions in this book that are concerned with the regional, national and European aspect of innovation policies, one becomes confused as the transferability of the specific results seems limited. We conclude from this that it is more important to take account of the consistency of the efforts of the various players. Thus interrelationship should be built into the decision-making mechanisms at all levels for all actors.

- The various elements of the innovation system have traditionally been developed in isolation, minimising the effort of coordination. This has been identified as a major hindrance to effective and efficient innovation systems at the European, national and regional level. We argue that the mere stepping up of coordination is likely to add to inefficiencies and unlikely to be effective without adequate frameworks and without financial stimuli. We find the EU systems for innovation policy lacking on both scores. However, the integration of innovation into the EU cohesion system is a promising way to increase effectiveness.

- Coordination that overrules the departmental (sectoral) approach to decision making seems to be a key factor for success for national public authorities in their efforts under the heading of innovation policy. The challenge is to 'overrule' the traditional governmental structure and find a form that can prove workable. Although we find the pace with which such forms come to life too slow, there is a positive tendency in this respect.

- Benchmarking exercises have traditionally been promoted with the idea that the making of a typology of regions could provide a menu of specific models of innovation and policy interventions. Notwithstanding the importance of benchmarking as an instrument, we argue that cultural components such as untraded interdependencies are almost impossible to quantify. So a more 'personalised' approach to each area based on detailed SWOT (strengths, weaknesses, opportunities and threats) analyses is needed for each national and regional authority.

NOTES

1. We acknowledge the support of Roderick van 't Hoff for effective literature search.
2. Not only DG Research but also various other Directorates General such as Employment and notably the one with an important spending capacity, i.e. Regional Policy (see Molle, 2007, ch. 12).
3. For a historical overview of the development of the concept see Freeman (1995); for a description of a set of national systems see Nelson (1993); and for some best practices in the application of the concept see OECD (1997a).
4. For the role of innovation in the economy, see, e.g., Freeman and Soete (1997). For the role of government, see, e.g., OECD (1997b); von Hippel (1988). A good example of why policy makers need to have a more inclusive understanding of innovation is the case of Ireland. Ireland has traditionally had low levels of R&D spend per capita and yet is one of the most successful economies in the EU, in terms of GDP growth and GDP per capita, and is rightly termed the 'Celtic Tiger'. Ireland's success is built on the prudent application of Structural Funds for skills development and infrastructure, fiscal reform, foreign direct investment and the presence of a cohort of indigenous internationalised

companies whose innovation models relate to redesigning their business processes. See in this respect, e.g., Aho et al. (2006).

5. It has been shown that differences in innovative capabilities can explain in large part the diverging trends in economic growth in European regions (Fagerberg et al., 1997).

6. See, e.g., Lambooy (2004). In the USA the tradition of commercialisation of university knowledge is older than in the EU. Many universities have well-organised transfer organisations. They generate substantial revenue from licences. The amount of this revenue is determined to a large extent by the speed of commercialisation of patent-protected technology. Speed itself is determined by the resources available to the transfer organisation to identify potential licensees and by the involvement of the inventors in the adaptation to the needs of the licensee (Markman et al., 2005).

7. There is a second form of spin-off: that is, by students; they tend however to create more service-oriented firms that do not in general have the potential impact of the research-based spin-offs (Pinay et al., 2003). Other paths between university and enterprise can be identified but have not yet been thoroughly explored (e.g. Shinn and Lamy, 2006).

8. For that reason USOs that are done in the form of joint ventures with an existing company or with a venture capitalist tend to have better chances of a good performance than USOs that lack these links (Wright et al., 2004). Unfortunately both options have negative sides to them. The joint venture may tend to become dominated by the existing experienced company, making the rewards for the inventors for their efforts small. The market for venture capital that is interested in USOs is very opaque and there is in most places mismatch between demand and supply. Venture capitalists tend to shy away from companies that do not present sufficient capabilities in management and finance. This implies that an intermediary has to put together teams that can match the demands of these venture capitalists (Wright et al., 2006).

9. In presenting the cases of Cambridge (UK) and Leuven (Belgium), Wissema brings useful background information to the contributions of Adrian Healy (the case of the South East of England in Chapter 4), and the cases of Flanders described by Geert Steurs et al. (in Chapter 6) and Arnold Verbeek et al. (Chapter 3).

10. See in this respect also the results in universities that are not part of the top set in the EU, e.g. in Ireland (Dineen, 1995).

11. IDEA Consult is part of ECORYS Group, a multidisciplinary group of European research and consulting companies that includes NEI and Kolpron Consultants in the Netherlands and ECOTEC Research & Consulting in the UK.

12. For instance, the attractions of the scientific knowledge infrastructure in the UK explain how the technological efforts of non-UK businesses tend to be drawn relatively strongly to these regions (Cantwell and Iammarino, 2000).

13. Equating innovation with the development of new products results in a sort of 'quality ladder'. Firms, and consequently countries, that climb up the quality ladder can afford higher wages by offering higher quality. Important insights are given by the product cycle model and its corollaries the profit cycle, the innovation cycle and the manufacturing process cycle. These models describe the typical pattern of a product's lifespan: from R&D investment to success, and ultimate decline and replacement by newer products. Generally, the four phases are described as innovation, growth, maturity and decline. This approach highlights the different labour and capital needs related to the product in different phases, and the ebb and flow of innovation activity.

14. See, e.g., Malecki (1997) and Deiaco (1992).

15. Although one commonly distinguishes between the intra- and inter-firm patterns of adoption, the main drivers of the diffusion processes are common to both (Battisti and Stoneman, 2003).

16. The essential role of finance is very visible in the case of USOs; see the contribution of Wissema to this volume (Chapter 2) and chapter 7 of the book by Wright et al. (2007).

17. Other instruments have also been used, such as tax credits (see, e.g., Bloom et al., 2002). An overview and analysis of a number of financial schemes for innovation can be seen in Djarova et al. (2007).

18. See for instance CE/ECORYS et al. (2003). See, for the local character of knowledge, Saviotti (2007).
19. HEIs are easily identified as sources of human capital within a region. However, the decision to stay and work in the region after graduation is highly dependent on location factors such as the quality of living and employment opportunities (Simmie et al., 2002). In empirical studies, the attraction and retention rates of those trained and educated, which might act as a measure of the return on investment in education, are often ignored (De Gaudemar, 1996). There is as yet little knowledge on how students flow into the labour market and how this affects economic performance and regional innovation (Goddard, 1997a, 1997b; Besson and Montgomery, 1993).
20. For a general introduction, see, e.g., Camagni (1991) and Aydalot and Keeble (1988), and for special cases, Johannisson (1998) for Sweden and Ritsilä (1999) for Finland.
21. First, it takes skilled professionals to perform R&D tasks. A second – and often neglected – reason is that only trained practitioners can interpret new knowledge and adapt it for profitable exploitation. For these reasons, surveys among entrepreneurs invariably list the availability of qualified personnel within a region as one of the most crucial factors for success (e.g. Simmie et al., 2002; ECORYS–NEI, 2001).
22. See Cooke (2003) and Leydesdorff and Meyer (2006) and the articles referred to in the latter.
23. Untraded interdependencies (Storper, 1995) contain not only labour market, regional knowledge infrastructure, business climate, but also regional conventions, norms and values, and public or semi-public policies. When these untraded interdependencies are concentrated, Storper considers them to be of pivotal importance in the supply architecture of innovation and learning, and as key determinants of regional innovation.
24. The business climate can spur firms to be more innovative. Important aspects are of course competition, market structure and cooperation, as described above. But there is more. The prospect of profitable exploitation of the innovation is an incentive for the entrepreneur to innovate. The perspective of large market power, favourable technological opportunities, the availability of qualified labour and high demand expectations all have an unambiguous positive influence on innovation (Stadler, 1999).
25. From a government point of view, they distinguish the following three modes of technology transfer:

    ● Grassroots RISs are characterised by local initiatives, diffuse funding (banks, local governments, chambers of commerce), applied, near-market research, low level of technological specialisation and local coordination.
    ● Network RISs can be initiated at several levels: local, regional, federal or governmental. Consequently, funding is more likely to be agreed by banks, firms and government agencies. The research is mixed, aimed at both applied and 'pure' technology with flexible specialisation given the wide range of participants.
    ● Dirigiste RISs are more animated from outside and above the region itself, initiated and funded typically by central governments. The research is rather basic or fundamental, to be used in large firms in or beyond the region in question. As it is state-run, the level of coordination is high and the level of specialisation is also likely to be high.

REFERENCES

Aho, E., J. Coruse, L. Georghiou and A. Subira (2006), *Creating an Innovative Europe*, Report of the independent expert group on R&D and innovation, Brussels.

Antonelli, C. (2006), 'The business governance of localized knowledge: an information economics approach for the economics of knowledge', *Industry and Innovation*, **13** (3), 227–61.

Arndt, O. and R. Sternberg (2000), 'Do manufacturing firms profit from intra-regional innovation linkages? An empirically based answer', *European Planning Studies*, **8**, 465–85.

Aydalot, P. and D. Keeble (1988), *High Technology Industry and Innovative Environments: The European Experience*, London: Routledge.

Battisti, G. and P. Stoneman (2003), 'Inter and intra firm effects in the diffusion of new process technology', *Research Policy*, **32**, 1641–55.

Bergemann, D. and U. Hege (2005), 'The financing of innovation; learning and stopping', *The RAND Journal of Economics*, **36** (4), 719–52.

Besson, P. and E. Montgomery (1993), 'The effect of college and universities on local labour markets', *The Review of Economics and Statistics*, **75** (4), 753–61.

Bloom, N., R. Griffith and J. Van Reenen (2002), 'Do R&D tax credits work? Evidence for a panel of countries, 1979–1997', *Journal of Public Economics*, **85**, 1–31.

Braczyk, H.-J., P. Cooke and M. Heidenreich (1998), *Regional Innovation Systems*, London: UCL Press.

Camagni, R. (ed.) (1991), *Innovation Networks, Spatial Perspectives*, London: Belhaven Press.

Cantwell, J. and S. Iammarino (2000) 'Multinational corporations and the location of technological innovation in the UK regions', *Regional Studies*, **34** (4), 317–22.

Chang, Y. and M. Chen (2004), 'Comparing approaches to systems of innovation: the knowledge perspective', *Technology in Society*, **26**, 117–37.

CE/ECORYS et al. (2003), *Factors of Regional Competitiveness*, study commissioned by DG Regio.

Clarke, G.R.G. (2008), 'Has the internet increased exports from low and middle income countries?', *Information Economics and Policy*, **20**, 16–37.

Cooke, P. (2003), 'The governance of regional innovation systems', paper prepared for UNIDO conference on The Process of Innovation and Learning in Dynamic City-Regions in China, Cardiff.

Cooke, P. (2004), *Regional Innovation Systems: An Evolutionary Approach*, London: Routledge.

Cooke, P. and K. Morgan (1998), *The Associational Economy: Firms, Regions and Innovation*, Oxford: Oxford University Press.

Cooke, P., M.G. Uranga and G. Etxebarria (1997), 'Regional innovation systems: new models meeting knowledge economy demands', *Research Policy*, **26** (4/5), 475–91.

Cooke, P., P. Boekholt and F. Toedling (2000), *The Governance of Innovation in Europe: Regional Perspectives on Global Competitiveness*, London and New York: Pinter.

Debackere, C. and R. Vleugelers (2005), 'The role of academic technology transfer organizations in improving industry science links', *Research Policy*, **34**, 321–42.

De Gaudemar, J.-P. (1996), 'The higher education institutes as a regional actor: some introductory thoughts', paper presented at Centre for Educational Research and Innovation.

Deiaco, E. (1992), 'New views on innovative activity and technological performance: the Swedish Innovation Survey', *STI Review*, **11**, 35–62.

Dineen, D. (1995), 'The role of a university in regional economic development: a case study of the University of Limerick', *Industry and Higher Education*, **9** (3), 140–48.

Djarova, J. et al. (2007), *Creating Financial Incentives for Innovation in Bulgaria*, ECORYS Report.

ECORYS–NEI (2001), *International Benchmark of the Regional Investment Climate in North-western Europe*, Rotterdam.

EC (2003a), *Innovation Policy; Updating the Union's Approach in the Context of the Lisbon Strategy*, COM 2003; 112 final.

EC (2003) (DG Regio), 'Structural policies and European territories: Competitiveness, sustainable development and cohesion in Europe – From Lisbon to Gothenburg'. Brussels.

EC (2004), 'A new partnership for cohesion; convergence; competitiveness; cooperation', Third Report on Economic and Social Cohesion, Brussels.

EC (2007), 'Financing innovation and SMEs; sowing the seeds; main findings of four workshops', Brussels.

Etzkowitz, H. (1998), 'The norms of entrepreneurial science: cognitive effects of the new university–industry linkages', *Research Policy*, **27**, 823–33.

Etzkowitz, H. and L. Leydesdorff (1997), *Universities in the Global Knowledge Economy*, London: Pinter.

Fagerberg, J., B. Verspagen and M. Caniëls (1997), 'Technology, growth and unemployment across European regions', *Regional Studies*, **31** (5), 457–66.

Freeman, C. (1987), 'National systems of innovation: the case of Japan', in C. Freeman, *Technology Policy and Economic Performance*, London: Pinter Publishers.

Freeman, C. (1995), 'The national system of innovation in historical perspective', *Cambridge Journal of Economics*, **19**, 5–24.

Freeman, C. and L. Soete (1997), *The Economics of Industrial Innovation*, Cambridge, MA: MIT Press.

Furman, J., M.E. Porter and S. Stern (2002), 'The determinants of national innovative capacity', *Research Policy*, **31**, 899–933.

Goddard, J. (1997a), 'Universities and regional development: an overview', CURDS website: www.ncl.ac.uk.

Goddard, J. (1997b), 'The local and regional role of higher education: comments on the National Commission of Inquiry Report', CURDS website: www.ncl.ac.uk.

Grossman, G. and E. Helpman (1991), *Innovation and Growth in the Global Economy*, Cambridge, MA: MIT Press.

Hall, B. (2005), 'The financing of innovation', mimeo, available from the Internet.

Hall, B. and J. Van Reenen (2000), 'How effective are fiscal incentives for R&D? A review of the evidence', *Research Policy*, **29**, 449–69.

Hollenstein, H. (2004), 'Determinants of the adoption of information and communication technologies (ICT)', *Structural Change and Economic Dynamics*, **15** (3), 315–42.

Horst, A. van der, A. Lejour and B. Straathof (2006), 'Innovation policy: Europe or the member states?', CPB document no. 132, The Hague.

Huntingford, J. and P. Frosini (2007) (eds), 'Knowledge and innovation for regional growth; policy recommendations based on European good practices', available from info@eriknetwork.net and from the website of the EU Commission.

Johannisson, B. (1998), 'Personal networks in emerging knowledge-based firms: spatial and functional patterns', *Entrepreneurship and Regional Development*, **10**, 297–312.

Jordan, A. and A. Schout (2006), *The Coordination of the European Union: Exploring the Capacities of Networked Governance*, Oxford: Oxford University Press.

Klette, T.J.J., Moen and Z. Griliches (2000), 'Do subsidies to commercial R&D reduce market failures? Micro econometric evaluation studies', *Research Policy*, **29**, 471–95.

Lambooy, J. (2004), 'The transmission of knowledge, emerging networks and the role of universities: an evolutionary approach', *European Planning Studies*, **12** (5), 643–57.

Leydesdorff, L. and M. Meyer (2006), 'Triple Helix indicators of knowledge-based innovation systems: introduction to the special issue', *Research Policy*, **35** (10), 1441–9.

Lööf, H. and A. Heshmati (2002), 'Knowledge capital and performance heterogeneity: a firm-level innovation study', *International Journal of Production Economics*, **76** (1), 61–85.

Lundvall, B.-A. (1988), 'Innovation as an interactive process: from user-producer interaction to the national system of innovation', in G. Dosi, C. Freeman, R.R. Nelson, G. Silverberg and L. Soete (eds), *Technology and Economic Theory*, London: Pinter Publishers, pp. 349–69.

Malecki, E. (1997), *Technology & Economic Development: The Dynamics of Local, Regional and National Competitiveness*, 2nd edn, Amsterdam: Addison Wesley.

Markman, G., P.T. Gianiodis, P.H. Phan and D. Balkin (2005), 'Innovation speed, transferring university technology to market', *Research Policy*, **34**, 1058–75.

Molle, W. (2006), *Economics of European Integration: Theory, Practice, Policy*, 5th edn, Aldershot: Ashgate.

Molle, W. (2007), *European Cohesion Policy*, London: Routledge.

Morgan, K. (1997), 'The learning region: institutions, innovation and regional renewal', *Regional Studies*, **31** (5), 491–503.

Morgan, K. and C. Nauwelaers (eds) (2003), *Regional Innovation Strategies: The Challenge for Less Favoured Regions*, Regional Development and Public Policy Series 24, London: RSA.

Nauwelaers, C. and R. Wintjes (eds) (2008), *Innovation Policy in Europe: Measurement and Strategy*, Cheltenham, UK and Northampton, MA, USA: Edward Elgar.

Nelson, R.R. (1988), 'Institutions supporting technical change in the United States', in G. Dosi, C. Freeman, R.R. Nelson, G. Silverberg and L. Soete (eds), *Technology and Economic Theory*, London: Pinter Publishers, pp. 312–29.

Nelson, R.R. (ed.) (1993), *National Innovation Systems: A Comparative Analysis*, Oxford: Oxford University Press.

NESTA (2007), 'Innovation policy in the modern world: five big challenges', Policy Briefing, National Endowment for Science Technology and the Arts.

OECD (1997a), *National Innovation Systems*, Paris: OECD.

OECD (1997b), *Industrial Competitiveness in the Knowledge-based Economy: The Role of Governments*, Paris: OECD.

OECD (2001), *The New Economy: Beyond the Hype*, Paris: OECD.

O'Shea, R., T.J. Allen, C. O'Gorman and F. Roche (2004), 'Universities and technology transfer: a review of academic entrepreneurship literature', *Irish Journal of Management*, **25** (2), 11–29.

Peterson, J. and M. Sharp (1998), *Technology policy in the European Union*, Basingstoke: Macmillan.

Pinay, F., B. Surlemont and F. Nlemvo (2003), 'Toward a typology of university spin-offs', *Small Business Economics*, **21** (4), 355–69.

Read, A. (2000), 'Determinants of successful organisational innovation: a review of current research', *Journal of Management Practice*, **3** (1), 95–119.

Ritsilä, J.J. (1999), 'Regional differences in environments for enterprises', *Entrepreneurship & Regional Development*, **11**, 187–202.

Rodríguez-Pose, A. and R. Crescenzi (2006), 'R&D, spillovers, innovation systems and the genesis of regional growth in Europe', BEER paper, 5, available from http://www.coleurop.be/eco/publications.htm.

Rubalcaba, L. (2007), *The New Service Economy*, Cheltenham, UK and Northampton, MA, USA: Edward Elgar.

Saviotti, P.P. (2007), 'On the dynamics of generation and utilization of knowledge: the local character of knowledge', *Structural Change and Economic Dynamics*, **18**, 387–408.

Schumpeter, J. (1934), *The Theory of Economic Development: An Inquiry into Profits, Capital, Credit, Interest and the Business Cycle*, Cambridge, MA: Harvard University Press.

Shinn, T. and E. Lamy (2006), 'Paths of commercial knowledge: forms and consequences of university enterprise synergy in scientist-sponsored firms', *Research Policy*, **35**, 1465–76.

Simmie, J., J. Sennett, P. Wood and D. Hart (2002), 'Innovation in Europe: a tale of networks, knowledge and trade in five cities', *Regional Studies*, **36** (1), 47–64.

Spithoven, A. and P. Teirlinck (eds)(2005), *Beyond Borders: Internationalisation of R&D and Policy Implications for Small Open Economies*, Amsterdam: Elsevier.

Stadler, M. (1999), 'Demand pull and technology push effects in the quality ladder model', Tübinger Diskussionsbeitrag 172.

Storey, D.J. and B.S. Tether (1998), 'Public policy measures to support new technology-based firms in the European Union', *Research Policy*, **26**, 1037–57.

Storper, M. (1995), 'The resurgence of regional economies, ten years later: the region as nexus of untraded interdependencies', *European Urban and Regional Studies*, **2** (3), 191–221.

Vicente, M.R. and A.J. Lopez (2006), 'Patterns of ICT diffusion across the European Union', *Economic Letters*, **93**, 45–51.

Von Hippel, E. (1988), *The Sources of Innovation*, Oxford: Oxford University Press.

Wright, M., A. Vohara and A. Lockett (2004), 'The formation of high tech university spinouts: the role of joint ventures and venture capital investors', *Journal of Technology Transfer*, **29** (3/4), 287–310.

Wright, M., A. Lockett, B. Clarysse and M. Binks (2006), 'University spin-out companies and venture capital', *Research Policy*, **35**, 481–501.

Wright, M., B. Clarysse, P. Mustar and A. Lockett (2007), *Academic Entrepreneurship in Europe*, Cheltenham, UK and Northampton, MA, USA: Edward Elgar.

PART I

R&D

2. Creating wealth from university know-how: the role of technostarters*

Hans Wissema

INTRODUCTION

As the growth of Western economies is based increasingly on knowledge-based enterprises, the role of universities as sources of new technology-based firms has recently gained much attention. Although the phenomenon of technostarters – students or academics who start their own, technology-based firm – dates from the early nineteenth century, the subject has gained wide attention since the beginning of the age of information technology that saw the rise of new multinationals such as Microsoft, Intel, Dell, Google, Skype and many others.

The structure of this chapter is as follows. We first define the subject and its economic relevance. Next we describe several role models for universities that create technostarters. Third, we describe how universities can actively support technostarters. We round off the chapter with some conclusions.

DEFINING THE SUBJECT

Meet the Technostarters

Technostarters are students or academics who establish their own science- or technology-based firm. They are people who take initiative and who are willing to take responsibility and risk (e.g. Kuemmerle, 2002). They are optimistic, subscribing to the phrase attributed to Walt Disney: 'This goes to prove that nothing is impossible if you just put your mind to it.' They are walking learning-organisations, networkers who learn from others and from introspection, analysing their own progress. They have the instinct to spot combinations between technical possibilities and (latent) market

Table 2.1   Reasons why people want to be self-employed

I want to take responsibility for my own future	53%
I relish the challenge of going it alone	52%
I want to be my own boss	48%
I have a unique idea	43%
I want to make more money	28%
I am unhappy in my job	19%
I want flexible working hours	8%
I am unemployed	6%

Source: Shell LiveWire (2004).

needs. They have organisational talents and they are good recruiters; they can be charismatic as well as critical leaders and they have the skills to form a team (Richard, 2005). The dream of many technostarters is to lead their own life rather than be employed. Technostarters are passionate people; they are dreamers who do (Pinchot, 1985).

Technostarters often originate from universities, mostly from universities of technology and science; from medical faculties of general universities and from agricultural universities. Corporate R&D departments and independent research organisations also act as cradles for technostarters.

We may assume that the vast majority of technostarters fall into the category of so-called opportunity entrepreneurs (see next section). This assumption is supported by the results of an investigation (see Table 2.1) concerning the reasons why people want to be self-employed (which of course is not the same as being a technostarter).

The outcome reported above fits with the general observation that people in general, and students in particular, are more individualistic and more willing to take risks now than they were in the past. Forty per cent of the alumni of INSEAD, a Paris-based business school, sooner or later start their own enterprise. Twenty per cent of MIT graduates start their own business. Only 6 per cent of Harvard Business School graduates go on to work in large enterprises, a fact that has made the school trade their General Management Course, which it had run for 80 years, for an Entrepreneurship Course in 2000. The entrepreneurship electives are the most subscribed to at the University of Cambridge, UK. Making money is no longer considered a negative attribute. For a long time, self-enrichment was looked down upon in Europe and Asia, and entrepreneurs were not generally encouraged. In the American culture of 'unlimited opportunities', however, people would look proudly at successful entrepreneurs, with the idea that 'If he can do it, so can I'. It seems that this attitude is spreading over the world. The more liberal attitude towards entrepreneurship is not limited to Western cultures or affluent countries. In an interview, Mr Sunil Mittal, the founder and chairman of the Bharti Group in India and the uncrowned 'India's king of telecoms', notes: 'In India, businessmen were always looked down on. The view was that these guys cheat on taxes and make profits by sucking money from the poor. We were never given credit' (Ridding, 2005, p. w3). The change, he believes, has been gathering pace since the early 1990s, when a reformist economic team embarked on a policy of liberalisation in India. 'Wealth creation is being celebrated. People are coming out of colleges saying "I don't want to be a bureaucrat, I want to be an entrepreneur" and people like me are giving them hope that it can be done' (ibid.).

So, entrepreneurship is *in* all over the world, in the USA, in Europe, Asia and Latin America. We believe that this attitude is stimulated by many large corporations that offer programmes to help technostarters create their own company. To give some examples: Royal Dutch Shell has the successful LiveWire programme for external technostarters and its GameChanger programme for internal entrepreneurs. DSM offers a wide range of facilities on its research campus in Geleen, the Netherlands. Philips Electronics has created an incubator on its High Tech Campus in Eindhoven, the Netherlands, where technostarters can share the extensive facilities this campus offers. This list can be extended with a multitude of other examples. Large corporations open up their R&D facilities with the aim of sharing knowledge with other companies (even competitors), selling know-how and supporting starters. Universities follow this trend, albeit hesitatingly in most countries.

The Impact of Technostarters

Link between start-ups and growth

Since 1997, an international group of researchers, led by scholars from Babson College in Massachusetts and the London Business School in the UK, has tried to map entrepreneurial activities in 34 countries (Acs et al., 2005). The resulting Global Entrepreneurship Monitoring (GEM) reports not only provide interesting statistical data, but also analyse the relationships between entrepreneurial activity and national economic growth. To this end, the GEM reports define the total entrepreneurial activity (TEA) as the percentage of adults (18–64 years of age) who are active as starting entrepreneurs or managing a young business of which they are also an owner, divided by the total workforce. The outcome of the 2004 survey is that in the workforce of the countries investigated (566 million) there are 73 million entrepreneurs (total population between 18 and 64 years of age in these countries was 784 million). The average TEA level in these countries comes to 9 per cent, with variations between countries from 2 per cent (Japan) to 40 per cent (Peru). The TEA percentage was 11 per cent for the USA, 6 per cent for the UK and 4 per cent for Germany. The GEM report 2004 concludes that in the sample researched, 65 per cent of the entrepreneurs are 'opportunity entrepreneurs' (that is, driven to exploit a perceived business opportunity) while 35 per cent are 'necessity entrepreneurs' (driven by the absence of other (satisfactory) employment opportunities). According to the report, men are twice as likely to start a new enterprise as women. Most entrepreneurial activity is carried out by 25- to 34-year-olds, regardless of the level of income in the countries. It will be no surprise that these percentages vary widely between countries.

The TEA index is an aggregated compound that does not say anything about the number of starters, let alone technostarters. The GEM report 2004 notes that only 3 per cent of all start-ups qualify as 'business with high potential', defined as 'those that expect to have few competitors, intend to bring innovations to the market, and use state-of-the-art technology'.

This definition comes as close to technostarters as can be measured statistically. However, it includes both 'nascent entrepreneurs' (people in the process of starting a new business in the year of consideration) and also 'young companies', defined as 'led by owner-managers of a firm that has paid wages or salaries for more than 3 months, but less than 42 months'. Unfortunately, the reports give no data that distinguish between these categories. Nevertheless, the number of technostarters and 'technostarted' entrepreneurs number roughly 2.2 million in the 34 countries investigated or – even more roughly – almost 3 per cent of the adult population. That means that technostarters are not a marginal phenomenon; there are simply a lot of them. Surprised by the absence of studies on the economic effects of entrepreneurial activities in mainstream economics, the investigators from the GEM team tried to establish the link between entrepreneurial activity and economic growth at the country level (Stel et al., 2005). By linking the GEM variable of TEA to economic growth, they conclude that the TEA rate correlates negatively with economic growth for the relatively poor countries while it correlates positively for the relatively rich countries. The reason for this unexpected result may be that technostarters make only a small contribution to the TEA index, and a high TEA index in poor countries indicates a lack of larger enterprises, with the small enterprises rarely having growth potential.

The MIT example
Technostarters render an indispensable contribution to the economy by creating new employment of a high level. This employment should

offset the loss of mass-production-based employment. At a rough count, the world needs one million start-ups per year to offset the loss of jobs in mature companies. In addition, in the period 2003–08 two million entrepreneurs will be needed for reducing unemployment (Twaalfhoven, 2002). The effect that technostarters can have in the creation of wealth and employment was first brought to light by the now legendary 'BankBoston Report' (Economics Department of BankBoston, 1997). This study stated that if the companies founded by MIT graduates and faculty had formed an independent nation, the revenues produced by the companies would have made that nation the 24th-largest economy in the world. The 4000 MIT-related companies (located worldwide) that existed in 1997 employed 1.1 million people and had annual world sales of $232 billion. That was roughly equal to a GDP of $116 billion, which is comparable to the 1996 GDP of South Africa or Thailand. The study found that MIT 'imports' entrepreneurs, as many companies were not spin-outs of the university, but rather company founders who came to Massachusetts to benefit from the presence of MIT. The MIT-related companies are not typical for the economy as a whole: they tend to be knowledge-based companies active in software, manufacturing (electronics, biotech, instruments, machinery) or consulting (architects, business consultants, engineers) businesses. Firms involved in software, electronics and biotechnology are at the cutting edge of technology. They are more likely to expand and export while they need a workforce of skilled professionals. About 150 new MIT-related companies are founded each year. In the MIT sample, there are only 106 companies with 1000 or more employees, and these companies generate nearly 90 per cent of the jobs. There are 17 companies with 10 000 employees or more, including Hewlett-Packard, Rockwell International, Raytheon Co., McDonnell Douglas, Digital Equipment Co., Texas Instruments, Campbell Soup, Gillette, Intel and National Semiconductor (some of these companies have merged with others; only six of the 17 companies had their headquarters in Massachusetts). The BankBoston Report showed the vast economic benefits that a high-level university of technology can bring to a region and to the economy in general. It is no surprise that other regions have studied MIT (and similar experiences at Stanford University) and have tried to copy their success. The message is: strong universities can create impressive amounts of wealth, not only for the region, but also for the national and even global economy.

> Job creation is not an objective by itself. We have to understand that it is only with new products that we can participate in the international competition. Because of the open markets and globalisation, we will rarely produce mass-products in this country (Germany) . . . More economic growth can only be

created by innovation, and growth will translate itself into more jobs . . . Many enterprises have gone bankrupt because of their single emphasis on mastering the cost spiral . . . We will always be an expensive country. Therefore we have to get back to the front line of technical progress.

These statements, made by Ludolf von Wartenberg, President of the Bundesverband der Deutschen Industrie[1] (Germany's main employers' association) characterise the dilemma of most Western countries. Mass production is shifting to East Europe and Asia, creating a need for new, innovative and high-added-value production in the older industrial states. Von Wartenberg adds that this is a slow process. Although the major part of any new innovative business will have to come from established enterprises, many look at technostarters to fill the gap in economic activity and job creation.[2] All over the world, an impressive range of government- or EU-supported programmes is being launched;[3] these are aimed at stimulating technostarters to create new companies, especially in areas where the loss of employment in mass production is severe.[4]

THE CAMBRIDGE PHENOMENON

The Old Model: Spontaneous Emergence of a Cluster

Encouraged by the successes of MIT and Silicon Valley, the hubs of IT companies,[5] universities the world over are creating courses in entrepreneurship and facilities to help technostarters establish companies. In Europe, the focus is on Cambridge, UK. Thanks to the emergence of a substantial high-tech industry, the county of Cambridgeshire was transformed from one of England's poorest areas into its second richest. This extraordinary change occurred as a result of a strong interactive process between businesses and the University of Cambridge. Some time ago the University embarked on a modernisation process aimed at keeping it among the world's top universities. It was stimulated by private initiative to create and support new technology-based enterprises. The two transformations together resulted in what is commonly called the Cambridge Phenomenon.

Cambridge can trace its spin-out activities back to companies such as Cambridge Instruments, established in 1881 by Horace Darwin (Charles Darwin's son) and Pye Radio, founded in 1896 with links to Cambridge's Cavendish Laboratory. Just after the Second World War, other firms started to exploit the developments in electronics that occurred during the war. Cambridge then was a rural place with no other industry. In 1970, there were some 20 firms located there. Shortly after that, a new wave of enterprises emerged: ARC, Sinclair, Acorn Computers and others. In 1983, Cambridge was one of the three clusters of new industrial activity in the UK, the others being west of London and central Scotland (see Box 2.1).

BOX 2.1   THE BASIC COMPONENTS OF THE CAMBRIDGE MODEL

Several hundred small, high-technology firms around Cambridge have thrived on inventive people and ideas, many from the university. Cambridge was the first university in Britain – as Stanford was in America – to attract high-technology firms to a science park. Most recruits were from the mathematics and computer departments and from a government-funded computer-aided design centre where engineers, tired of wrangling about money, left to found their own firms . . . In Cambridge, the electronics manufacturer Pye was the local version of Silicon Valley's Fairchild: it had plenty of clever, disgruntled engineers who left for smaller firms. Commercial research laboratories also bred entrepreneurs: more than 20 companies having been formed by people leaving Cambridge Consultants, founded in 1960 by three alumni who returned to Cambridge after having served in World War II. Among its spin-offs was a second contract research laboratory set up with management consultant firm PA, which also became a nursery for entrepreneurs.[6]

Source: Editorial in *The Economist* (1983).[7]

In 1987 there were some 360 companies operating in Cambridge, many of them created by or from the consultancies that were founded in the 1960s with the objective of 'putting the brains of Cambridge University at the disposal of the problems of British industry'. The consultancies included Cambridge Consultants, PA Technology, Scientific Generics, Analysis and TTP. Cambridge is a networking hub and that network of personal relationships provides a safety net for start-ups that fail (Pesola, 2005). Some people call it the innovation and entrepreneurial 'ecosystem' (*The Economist*, 2004). The Cambridge experience shows that it is the serial entrepreneur that has the greatest impact (Vyakarnam et al., 2005). Right now, there are some 3000 high-tech industries in the 'Cambridge Technopole' (the area around Cambridge and the name of an informally organised network). These have created direct employment for about

60 000 people (indirect employment is about twice that); 98 per cent of these new companies are there because of the university, although only 10 per cent have been initiated by the university itself. In addition, many large international firms have operations or R&D activities in the area, including Philips, Microsoft, Motorola, Nokia, Novartis and many others.

The University of Cambridge as an institution was not involved in these activities. Cambridge was and still is a typical research university, collecting selected academics and students from all over the world. It has the highest number of Nobel Laureates (81 as of 2006) in the world and it has an incredible history. Newton and Darwin pioneered their theories in Cambridge; Rutherford split the first atom there (in the Cavendish Laboratory, still there, and amazingly small); Crick and Watson discovered the DNA double-helix structure. It is not surprising that commerce was anathema to such a university:

> Sir Clive Sinclair, whose company does much of its research in Cambridge, says attitudes towards business could not be more different than when he arrived in 1967. British prejudice against wealth creation lives on, even in Cambridge. The lack of a single business management course at the university is absolutely pathetic.[8]

Despite being a medium-sized university with 11 000 undergraduate and 4500 graduate students, 3800 academic and research staff, and 2700 support staff (figures from 2000), Cambridge covers a full range of faculties and specialisations in the arts and sciences, including academic hospital facilities at Addenbrooke's Hospital. The University of Cambridge has preserved its medieval structure, meaning that most students and staff members are incorporated in independent colleges through which the students get extra tuition in addition to housing and catering facilities. Colleges sometimes act as initiators of new scientific and other programmes financed by endowments. They also act as a link between the university staff and industrial researchers who work in the region. High-flying researchers from Microsoft's Cambridge team were, for instance, invited to be fellows of the colleges and thereby drawn into the academic community.[9]

The New Model: Active Involvement of the University

In the 1990s the university started its modernisation programme. In 1991 it appointed its first full-time vice-chancellor, i.e. the president of the university; previously the position was filled by the master of one of the colleges on a part-time basis for a period of two years. The second full-time vice-chancellor, Sir Alec Broers (vice-chancellor from 1996 to 2003; now

Lord Broers), began collaborating with industry on a large scale. Concerns about academic freedom were replaced by the view that cooperation with industry was an essential part of the development strategy of the university, both for scientific as well as financial reasons. Maintaining a leading role in research required far more funding than the government was willing to provide:

> funding from the UK research councils was felt by some of the leading scientists to be insufficiently strategic, overly egalitarian, risk aversive and short term. They will seldom, if ever, fund even eminent researchers outside their established fields, whereas industry may well be prepared to do so and, equally importantly, reach a quick decision.[10]

The collaboration with industry was favoured by the fact that high-tech enterprises started outsourcing their fundamental research activities in order to reduce their in-house research efforts. Indeed, the 1990s saw a sharp decline in such in-house research activities. A typical outcome was the combination of donations with so-called embedded research in which a team of researchers from an industrial firm co-locate with researchers from the university. The University of Cambridge has embedded research agreements with Microsoft, Glaxo, Rolls Royce, Hoechst, Hitachi, Toshiba, SmithKline Beecham, Unilever, BP Amoco, Seiko and others. Interdisciplinary research became more important, for instance in a new chair in medical materials in which the Medical School, Veterinary School, the Department of Engineering and the Institute of Biotechnology cooperate.

While the collaboration with industry gained speed, the university successfully bid for a host of new government grants, benefiting from its experience and reputation (the system did not hand out money proportionally to all universities, but was based on competitive bids and letting the best bids win. One fund gave ten universities £100 million and the other 121 universities £10 million between them).

When Gordon Brown became Chancellor of the Exchequer (Minister of Finance) in 1997, he initiated a government White Paper[11] stating that 'the ability to turn scientific discoveries into successful commercial products and processes is vital in the knowledge-driven economy'. This statement is of historic significance, because it made 'transfer of technology to the community' the third formal objective of institutes of higher education, next to research and education.

The White Paper also announced a range of measures including the creation of Higher Education Innovation Fund (HEIF) and later the Higher Education Reach-Out to Business and the Community Fund (HEROBC) to enhance the links between higher education and business

– all financed by the Treasury. With these funds, eight entrepreneurship centres were created, one at the University of Cambridge. In addition, money was allocated to establish seed funds (university challenge funds) and technology transfer offices. In 1999, Cambridge University merged its Entrepreneurship Centre with its Challenge Fund, its Corporate Liaison Office and its Technology Transfer Office, creating a new entity: Cambridge Enterprise. Cambridge Enterprise was and is to provide for incubation, seed funding and teaching. It administers the intellectual property rights (IPR) of the university through Cambridge University Technical Services Ltd and acts as the vehicle for commercial activities related to IP. As such, it concludes licensing agreements and helps create new enterprises, whether based on the university's IP or otherwise.

The establishment of Cambridge Enterprise followed earlier activities. These are detailed below:

- *Cambridge Science Park* was established by Trinity College in 1970, on land given to the college by Henry VIII in 1546. It was the first science park in the UK and now houses some 71 high-tech enterprises that employ some 5000 people. Cambridge Science Park also began to accommodate spin-outs from tenant companies such as Cambridge Consultants. The initiative was followed by the establishment of private technology parks such as Babraham Bioincubator, Granta Park, Melbourn Science Park, Peterhouse Technology Park and Cambridge Research Park (Herriot and Minshall, 2003).
- *St John's Innovation Centre* was established by St John's College in 1987 for early-stage knowledge-based companies. It was the first business incubator in the UK. It offers accommodation, shared facilities such as conference rooms and a restaurant. Advice on business issues is free. The centre organises programmes with university departments and government bodies, and gives assistance in gaining access to funding through the Business Angel Network and venture capital funds. The centre now houses some 65 companies employing over 500 people. Over a five-year period the survival rate for companies is close to 90 per cent, compared to about 50 per cent for other similar businesses in the Cambridge area, and 45 per cent for businesses generally in the UK. In and around Cambridge there are now well-established groups of· business angels such as Cambridge Angels, Cambridge Capital Group and the Choir of Angels, meeting platforms such as Great Eastern Investment Forum, and research and data service companies such as Library House.

- In 1990 the *Judge Management School* was established, following an initial donation and expanding as further donations were received. A successful bid for government funding helped create the Centre for Entrepreneurial Learning in 2003; this currently gives some 30 courses on entrepreneurship a year, including a course that helps technostarters write their business plan and establish their company. With government support, the management school established collaboration with MIT on education, research, faculty exchange and post-experience programmes, including programmes in innovation and entrepreneurship. Another major event in the context of this chapter was the establishment of the Institute for Manufacturing with research and educational activities at the engineering–management interface.

- *The Cambridge Technopole Group* acts as an informal network of business support organisations with the aim of improving the range and quality of such organisations with a focus on technology-based firms. The success of the Cambridge Phenomenon is not so much a top-down, centralised approach, but rather a 'constructive chaos and a sense of community and collaboration' (Herriot and Minshall, 2003). An essential element is the fact that the university leaves much of the IPR to academics and students. This stimulates academics to set up new enterprises – one professor is said to have made £250 million – from which the university benefits in return.[12] The idea of entrepreneurship is very much supported by students, who established Cambridge University Entrepreneurs (CUE) as 'A passionate student organisation created to inspire and educate, and to facilitate the creation of real businesses from the university. This is mainly achieved through the organisation and running of various business plan competitions (BPC)' (see www.cue.org.uk).

What Have We Learned?

In conclusion we can say that the Cambridge Phenomenon was not designed, it emerged. Only at a later stage was it deliberately supported by the university, the colleges and the local administrations. There were three interacting stages: the development of a community of high-tech enterprises; the process of modernisation of the university; and the development of technostarter facilities.

- The development of a community of high-tech enterprises is the spontaneous creation of new technology-based firms that benefit from proximity to the university. They were created either by academics and (former) students or by companies that moved in from other areas, including international enterprises. Their emergence or arrival provided a dynamic environment, common to the early stages of the era of the Industrial Revolution, in which employees leave their companies in order to start their own.[13]

- The modernisation of the university started from the realisation that traditional ways of financing would be insufficient to stay at the leading edge of science and technology. The ambition to stay in the premier league, combined with a strong vision and leadership, could move the university beyond the age-old tradition of value-free, pure science into an era where the university creates value to society and starts cooperating with industry.

- Finally, the development of technostarter facilities was initiated by some of the university's colleges, later supported by government grants. Private capital moved in as business angels and venture capital funds. The result is a rich and varied range of incubators, shared accommodation facilities, financiers, and all kinds of professional support.

The three streams together have created a sustainable cluster for innovation and entrepreneurship and an entrepreneurial culture, the critical success factors of which are given in Box 2.2.

BOX 2.2   SUCCESS FACTORS FOR THE CREATION OF AN INNOVATION CLUSTER

1. *You need exemplars*, local heroes who have pioneered the way and shown it can be done without putting your home or family at risk, people the starter can associate with.
2. *It must be acceptable to fail.* Many US venture capitalists will not invest unless the founders of the company have failed before. It is part of their education as an entrepreneur. Sometimes one can have a soft start – using, for example, a sabbatical break or a period of part time work to test starting a company, and if it doesn't work returning to the academic treadmill. It is also easier to spin out in a growing economy and high skill employment demand, since if it doesn't work it is easier to find another job.
3. *The job of setting up a company should be within the reach*

of what an individual or small team can do. That means for example that local support of all kinds should be available that truly understand and are sympathetic to new companies. The starter needs to be able to get whatever is required to get his or her enterprise going: funding, broadband connectivity, people, liquid helium etcetera, with a minimum of fuss and delay so that they can concentrate on the core business problems like technical development and sales.

4. *Starting a business must be compatible with one's lifestyle.* The starter should not need to lose their soul or put their family at risk. Part of this is societal acceptance but there are also more practical things such as loan guarantee schemes, mortgage and rates holidays, childcare facilities, late night shopping etcetera.

5. *The rewards need to be there.* Measures here include suitable tax incentives and sensible IPR policies, either from an employer or academia. If the university insists on a major cut of any exploitation of the research they did at the university, the incentive for them to work hard and spinout a company is much reduced. The game has to be worthwhile

Source: Jack Lang, entrepreneur in residence at the Centre for Entrepreneurial Learning and business angel.[14]

Note that it took Cambridge 30 years to establish the cluster and that many people have made a great deal of effort to get it going. The driving forces were the university's outspoken desire to remain a top establishment for the development of science and technology, and many private (and college) initiatives to create high-tech enterprises linked to the university's rich sources of science and technology.

LEUVEN – THE OTHER ROLE MODEL

Cambridge, with its top-down orchestrated collaboration with large, technology-driven enterprises and its bottom-up activities concerning techno-starters, is but one role model for universities that want to turn themselves into what we have called a know-how hub, defined as:

the synergistic combination of traditional academic research and education, R&D institutes of enterprises, independent (often specialised) R&D centres, facilities for technostarters, financiers of many kinds and professional services of many kinds (accountants, management consultants, marketing consultants, intellectual property specialists and so on) that collaborate in the creation and exploitation of know-how, preferably on the grounds of the university or near it. (Wissema, 2009: 232)

Such a know-how hub is Eldorado for entrepreneuring students and academics, as well as for those who want to pursue deep science. Many universities pursue a role as a centre of a know-how hub and that implies an active role of the university.

As a role model for a more top-down approach – contrasting with the mainly bottom-up approach of Cambridge – we would like to suggest the Catholic University of Leuven (KU Leuven) in Belgium (Debackere, 2000), set up with ample funds from the regional government. In 1972, this university established KU Leuven Research and Development (KUL R&D), as an organisation responsible for the commercialisation of the university's know-how, either by licensing or by establishing new ventures. It owns and manages the property rights. With KBC and Fortis, two commercial banks, it has set up the two Gemma Frisius investment funds of €12 million each (the banks hold 40 per cent each in these funds and the university 20 per cent) as the business angel; the venture capital structure was far less developed in Leuven than it was in Cambridge. The position of KUL R&D is stronger than that of Cambridge Enterprise as Leuven always and fully owns the university's IPR (see Looy et al., n.d.). KUL R&D supports itself by retaining 8 per cent of revenues. The university gets another 8 per cent and the rest is shared by the department and individual researchers, who can receive up to 50 per cent of revenues.

KU Leuven has incorporated 'service to the community' as its third objective (next to teaching and research). To give effect to this objective it has taken a series of initiatives, as listed below:

- *Science parks* The Haasrode Science Park, for example, is a 120-hectare site that houses several dozens of university spin-offs and international high-tech firms that together employ some 5000 people. Haasrode includes a business incubator with office space for 70 companies and the Business Centre, a shared accommodation centre that houses not only IT companies, but also multi-media, communication and industrial coating firms, human resource bureaux, import/export firms, a print shop and a translation bureau. The Arenberg Science Park offers 90 000 m² of working space and the Termunck Science Park 120 000 m² and 35 hectares of land. Two more centres are being prepared in former company offices, the Ubicenter and Campus Remy.

- *Specialised centres* Perhaps the most impressive creation of KU Leuven is IMEC (Interuniversity MicroElectronics Centre), which claims to be Europe's leading independent research centre in the field of microelectronics, nanotechnology, enabling design methods and technologies for ICT systems. Founded in 1984 by the legendary Professor R. van Overstraeten, it carries out pre-competitive research with virtually all the world's major ICT corporations, which can also use the facilities for their own research. IMEC's research budget was €230 million in 2006 with €35 million coming from government grants and the remainder from industries such as Intel, Samsung, Philips, ASML and ASMI. These companies expect the research component of the cost price of electronic devices to go up to 40 per cent of revenue in 2020. In addition, the semi-conductor industry is going through a transition phase, incorporating nanotechnology and transdisciplinary research. These factors make collaboration more a necessity than an add-on, and this explains the interest of these enterprises. IMEC offers many services. In addition to the facilities mentioned, it gives many courses and seminars; its population is highly international.
- *Networks* Finally, KU Leuven operates a number of high-tech networks, including DSP Valley (DSP is digital signal processing), the Leuven Security Excellence Consortium and others. For ambitious students it is paradise.

HOW TO SUPPORT TECHNOSTARTERS?

The Four Flow Model

In the previous sections we have seen that technostarters can provide a strong stimulus to growth. We have given two examples of universities that are successful in promoting technostarters. Can these successes be reproduced elsewhere? Can we indicate the ways in which universities stimulate the emergence and growth of technostarters?

We would postulate that a good supply of four kinds of 'raw materials' (Figure 2.1) is required in order to create a successful university 'factory' for new technology-based firms (NTBFs); we have called this the four flow model.[15]

Before we move on to a more detailed description of each of the four flows, note that if any of the four flows is lacking, the 'factory' will not

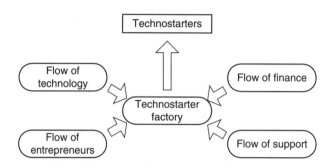

Figure 2.1   The four flows of 'raw materials'

work, however well the other flows have been organised. Many attempts by universities to create technostart facilities fail because an organisation to attract financiers is missing or because the flow of support lacks vital elements. The winners in this game are those who have it all. Let us now look at the four flows in more detail.

The flow of technology
The need for technology (know-how) is self-evident as one cannot create new technology-based firms (NTBFs) without new technology. Traditional universities regard the commercialisation of know-how and the creation of NTBFs as a side-effect rather than an objective. University researchers and inventors regard a publication or patent as the end-result of the research project. Much know-how that could have been commercialised therefore never reaches the market. The creation of a flow of technology on which NTBFs can be established requires a change in the mind-set of the academic. Right now, researchers can spot a publishable piece of research, as carried out by students for instance, at a great distance, and they are motivated to put time into the conversion of a thesis into a publication. They can also identify a potentially successful PhD student if they see one. Academics should develop a similar instinct for spotting commercialisation options for their research. This can start even before the actual research begins, as the research project can be redesigned to serve a scientific as well as a commercial purpose. The extra effort to serve two objectives is usually relatively small. In any case, the idea that a research project is not finished until the two questions:

● Have the results been properly published and patented?
● Have the options for commercialisation been charted?

have both been answered must become part of the DNA structure of every single researcher, implanted during early scientific training.

Apart from this change in culture, the university should also give researchers who are the cradle of a spin-out a financial incentive. This incentive may benefit the individual researcher, the section he or she is part of, or – preferably – both. If there is no financial reward, then there is no incentive to compensate for the hassle inevitably involved in transferring know-how to a spin-out. Some inventors want to keep an active role in the spin-out; others just want to throw the idea over the wall to others. Both options should be respected and for each an appropriate reward scheme should be designed. If the researcher or inventor is to play an active role in the new venture, then it is logical that he or she should be awarded free shares in the enterprise.

The flow of entrepreneurs
It is also self-evident that new companies cannot be created without entre-preneurs. In the case of technostarters, the student or academic is himself the entrepreneur, as it is s/he who takes the initiative to start the company. In the case of university spin-outs, the university has to recruit a CEO with entrepreneurial qualities who will be able to get the new venture off the ground. Note that technostarters may need to recruit a CEO different from the founder(s) as not all founders/entrepreneurs are the best CEOs for the newly created firm. Different stages of the development of a firm require different types of leader (Greiner, 1972; see also Penrose, 1959; Kor and Mahoney, 2000 and the literature cited therein), and only in rare instances will the original entrepreneur manage to transform himself into the ideal leader for the next stage. Even when the entrepreneur decides to hand over the leadership of the firm to an appointed CEO, this CEO will have to have strong entrepreneurial capabilities, certainly in the early phases of the enterprise. So, whatever the ownership position or whoever takes the initiative, enterprises need entrepreneurs to get them off the ground, and the question is: how to motivate potential entrepreneurs?

Only a few students enter a university with the explicit aim of finding a subject to study with which they start their own enterprise. The same applies to academics. Most students have to become aware of the option to become an entrepreneur by what we will call the funnel model, meaning a programme comprising of a number of stages in which the entrepreneurial intent increases after each stage while the number of students decreases (Figure 2.2).

'Awareness' and 'education' are the buzz-words to get the flow of entre-preneurs moving. The programmes can be partly followed by students or academics who have not yet chosen a subject for their new enterprise

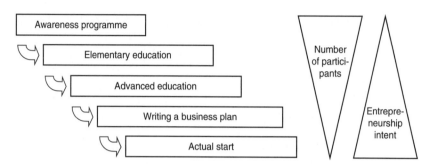

Figure 2.2   The funnel model to create a flow of entrepreneurs

and they can be matched with opportunities created by others at a later stage.

The flow of finance
Many technostarters and, indeed, many universities underestimate the flow of finance as a critical factor for success. The success of Silicon Valley as a know-how hub for information and communication technology (ICT) is as much due to the presence of a variety of financial offers as it is to know-how, generated to a great extent at Stanford University. Such know-how was also available in other places, but Silicon Valleys did not develop there because of the lack of this variety of financing sources.

As it develops, a start-up needs an increasing amount of money. We need an insight into this process if we are to design tools for university-driven technostarters. There are many ways of characterising the development phases of a new firm and, compromising between literature and practical experience, we use the following (Figure 2.3; cf. Van Osnabrugge and Robinson, 2000):

1. *Design or pre-seed phase*   For technostarters as well as spin-outs, this phase includes attempts to design the product or service and to check out its feasibility by addressing the market and finally writing a business plan. There is not yet a commitment to go ahead with the enterprise and the design phase is usually playful in nature. The entrepreneurs need little money at this stage. They study on a grant or the university employs them and they don't yet need an income from the company. Their technical design is part of their university project, and hence paid for by the university. The money they need is for business cards, a website, expenses, IP research, acquiring some indications about the market, etc. The design phase carries a very high risk as it

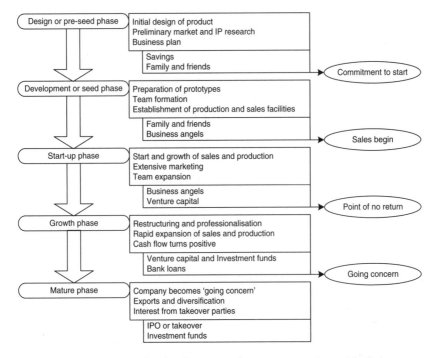

Figure 2.3   Phases in the development of a new enterprise, with their activities, ways of financing and transition points

is still uncertain whether the firm can go ahead. It ends with a firm decision to do so.

2. *Development or seed phase*   During this phase, a commercial prototype is developed, patent requirements are completed, marketing surveys and promotional activities such as presenting the product at an exhibition are carried out, promotional materials are prepared, time is taken for talking to launching customers. The team is recruited and office and/or production facilities are prepared. No products or services are being sold at this stage; it is still a preparatory phase but the basis is deadly serious. The risk is high as the new enterprise has not yet seriously met its market. The phase ends when regular production and sales have begun.

3. *Start-up phase*   Now the entrepreneurs have launched their product or service. Money is needed to follow up the product's introduction by carrying out marketing activities, de-bottlenecking production, setting up customer services, and hiring more people. The risk is medium or still high. This phase ends when there are clear signals that the

company is breaking through, that it has passed a point of 'no return', that 'it will make it'.

4.   *Growth phase*   We now have an early 'going concern' that is heading for growth. The company needs to reorganise itself, moving from *ad hoc*, improvised management to a more professional organisation with clearly delineated responsibilities, professional planning, professional attention to quality, procurement and logistics, plant expansion and expansion of the sales organisation. The excitement of getting the company off the ground is replaced by increasing professionalism. Money flows in but the working capital expands rapidly and investments are needed, resulting in a continued negative cash flow. Profits are rare at this stage and, if the company is in the black, the amount of profit will still be insignificant. During the growth phase, the entrepreneurs discover that now and then they have a free moment, a luxury they did not have during the previous two phases. The phase ends when the company becomes well established, the cash flow turns positive and the owners start having time to think about other things. The risks at this stage are significantly less than in the previous phases and begin to approach the normal business risks of established firms.

5.   *Mature phase*   In the mature phase the company will still be growing. It now has a good financial track record, especially one for payments from debtors, and it can finance itself, and even pay off loans. Activities concerning export, diversification and innovation of subsequent products are initiated. The mature phase can last forever but often start-ups are bought out by large enterprises.

Although the financing of the design phase can be difficult for the starters, the real problems start when they go into the development and start-up phases. Financiers are reluctant to invest in these phases. Venture capital firms usually require a track record of several years of sound financial performance (especially debtors' performance) and they usually work with larger amounts of money than are needed for the development phase. When the start-up phase has turned into the growth phase, venture capital firms or regular investment funds are more likely to enter the game. Banks will then – at last! – be willing to provide loans. Share participation from an existing firm in the same field is an option that is often used; this also brings in branch and technical know-how. When the company has matured, it can move from venture capital financing to investment funds while creating more leverage from bank loans. Alternatively, it can go public or be sold to an existing company that offers better opportunities for continued growth.

The gist of this overview is that financing in the design, growth and mature phases does not present insurmountable problems. Problems may

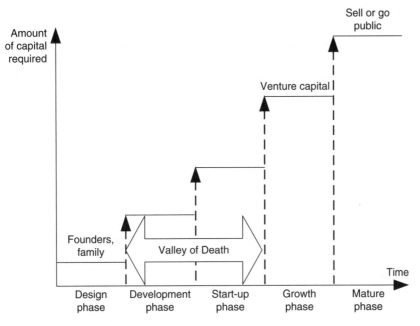

Figure 2.4   Growing capital need and different capital sources as the firm progresses

occur, however, in the development phase and, to a lesser extent, in the start-up phase. These phases are often called the Valley of Death[16] (Figure 2.4), as some potentially successful enterprises don't make it because of lack of money/water.

The Valley of Death is characterised as follows:

- More capital is needed than the founders, family and friends can provide.
- Not enough capital is needed to attract venture capital firms or investment funds.
- The risk for these and other financiers is too high to consider investment.
- Banks cannot be used as there is no collateral.
- In the development and start-up phases, the founders have to go through a process of extensive learning. They have to become entre-preneurs who know the tricks of the trade. In other words, they not only need capital, they also need training and they need to build their commercial, technical and financial networks.

The Valley of Death can be avoided by experienced entrepreneurs/investors who have a more than average knowledge of the branch the start-up is working in, as well as of enterprise generally. For them the risks are lower than for other investors as they are in a better position to judge the risks and merits of the new enterprise. If they bring in capital, branch and entrepreneurial know-how, and if they are willing to open their commercial, technical and financial networks to the start-up, we call them 'business angels' or 'informal investors'.[17] Business angels are often seasoned entrepreneurs who have sold their own company or drawn capital from it. Rather than go fishing, they enjoy putting their skills and experiences to use by financing and guiding start-ups. In this way, they can maintain their network, enjoy the satisfaction that comes with guiding young people and also make good money. For the start-up a good business angel is a blessing: the starter can work with people who have been there before. A typical example is a friend of mine who lives in San Rafael in Silicon Valley. He started an IT company in the 1970s and sold it 20 years later. He spends about 20 per cent of his capital on high-risk ventures; the rest is for his pension, as he says. He invests only in IT companies because he knows that business and the people that matter. He says he can manage only about six investments at a time. He has the management team of a new investment visit him at his home on Sunday mornings to discuss business and progress. He will join the founders/managers in important meetings with customers or other concerned parties, evaluating the team's performance afterwards. 'With the phone calls and meetings I share with them during the rest of the week, I spend about a day a week working for them', he states. He will only invest in a company if he is reasonably sure his investment will be paid back ten times over in a few years.

Informal investors are crucial to university start-ups and technostarters. But the problem is that, at least outside the USA and the UK, the concept of informal investing is only just beginning to develop, and the market between informal investors and starters is still emerging. Universities cannot wait for an informal investment culture to develop. Therefore they have to develop other means of financing start-ups – for the benefit of university spin-outs as well as for technostarters – such as establishing a commercial investment fund (see below). At the same time, they can initiate match-making sessions where start-ups can present their business plans to an audience of investors who will 'roast' them with critical questions. Such sessions can be attractive for informal investors. The university should carefully select the serious and professional informal investors who are going to put in some effort and not just money. Such investors can be registered by what can be called the Platform, a body that organises match-

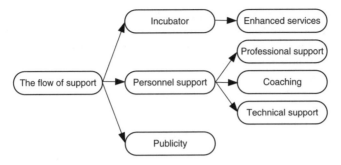

Figure 2.5   The flow of support

making sessions and that also carries out a pre-selection of start-ups that are permitted to present their business plans.

The flow of support

Last but not least is the flow of support. This is delivered in several ways, schematised in Figure 2.5. We discuss each form of support in some more detail.

Incubator facilities   There are as many definitions of 'incubators' as there are incubators (for an overview, see Adkins, 2002). Expressions such as incubator-plus and 'accelerator' are used for basic incubators with enhanced services. We define a basic incubator as an office or work space that can be rented by start-ups and technostarters on favourable terms. The rent includes heating, cleaning, power (electricity and sometimes high-voltage electricity and steam) and a high-speed network. This package can be extended by porter services, parking, security, common administrative services, common switchboard, canteen and other facilities that have to be paid for separately. We prefer to list professional services as a separate entity, but some universities include them and then call the incubator an accelerator. Incubators have been created all over the world by municipalities and institutions of learning; the universities of Cambridge, Leuven and many others have complete parks of incubator buildings (at Cambridge, these are owned or administered by the central university administration). The residence time for start-ups can be limited and sometimes rents increase annually to create an up-or-out system. The value of incubators is that start-ups can rent space at low cost in the design and development phases while being freed from the need to arrange for the extra services. An important side-effect of incubators is that the tenants can exchange experiences and benefit from each other's advice; this is often as valuable as the advice given by professionals. The danger of an incubator is that the authorities that establish them may think that this is all they have to do to support starters. Incubators are useful, but they are only a small part of the whole story. In addition, incubators (and the services around them) must be tuned to local circumstances. An incubator in Veles, Macedonia, failed because:

- there was a lack of a strategy for economic development at the local level;
- there was no well-targeted approach within the incubator;
- cooperation between the partners involved was lacking (the government, the state and the local authorities, private communities, research institutions, educational institutions, etc.);
- there was no 'network of competence';
- no objectives were set in an explicit manner and based on a thorough analysis of the local economic circumstances;
- cost and efficiency were not determined properly;
- the incubator was structured as an independent corporation, not as a part of a larger local structure for development (see Danilova, n.d.).

Professional support

University start-ups and technostarters, like all entrepreneurs, need specialised advice on topics such as marketing and market research, IPR, finance, administration and reporting, quality management, logistics, procurement and others. During the early phases of the enterprise, the founders will have problems in paying for these services and they should have the opportunity to get them free of charge, at least during the initial stages. At TU Delft, we created the 'Foundation Network Young Entrepreneurs Delft', in which professional auditing, marketing, management consultancy and IPR bureaux and a bank participate. These parties offer free lectures and assessment in the 'Writing a Business Plan' lectures, and they offer free advice during the early stages. Their interest in doing this is a mixture of good publicity, access to potential new clients, training for their young experts, keeping in touch with high technology, and just plain fun.

Coaching

In addition to the specialist support discussed above, start-ups need support from generalists who can help them become true entrepreneurs. In the design, and often still in the development phase, when there is not yet an informal investor or an investment fund and its management company to take on that role, management consultants from an international management consultancy will become involved. Preferably, these consultants are alumni of the university and they like doing this job although they mostly do it in their own time, stimulated by their managers. The coaching activities offer them development opportunities. The coaching activities start with the 'Writing a Business Plan' lectures and continue afterwards in an informal way, sometimes over several years. Coaching has become quite an important issue in the world of management. In a way, everyone, even the CEOs of large enterprises, needs professional coaches to prevent them from overlooking information or opportunities and to give feedback on their performance (Wissema, 2002). The idea of coaching sometimes collides with the ego ('I can do this myself'), but wise people realise that despite long and varied careers, everyone can make mistakes and needs feedback on what they are doing.

Coaching is one of those activities that most people think they can do without any training, but good coaching is actually a profession in itself. We therefore suggest that coaches are selected and trained, even if they are not paid. Coaches should exchange experiences from time to time; they should be willing to invest time in their development as coaches.

Technical support

Technostarters often, but not always, use their thesis (MSc or PhD) as the technical foundation for their enterprise. As this is part of their course, the technical support and supervision are included and free of charge. This support, however, should not end when the course is finished. If the academics remain active supporters after the degree has been awarded, they should have a share of the value created. The same applies to university spin-outs. Although the staff members are on the pay-roll of the university, it is wise to offer active contributors a bonus when there is an exit or when the company makes money. One need not be afraid that bonuses will turn the university staff into bounty hunters: the academic tradition is too strong for that. On the contrary, such bonuses can help to change the university's culture, and one should not be afraid to offer a good bonus system. If the value created is large, university staff may receive bonuses exceeding their annual salaries, and administrators might be afraid that this could cause jealousy. It is important, however, not to give in to this fear. In one case, a university designed a reasonable bonus system for its staff and then found that one academic would receive a bonus five times his salary. The university backed off, saying that this was not the intention etc., and limited the bonus in hindsight to one year's salary. This was obviously a violation of the agreement and, worse, sent out the wrong sort of signal.

Publicity

In our complex society, publicity is of paramount importance in creating a good image for the university as well as for its start-ups. Such publicity helps to gain customers for the start-ups as well as support in a general sense. Many universities offer a journal for alumni and others interested in its progress. Such journals could include well-written contributions about successful technostarters. The university website should have a web address on its home page referring to all its entrepreneurship activities, thus stimulating networking and promoting the image of the university. The university's press agency should issue press releases with news about starters and make every endeavour to get them published.

CONCLUSIONS AND RECOMMENDATIONS

Technostarters are daring young (or not so young) men and women who create their own, technology-based firm. In doing so, they bring knowledge that is often created by, or in association with, a university to the market. The economic effect of such firms can be substantial, as shown by documented cases of MIT and the universities of Cambridge and Leuven, Belgium, and this is one reason why universities should support technostarters.

A second reason to do so is the worldwide interest of young people in creating their own company rather than seeking employment in an established firm or other organisation. The third reason why universities should support technostarters lies in the competitive position of universities themselves. Universities and enterprises used to be separated worlds. All nineteenth-century innovations that created large enterprises, from James Watt's steam engine to Alexander Bell's telephone and Thomas Edison's electric light, were developed outside universities with no involvement from universities. As the case of the University of Cambridge shows, universities that want to stay at the edge of scientific development need more money than any government will give them. For this and other reasons, they seek collaboration with industry in order to develop and commercialise know-how. Such collaboration can lead to the emergence of an international know-how hub and technostarters are an indispensable part of such a hub. Universities that manage to manoeuvre themselves into the nucleus of a know-how hub will be the winners in the increasingly competitive race between universities. They can stimulate the emergence of technostarters by establishing awareness and education programmes for students, platforms with financiers, easy access to know-how and support from various professional service firms as well as incubators.

NOTES

*   This chapter is based on J.G. Wissema (2009), *Towards the Third Generation University: Managing the University in Transition*, Cheltenham, UK and Northampton, MA, USA: Edward Elgar.

1.   See Niejahr and Vorholz (2005), p. 25. See also von Wartenberg and Haß (2005).
2.   An interesting study linking entrepreneurship and economic growth is to be found in Stel (2006).
3.   In February 2006, EU Commissioners Verheugen (enterprises and industry) and Figel (education) issued a list with recommendations to stimulate entrepreneurship in the EU. Half of Europeans will not start an enterprise if there is risk involved, compared to 30 per cent in the USA.
4.   For an overview of policies in different countries see Lundstrom and Stevenson (2005).
5.   SUN Microsystems, one of the largest IT companies in the world, emerged from the university's network facility, 'SUN' meaning originally Stanford University Network.
6.   The technical component of PA Consultants was created by Gordon Edge and others when they left Cambridge Consultants.
7.   Anonymous but no doubt written by its then deputy-editor Norman McCrae, 'Business – The new entrepreneurs', *The Economist*, 24 December 1983, pp. 59–71.
8.   Ibid.
9.   *The Cambridge Phenomenon* and *The Cambridge Phenomenon Revisited*, prepared by Segal Quince Wicksteed, 1985 respectively 2000. Some other data in this paragraph are also drawn from these publications.
10.   *The Cambridge Phenomenon Revisited*, op cit.
11.   *Our Competitive Future: Building the Knowledge Driven Economy*, White Paper, UK Department of Trade and Industry, The Stationery Office Ltd, 16 December 1998.
12.   Carl Schramm, head of the Ewing Marion Kauffman Foundation, which fosters entrepreneurship in American universities by giving grants of $70 million a year, is seriously worried that 'universities are becoming too bureaucratic in their approach to intellectual property, creating a new bottleneck in the transfer of technology to start-ups. Several big firms told [him] recently that they are considering switching research to universities in some development countries, because there will be no question over who owns the rights to a breakthrough in those countries.' 'Face Value – The evangelist of entrepreneurship', *The Economist*, 5 November 2005. Josh Lerner (2005) of Harvard Business School voices similar warnings.
13.   This phenomenon is familiar from the development of the IT industry in Silicon Valley and the Boston area, but it was equally present in the development of the book printing industry, following the first successful book printing with movable type by Johannes Gutenberg in 1454 in Mainz. His financier, Johannes Fust, can probably be regarded as the world's first business angel.
14.   J. Lang (2003), 'Creating the climate for innovation', handout, the University of Cambridge, quoted and edited with permission.
15.   The (US) National Business Incubation Association (NBIA) publishes interesting reports on this issue. See, e.g. Wolf et al. (2002) and Lewis (2002).
16.   The term is in general use. See, e.g., Markham (2002).
17.   Angel capital is a form of private equity. Other forms are venture capital (funds that finance the growth of young firms that have passed the start-up phase) and buy-out capital (funds that buy even very large companies with the aim of breaking them of or forging mergers, thus creating shareholder value).

REFERENCES

Acs, Z.J. et al. (2005), *Babson College and London Business School*, Global Entrepreneurship Monitor 2004, available from http://www.gemconsortium. org.

Adkins, D. (2002), *A Brief History of Business Incubation in the United States*, Athens, OH: National Business Incubation Association.

Danailova, I. (n.d.), *Local Economic Development and the Efficiency of its Instrument – Incubator in Transition Countries*, MSc thesis, ESCEM, School of Business and Management, New York College, Thessalonica.

Debackere, K. (2000), 'Managing academic R&D as a business at K.U. Leuven: context, structure and process', *R&D Management*, **30** (4), 323–8.

Economics Department of BankBoston (now Bank of America) (1997), *MIT: The Impact of Innovation*, BankBoston, March (available from the MIT website).

The Economist (2004), 'Clustered cloisters', 21 February.

Greiner, L.E. (1972), 'Evolution and revolution as organisations grow', *Harvard Business Review*, July–August, 64–73.

Herriot, W. and T. Minshall (2003), *Cambridge Technopole: An Overview of the UK's Leading High-Technology Business Cluster*, St John's Innovation Centre, Cambridge (updated biannually).

Kor, Y.Y. and J.T. Mahoney (2000), 'Penrose's resource-based approach: the process and product of research creativity', *Journal of Management Studies*, 109–39.

Kuemmerle, W. (2002), 'A test for the fainthearted', *Harvard Business Review*, **80** (5), 126–7.

Lerner, J. (2005), 'The university and the start-up: lessons from the past two decades', *Journal of Technology Transfer*, **30**, 46–56.

Lewis, D.A. (2002), *Does Technology Work? A Critical Review*, Athens, OH: NBIA.

Looy, B. Van, J. Callaert and K. Debackere (n.d.), 'Publication and patent behaviour of academic researchers: conflicting, reinforcing or merely coexisting?', Paper, KU Leuven's Research Division INCENTIM

Lundstrom, A. and L.A. Stevenson (2005), *Entrepreneurship Policy: Theory and Practice*, Series in International Entrepreneurship, New York: Springer.

Markham, S.K. (2002), 'Moving technologies from lab to market', *Research and Technology Management*, **45** (6), 31–42.

Niejahr, Elisabeth and Fritz Vorholz (2005), 'Die Politiker machen unrealistische Versprechen' ('Politicians make unrealistic speeches'), interview with Dr Ludolf von Wartenberg, *Die Zeit*, 2 June, p. 25.

Penrose, E.T. (1959), *The Theory of the Growth of the Firm*, New York: John Wiley.

Pesola, M. (2005), 'Cultivated in Silicon Fen's ferltile soil', *Financial Times*, 9 February.

Pinchot, G. (1985) *Intrapreneuring: Why you Don't Have to Leave the Corporation to Become an Entrepreneur*, New York: Harper & Row.

Richard, D. (2005), 'Start-up secrets, Part II, Creating a team', *Financial Times*, 1 June.

Ridding, John (2005), 'Lunch with the FT', *Financial Times*, 5 February, p. w3.

Shell LiveWire (2004), 'Young Entrepreneurs of the Year Awards, Finalists Report 2004', quoted in *The Financial Times*, 9 November, p. 8.

Stel, A. van (2006), *Empirical analysis of entrepreneurship and economic growth*, Series in International studies in Entrepreneurshi, Springer, New York

Stel, A. van, M. Carree and R. Thurik (2005), 'The effect of entrepreneurial activity on national economic growth', Scales Paper N200419, EIM Business & Policy Research and Scientific Analysis of Entrepreneurship and SMEs (Scales), unpublished version, January (available from www.eim.net).

Twaalfhoven, Bert (2002), 'Choice for life: European entrepreneur', speech at opening of the academic year, Vlenick Leuven Gent Management School, 30 September.

Van Osnabrugge, M. and R. J. Robinson (2000), *Angel Investing*, Jossey-Bass, San Fransisco,

Von Wartenberg, Ludolf and Hans-Joachim Haß (2005), *Investition in die Zukunft: wie Deutschland den Anschluss an die globalisierte welt findet*, Weinheim, Germany: Wiley–VCH.

Vyakarnam, S. et al. (2005), 'Research parks and incubators: re-defining the role of the incubator', Research Paper, Centre for Entrepreneurial Learning, Judge Institute of Management Studies.

Wissema, J.G. (2002), 'Driving through red lights – how warning signals are missed or ignored', *Long Range Planning*, **35**, 521–39.

Wolf, C. et al. (2002), *Best Practices in Action: Guidelines for Implementing First-class Business Incubation*, Athens, OH: NBIA.

3. Assessing the impact of centres of excellence on business innovation: the Flemish case

Arnold Verbeek, Elissavet Lykogianni, Valentijn Bilsen, Veerle Minne and Geert Steurs

INTRODUCTION

Knowledge creation, diffusion and absorption are key elements in the present debate on economic growth. Knowledge is usually the result of research, but research cannot be carried out if there is not a certain knowledge base to start with. Once knowledge is generated, it can materialise, in due time, in new applications, such as new products and processes. In that case, when the market is entered, one may speak of an innovation that at some point in time may lead to a competitive advantage and perhaps generate 'extra' returns to the innovator. On the firm level, innovation is a central 'element' of the behaviour of successful firms, essential for the improvement of social welfare and well-being, and closely related to the creation of a competitive and dynamic economic environment. This view on economic growth is subject to a number of uncertainties, especially on how the process or interaction between science, technology and economy evolves over time.

From a policy perspective this uncertainty becomes manifest when we look at the ongoing initiatives (in Europe and in the USA) to better understand and influence this interaction, for example through the organisation of the national innovation system, the stimulation of linkages between industry and academia (think of the Triple-Helix notion), and the support of universities to become entrepreneurs in applying and valorising their knowledge. But the main question is whether policy makers should aim to steer this kind of interaction or whether they should limit their role to monitoring the developments and mainly let the invisible hand of the market play its role.

Fundamental to answering this question is our understanding of the various effects of innovation policy. Taking into consideration the increasing appeal to public accountability and the increasing rationalisation of public funding of RDI (research, development and innovation) faces policy makers with a rather daunting task: to understand and rationalise innovation policy through an 'evidence-based approach'.

By taking this approach one looks for 'evidence' of success or failure of specific policy interventions (measures, programmes, institutes etc.) through a structured process referred to as 'evaluation': a highly complex, socially embedded and thus time-consuming process. One can also observe several shifts with respect to the emphasis of evaluation in general, e.g. a shift from 'input'- and/or 'output'-driven evaluation to more 'impact'-driven evaluation, from focusing on short-term results to focusing on longer-term results and impact. These developments involve specific methodological challenges as well.

Our objective in this chapter is twofold. First, we present the main features of the methodological impact assessment framework that we have developed and applied to a number of specific cases. We relate this to the ongoing international debate on appropriate impact assessment methods. Second, we make a 'tour' among a selection of Flemish cases where we have applied our methodology. Some of the results of these studies are confidential, so we have made a careful selection of those items that we can disclose. We have used the usual academic standards to make sure that the results presented here accurately reflect the findings of the various studies.

The structure of this chapter is as follows. First we present some recent policy developments in the evaluation of public funding. In the next section we present an overview of the evolution and the role of the centres of excellence in Flanders. The following section focuses on our methodological framework for the impact assessment of innovation policies (the MI²A framework). The subsequent section provides a detailed description of the application of the MI²A methodology in real cases in which IDEA Consult[1] has performed evaluations. Finally, the last section concludes.

Our main finding is that the aforementioned centres of excellence play a role of major importance in strengthening the knowledge base in specific areas (sectors) and in stimulating international competitiveness of Flemish industry.

METHODOLOGICAL ASPECTS

From Output to Outcome and Impact: A Transition

In the analysis and evaluation of publicly funded innovation actions (specific measures, programmes, institutes etc.) we can observe a shift from input-oriented measurements to output- and even impact-related measurements (e.g. Ertl et al., 2006). Whereas the output-related measurements focus on the direct results of public spending, impact measurements go a step further. They take into account more indirect results as well, results related to the policy intervention but considered as an indirect result. The output or the result of a certain action functions as a catalyst for additional effects consistent with higher-level policy objectives and ambitions. This shift is highlighted by experts in the USA and the EU.

In the USA, the director of the Office of Science and Technology Policy (OSTP) referred to a number of relevant policy developments in evaluation and general appraisal of public funding (Marburger, 2006). He emphasised the need for an adequate and sophisticated empirical basis in order to develop a more effective science, technology and innovation policy.

In Europe the notion of empirical-based assessment is also gaining ground and importance. Evidence-based policy has become a rallying call for modernising politicians. Governments are under pressure to justify their expenditure decisions to the media and to the population at large (Miles and Cunningham, 2006). Innovation policy can be improved by a better analysis and diagnosis; specific policies are needed to support analysis, monitoring and evaluation practices, which should then feed back into the policy-making process (Veugelers, 2006). Nevertheless, an important precondition for an effective evidence-based innovation policy is the availability of adequate data and studies relevant and accessible to policy makers (see, among others, Arundel, 2006; Veugelers, 2006; Anderson et al., 2006). A pilot initiative of DG Enterprise (EC) on a European modular approach to impact assessment states as one of its most important objectives to 'help to implement the shift from today's focus on the innovation support programme evaluation concept to a focus on innovation policy impact analysis' (Enqvist et al., 2006, p. 8).

Two Trends

In the entire evolution towards impact/outcome measurement one can identify two large/simultaneous trends. First of all, we see a certain field-specific specialisation concerning indicators and methods; for example, consider the areas of biotechnology and nanotechnology, where we find different indicators capturing similar effects, due simply to the intrinsic differences and characteristics of these fields (cf. Bernstein et al., 2006).[2]

Second, we see an increasing interest in the concept of additionality, and specifically behavioural additionality (Miles and Cunningham, 2006). It is argued that emphasis is laid on effects rather than on output; the concept of additionality comes to the foreground.

Additionality lies at the heart of justification of (policy) intervention (Georghiou et al., 2002, p. 6; Buisseret et al., 1995). This concept refers to the net effect of a policy intervention in comparison with the counterfactual situations in which the intervention would not have taken place. In other words, it does not suffice to consider the direct output and outcome only; the results without the policy intervention also need to be considered. The discrepancy between the two indicates the value added of the intervention.[3]

At the same time, evaluation of the impacts of innovation policies requires taking into account the direct or indirect interaction of innovation policies with other public policies (e.g. IPR and competition policies, science–industry collaboration-promoting policies, entrepreneurship-strengthening policies, ICT support policies etc.).[4] A system of evaluation of policy measures is therefore essential in order to ensure the most efficient use of public funding, thereby controlling for the most desirable impact of the policy on the economy/society.

CENTRES OF EXCELLENCE: A 'CORNERSTONE' OF FLEMISH INNOVATION POLICY?

Start and Subsequent Development

The creation of knowledge centres for stimulating innovation in Flanders has its own history within a moving framework of policy priorities and ambitions. The sectoral 'collective centres' were created just after the Second World War as a result of the 'De Groote' law (1947). The ambition was to stimulate and strengthen sector-oriented collective research and technological capabilities, mainly targeting the Flemish SMEs. In 2002, this initiative was integrated into and complemented by the VIS (the Flemish Innovation Collaboration programme), which offered a wider supportive framework to new institutions and actors in the field.

IMEC, the Inter-university Microelectronics Centre, was created in 1984. Microelectronics was regarded as one of the 'cross-road' technologies for the economic future of Flanders. IMEC was an initiative in the context of the Third Industrial Revolution in Flanders (DIRV), initiated by the first Flemish prime minister Gaston Geens. VITO, the Flemish Institute for Technological Research, was set up in 1991 by an initiative of the federal government. VITO deals with energy, environmental and materials technology.

VIB, the Flemish Interdisciplinary Institute for Biotechnology, was set up in 1995 as a response to the increasing need for structural support of university research in the life sciences. At that time, Flemish universities already had a strong (national and international) track record in biotechnology. The underlying principle was again a science/technology 'push' approach with, at that time, a still limited industrial absorptive capacity in the field of biotechnology in Flanders.

By the end of the 1990s, the European Structural Funds (EFRO) made it possible to set up a number of centres with specific objectives, such as VIGC (a centre in the graphics sector), EDM (a centre in the multimedia sector), and Flanders Drive (a centre for the automotive industry). In 2003 a number of *ad hoc* initiatives got support from the Flemish government: the Flemish Institute for Logistics (VIL), the Incubation point Geo-information (IncGeo), and the Flanders Mechatronics Technology Centre (FMTC).

Developments since 2000

In the present decade we see a certain 'horizontalisation' of the science, technology and innovation (STI) support system in Flanders, with the establishment of different support schemes independent of sectors and/ or technologies. In due time the policy makers became aware of the need for more focused support in order to provide the necessary 'critical mass' to make a 'real' difference. As a consequence, a certain rationalisation replaced the more *ad hoc* initiatives seen so far. At this time the term 'poles of excellence' was coined, referring to a selection of institutes dealing with specific technologies/sectors.

In the course of 2004, the initiative was taken to set up the Interdisciplinary Institute for Broadband Technology (IBBT) as a response to the economic crisis in the ICT sector. This clearly has been a 'bottom-up' and 'demand-driven' initiative to strengthen the economic potential of the ICT sector in Flanders. Looking at the size of the support that IBBT receives (about €17 million/year), the institute falls in the category of research centres such as IMEC, VIB and VITO. The concept underlying IBBT is unique: it is a virtual institute like VIB, but with the difference that IBBT funding is allocated on a project instead of a departmental basis (VIB).

The first half of 2004 was characterised by a series of initiatives for new 'poles of excellence'. This was largely due to the agreements made at the 'Entrepreneurship Conference' in 2003. Without intending to be exhaustive we mention the following initiatives: Flamac (Flanders Material Centre), MIP (Environmental Innovation Platform), Flanders FOOD (knowledge diffusion in the food sector), and Flanders DC (Flanders' District of Creativity focusing on international and interregional collaboration on creativity and innovation).

Recent Policy Changes

Recently, the Flemish government took the initiative to develop a more coherent strategy and policy framework. Questions have been raised, mainly due to the *ad hoc* character of several of these initiatives. Furthermore, it seems that the rather fuzzy concept of 'poles of excellence' has led to an unconditional growth of initiatives. Obviously, strategic knowledge centres are important to Flanders, but the issues of critical mass and transparency are of major interest as well. In rethinking its strategy, the Flemish government has taken the following issues into account:

- The notion of 'open innovation systems', in which there is intense interaction between the knowledge actors.
- The fact that companies increasingly pull back from (internally funded) basic research; a more collective approach should compensate for this development.
- Combining and interrelating existing institutes prevails over the creation of entirely new institutes.
- The collective dimension justifies government intervention (collective advantage).
- The strategic dimension points mainly to the economic and/or societal benefit of this type of (longer-term) knowledge investments.
- Larger knowledge centres are not only a Flemish insight; on the international scene this is also being discussed (e.g. the creation of a European Institute of Technology).

As a result of these discussions and challenges, the policy makers in Flanders have adopted the terms 'poles of competence' and 'strategic research centres', into which the above-mentioned initiatives were classified. The poles of competence aim at bundling strengths and stimulating collaboration between actors focusing on research and innovation in relevant topics/themes.

Strategic research centres are expected to include a more international dimension of excellence as well. It has become clear that Flanders must still make motivated choices about the initiatives that will be prolonged, integrated, reshaped and perhaps discontinued. In this process attention has to be paid to the cost–benefit ratio between government funding on the one hand and the economic (societal) value added that can be achieved on the other. Also the percentage of subsidies that is acceptable will have to be considered. The 'sky is not the limit' is a statement that is not to be misunderstood in this context.

As referred to above, making choices must be based on clear and transparent criteria. Setting such criteria is by no means a straightforward task.

Besides objective criteria, more subjective criteria (e.g. political interests) also play a role. Moreover, we see that the complexity of both sets of criteria has increased. Whereas in the past allocation decisions were often based on straightforward 'performance' (read 'output'), today there is more emphasis on 'value added' or longer-term 'impact'. The relation between the Flemish government and the strategic research centres (or centres of excellence) is described and formalised in specific contracts. Different types of indicators and expectations are developed and stated in this context, reflecting the economic but also the societal value added. An additional challenge is the change in the time horizon considered to achieve results. There is increasing interest in longer-term results and the impact of public funding that introduces the very specific problem of 'attribution' of results to well-defined 'interventions'.

In summary, the entire rationalisation of public funding of RDI appeals to new and more sophisticated indicators and methods to monitor and evaluate the results achieved.

THE MULTIDIMENSIONAL INNOVATION IMPACT ASSESSMENT (MI²A) FRAMEWORK

Impact Assessment of Innovation Policies

This section presents a methodological framework that helps to deal with several of the challenges posed above.

Impact assessment of innovation policies is a process that identifies the impacts of a policy intervention on a set of factors that the policy is designed to affect. These factors can be economic, social or other factors underlying the socioeconomic environment. The policy intervention may involve a policy measure to promote private R&D, or the development of an institute that fosters innovation-related activities. The assessment of the impacts of such policies entails a comparison with the situation in which the policy was not undertaken (the 'counterfactual' case) and identifies the differences, using indicators for the intervention and non-intervention cases. For instance, if the intervention concerns a public subsidy to a firm for research, the counterfactual could be a similar firm in the industry that has not received such financial support (the concept of 'additionality').

After the impact of particular policy interventions on the economy has been assessed,[5] it should be indicated whether this specific impact was indeed an effect of the implementation of the initiative under consideration rather than a (partially) coincidental effect that might be attributed (fully or partially) to other circumstances. The notion of causal chain analysis can help overcome this difficulty and provide more detailed evidence on the magnitude of the different impacts. This is relevant when an impact generated by an intervention becomes a 'cause' in its own right, generating further effects. This notion is taken into account when dealing with direct, indirect and induced effects, as already discussed in the previous paragraphs.

In addition, the fact that innovation policies are closely (inter)related to other public policies adds to the importance of 'attribution' issues. An effect caused by an innovation policy intervention can be augmented by the effects of other policies.

Introduction of the MI²A

Impact assessment has so far focused on three main categories of impacts: economic, social and environmental (Lee and Kirkpatrick, 2006; Bond et al., 2001; Eales et al., 2005). Such assessment focuses on the effects of particular policies (or specific measures) on factors directly linked to one category of impact: either to the economy or to the social life or to the quality of the environment. This can be considered as a one-dimensional view of impact. However, reality is far more complex, with interactions, interrelations and cross-fertilisations lying at the core of today's economic and technological development. A one-dimensional perspective (even though considering many dimensions sequentially) unfortunately does not grasp this complexity. Therefore integrated impact assessment methodologies have also been developed (Papaconstantinou and Polt, 1997; Georghiou, 1997; Miles and Cunningham, 2006). However, these assessments cover a range of impacts that are restricted to the three aforementioned categories: economic, social and environmental impacts.

The multidimensional innovation impact assessment (MI²A) methodology, on the contrary, focuses on the identification of the impacts in four domains: economic, fiscal, science and technology (see Figure 3.1). It therefore provides the new feature of a consolidated impact assessment of innovation policies that takes into account a variety of links between technology and economic growth (cf. Verbeek and Debackere, 2006).[6]

The two domains of science and technology are highly interrelated and have direct and strong links to innovation policy measures. The economic domain is heavily influenced by the previous two domains and receives feedback from the implementation of innovation policy measures. The fiscal domain is a new feature of the MI²A approach: it includes impacts of innovation policy measures on public revenues. Such revenues are generated mainly from taxation on the various components of value added that

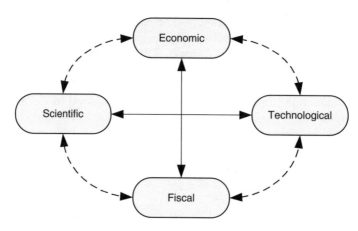

Source: IDEA Consult.

Figure 3.1 Types of impacts (MI²A)

have resulted from the intervention (e.g. wages, profits). If these increased revenues are used for the implementation of additional policies, then they flow back into the economy, inducing further economic impacts.

Economic Impact

For the assessment of the economic impact resulting from a policy intervention (e.g. the creation of a research institute), the main underlying concept is the comparison of the current situation with the counterfactual situation of the economy without the particular policy intervention (e.g. the institute in question).

For the measurement of the economic impact, the analysis focuses on the impacts of the factors that are more directly linked to output and employment. These elements are interrelated and often represent priority target variables for policy makers: economic and employment growth.

We distinguish between 'direct', 'indirect' and 'induced' economic impacts.[7]

- *Direct economic impact* refers to the immediate impact of the activities of the policy intervention on the economy (in terms of value added and job creation that are generated directly to serve the institution's activities).
- *Indirect economic impact* refers to the impact of the intervention on the operations and activities of firms and individuals due to inter-

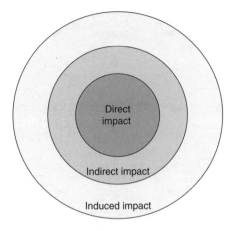

Source: IDEA Consult.

Figure 3.2   Types of economic impact

industry (supply) linkages (e.g. increase of employment for suppliers in order to satisfy increased demand for intermediate products for the organisation/project in question).

● *Induced economic impact* refers to the spending of income that is generated by the activities of both the direct and the indirect effects (e.g. increased consumption for people who are employed as a result of the intervention, due to income increases).

This discussion on the different economic impacts is illustrated by Figures 3.2 and 3.3.

An important issue that arises at this point is the measurement of these impacts. Two indicators are frequently used. The first is 'value added', used mainly for the measurement of the contribution of a policy intervention to the economy. In economic terms (the notion used here) value added equals sales minus intermediary purchases for goods and services needed to produce the goods and services that have been sold by the firm.[8]

The second indicator is the number of people employed. Since both full-time and part-time jobs can be involved, for a correct interpretation it is better to use a unified measure: full-time equivalents (FTEs).

Fiscal Impact

Many policy interventions have a fiscal impact. More specifically, policy measures such as the creation of a research institute or the attribution of

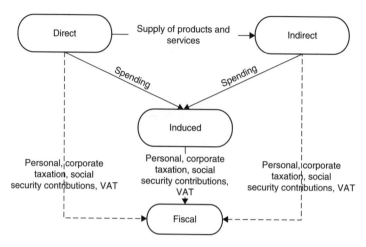

Source: IDEA Consult.

Figure 3.3   Types of economic and fiscal impact

a tax incentive to a firm will lead to the employment of more people in R&D. The incomes earned by them lead to higher tax returns (e.g. higher labour tax) for the government. The assessment of these fiscal impacts aims at the quantification of the various components of these effects in terms of government revenues. These revenues stem mainly from:

- *Financial feedback via the additionally generated employment, focusing on employment-related taxes.* This component of fiscal impacts includes mainly personal income tax and social security contributions. The employment-related taxes have been estimated on the basis of the number of FTEs that have been generated by the intervention in the domestic economy. These include direct employment, as well as the indirect and induced type of employment.
- *Financial feedback via the extra output, measured by production-related taxes* (taking the form of corporate taxes and other taxes paid by companies). These have been approximated using an average effective tax rate based on historic data of companies in different sectors.
- *Financial feedback via the taxation of the value added, measured by VAT.* This component has been estimated on the basis of a weighed-average VAT rate.

These fiscal impacts are (inter)related with the various (direct, indirect, induced) economic impacts (see Figure 3.3).

The fiscal returns to the government compensate to some extent for the (recurrent) public funding involved with the policy intervention. The objective of the assessment of fiscal impacts of policy interventions is the estimation of the difference between the public investments disbursed for the implementation of the intervention and the fiscal resources (returns to) generated by the intervention. In the extreme case one can find a zero-operations outcome: this may occur where the fiscal feedback to the government is equal to the initial public investment.

Scientific Impact

In matters of development and progress of science, and the transfer of knowledge, a range of impacts should be acknowledged and estimated. In the traditional 'linear' thinking, scientific development and progress were considered as a prerequisite for technological development and follow-up of economic exploitation. Today, such linear thinking is no longer believed to grasp the complexity that we are dealing with, although scientific development is still considered an essential ingredient of technological and economic progress. Therefore the effects on science and the pool of scientific knowledge in a broader perspective resulting from a certain policy intervention need to be taken into account as well.

In order to evaluate the impact on science we again distinguish between the following main types of impact (see Figure 3.4 and Box 3.1):

- *Direct scientific effects or contribution to science effects* refer to the straightforward contributions to the existing pool of scientific knowledge. They can be measured, for example, through the number of international publications in, among other things, peer-reviewed journals. A quality parameter related to this contribution is given by the number of citations to those publications, generally considered as an indication of appreciation by the (academic) community. Furthermore, the publishing journals' impact factor also allows us to take into account the 'quality' of the journal and thus of the publications (Verbeek et al., 2002). The measurement of the scientific impact of a project is a rather controversial issue since it concerns the provision of measurable indicators of scientific quality. However, there is general agreement that a peer review – in which independent experts evaluate the performance of a (group of) researcher(s) – is a necessary ingredient in the evaluation of scientific work. Therefore, in our methodological framework, when measuring the direct scientific effects in terms of publication and citation records, we pay attention to the involvement of 'peers'. In other words, we aim to find a balance between a quantitative and a qualitative analysis.

- *Indirect scientific effects or utilization effects* refer to the potential take-up and usage of new scientific insights. For example, this varies from a simple analysis of the collaboration intensity with industry, because of the potential value to industry, to the analysis of the contribution to new breakthrough scientific discoveries.

BOX 3.1   TYPES OF SCIENTIFIC AND TECHNOLOGICAL IMPACTS

The assessment of the scientific and technological impacts will be based on a framework that considers three types of impacts: direct, indirect and induced. This is similar to the approach followed in the assessment of the economic impact.

- *Direct impacts* refer to 'under-the-roof' activities of an institution (also applicable to broader policy measures). In the case of a publicly funded institution, these include the impacts on science and technology caused by activities carried out within the institution (or linked directly to the activities caused by a broader policy measure). For example, they can include publications or patented technologies of researchers working for the institution.
- *Indirect impacts* concern activities that are indirectly linked to the direct impacts. For example, indirect scientific impacts include the organisation of conferences and workshops, or the development of scientists' networking as a result of their publications (linked to the direct impact). Similarly, the creation of spin-offs can be considered as an indirect technological impact caused by the technological developments of an organisation (also linked to the direct impact).
- *Induced impacts* of science and technology refer to those impacts that can been realised in a wider time-frame, such as the creation of location effects through the attraction of centres of excellence or of foreign companies in the geographical area where the policy measure has taken place (e.g. around the location of a publicly funded institution).

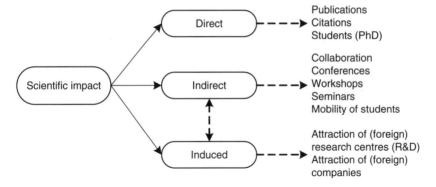

Source: IDEA Consult.

Figure 3.4   Types of scientific impacts

These effects are considered as direct and indirect scientific effects contributing directly and indirectly to the 'size' and 'value' of the science base of an economy. However, the more induced effects of scientific performance cannot be neglected either. These induced effects are, for example:

- *'International-visibility effects'*, or contributions to the attractiveness of the science base. These refer to the increasing attractiveness of networking, for example as a result of the creation of centres of excellence in the context of a particular policy.
- *'Societal effects'* or contributions to societal challenges. These concern mainly the effects of a particular policy on day-to-day life.

Technological Impact[9]

The scientific output developed is expected to have a positive influence on technological output. However, this relationship is not as straightforward as it sounds, and it is unlikely to be a linear one. The aim of the evaluation of the technological impact of a policy or an institute concerns mainly the consideration of knowledge and technology transfers to the market and thus to the broader economy. As illustrated in Figure 3.5, the main effects considered in this respect are:

- *Direct technological effects or contribution to technology effects*   These refer to the existing 'pool' of technologies in the economy and have a direct impact on the development of new products, processes and/

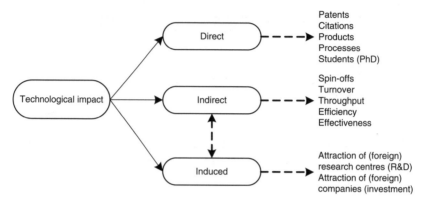

Source: IDEA Consult.

Figure 3.5   Types of technological impacts

or markets, or on the increase of the efficiency of existing processes. Indicators to measure this contribution are patents (cf. Debackere et al., 2002), citations, new products and/or processes, qualified engineers etc. The output is a direct result of ongoing technological activity.

● *Indirect technological effects or valorisation of technology effects* These refer to the applications of new know-how or new technological developments to, for example, new spin-offs, higher turnover, throughput reduction effects etc. (take-up and usage). One may say that environmental factors other than technology are at play here, but technological progress still provides the real value added.

These direct and indirect effects influence the 'size' of the 'pool' of technologies and know-how in the economy. However, they are also indirectly augmented through spillover effects or societal effects. As a result, a number of effects appear that are 'induced' in nature. Examples are:

● *Spillover effects*   These refer to effects on the technology base of the economy through the supply chain by increasing the know-how or improving the quality for other agents (suppliers, competitors, clients etc.) in the economy. Spillover effects on the technological impacts can also be produced through clustering effects when agents (other firms, institutions) are attracted into the same geographical area, providing more opportunities for networking and cooperation in research and technology development.

- *Societal effects* (as in the case of scientific impact)   These refer to the effects on the quality of day-to-day life.

For the assessment of knowledge transfers, the empirical literature often uses the notion of the so-called 'technology-multiplicator' (Peeters, 1998; Papaconstantinou and Polt, 1997). The technology-multiplicator gives the relationship between the total embodied R&D and the internal R&D, taking into account the direct and indirect technological spillovers (or diffusion) in the economy. Calculations in Flanders, The Netherlands and Denmark suggest a value of 2, which means that for every euro of internal R&D, 2 euros of embodied technology are created.

APPLYING THE MI²A METHODOLOGY: THE CASE STUDIES

Introduction

In this section we illustrate the application of the methodological framework described in the previous sections. Flemish innovation policy is strongly based on the creation and support of so-called strategic research centres. Although one cannot yet speak of a true Flemish evaluation culture, there are definitely indications that evaluation is becoming a tool for providing public accountability and transparency in the results of Flemish innovation policy.

The methodological framework presented above can either be part of a formal evaluation process initiated by the government in the context of a prolongation of public financial support, or part of a self-evaluation process carried out by a research institute (or a programme manager in case of a programme) in order to obtain insight into the broader performance and the different optimisation possibilities.

We chose to discuss three cases operating in different sectors: ICT and microelectronics (including nanotechnology) – IMEC; life sciences – VIB; and energy, materials and environmental technology – VITO. The VIB case was part of a formal evaluation process initiated by the Flemish government in 2006 in the context of the renewal of its contract with VIB (AWI, 2006). Two other cases come under the category of 'self-evaluation', – VITO and IMEC (VITO, 2006; IMEC, 2005). Before proceeding with a description of the application of the MI²A methodology in the three above-mentioned institutions, it is useful to mention particular differences in the structure of those institutions.

IMEC is an institution in which all activities are carried out 'under the roof'; in other words, it is a physical entity to which all activities can be allocated.

VIB, on the other hand, is a 'virtual' entity, an inter-university decentralised structure in which nine VIB research departments are physically located on the university campuses and structurally embedded (linked) with the partner universities.

VITO is an independent research centre conducting customer-oriented contract research in the fields of energy, environment and materials.

Taking into account the differences in the structure and organisation of each institution is crucial for the application of the MI²A methodology, since adjustments are often necessary. For example, in measuring the direct economic impact of a physical 'entity' (such as IMEC) the allocation of invoices to activities is more straightforward compared to allocating such evidence to a virtual entity (such as VIB). In the latter case, the direct economic impact should take into account the different 'streams' of financing: the financing that goes directly to the 'virtual' institution and the financing received from the partners of the network involved in the virtual institution.

We illustrate the results of the analysis for each dimension with only one case, in order to avoid unnecessary duplication. We use the case of VITO to illustrate the analysis of the economic and fiscal impact; VIB is used to exemplify the analysis of the scientific impact, and finally, IMEC is used to illustrate the analysis of the technological impact. Please keep in mind that due to confidentiality considerations, we can only rarely provide accurate quantitative information.

VITO: Economic Impact

VITO (the Flemish Institute for Technological Research) is an independent research centre that conducts contract research and develops innovative products and processes in the fields of energy, environment and materials, for both the public and the private sector. Central to its mission is the provision of innovative, technological solutions and scientifically based advice and support, to stimulate sustainable development and to reinforce the economic and social structure in Flanders.

For the quantification of the direct economic impact of VITO, the first step in the analysis concerns the growth of employment within VITO, using data on the total number of full-time and part-time employees, as well as translating these results into the full-time-equivalent (FTE) number of employees. The second step concerns the income/profits of VITO. This includes analysis of the growth in state subsidies received, and other receipts, making a distinction between receipts for projects financed by the Flemish government and those for projects resulting from contacts with private firms. Finally, the value added generated from the activities of VITO is defined as the turnover minus the value of products/services purchased or used for its activities. This amount is also calculated as a percentage of turnover and of the total number of employees.

The indirect economic impact of VITO has been estimated in two ways. First, the number of jobs created due to the supply of products and services of other firms/organisations was estimated. Then the first-level indirect economic impacts of VITO were estimated on the basis of invoice information: all purchases of VITO were aggregated and classified by sector, which is a unique feature of the methodology and approach proposed. While it is common practice to assume that the spending pattern of VITO is the same as that of other organisations and firms in its sector, we used a more refined approach by calculating explicitly the intermediate purchases of VITO for the relevant time period. All purchases of VITO were classified and aggregated by sector. Also, a classification was made according to purchases made in Belgium and those made abroad, while special care was taken to avoid double counting. Subsequently, for each sector the change in employment due to the activities of VITO was calculated based on employment-to-output ratios for each sector. In the same way, for the assessment of the changes in the value added, the value-added-to-turnover ratios of each supplier were used.

Second, the higher-level indirect effects were calculated: these concern the upstream employment effects in the supply chain through the purchases of products/services of VITO. For the estimation of the higher-level effects (e.g. the intermediary purchases of the suppliers of VITO), information from national input–output data were used in order to estimate the intensity of inter-industry relations. On the bases of these data, higher-level indirect effects in employment and value added were calculated.

The summation of the first-level and higher-level indirect effects provided the overall indirect economic effect of VITO in terms of employment growth and value added.

Finally, the induced economic impact of VITO was calculated. We recall that the induced impact concerns the spending into the economy due to the direct effects (wages/incomes of the personnel of VITO) as well as the indirect effects (e.g. of the people employed by the suppliers of VITO). The induced effect was estimated on the basis of the average gross wages of the sectors where VITO creates direct and indirect employment. These gross wages were translated into net wages using a weighted average of different household types. Using the average consumption and savings pattern in Belgium as an approximation for the spending/savings behaviour of all

FTEs employed due to VITO, the amount of the purchases that are the result of VITO activity was estimated.

The results of the economic impact assessment of VITO highlight the importance of its contribution to the local society and economy. An important part of this contribution stems from the higher-level effects. The indirect impact can be expressed as being close to 50 per cent of the direct impact of VITO. These results emphasise on the methodological level the importance of considering not only direct impacts but also indirect and induced impacts. At the same time, they emphasise on the policy level the importance of public investment in institutions that have a significant impact on income creation and employment growth in the economy.

VITO: Fiscal Impact

For the calculation of the impact of VITO on governmental revenues, employment-related taxes, value-added taxes and production-related taxes are taken into account. The employment-related revenues are calculated based mainly on personal income tax and social security contributions and on the number of FTEs generated by VITO in the domestic economy. These include direct employment, as well as indirect and induced employment. The value-added taxes are estimated on the basis of a weighted-average VAT rate of 12.5 per cent. Finally, corporate taxation and other taxes paid by companies have been approximated using an average effective tax rate based on historic data of companies in different sectors.

The quantitative results on the fiscal impact of VITO show that a significant percentage of the annual grant to VITO is earned back by the state. Summarising the main results on the fiscal impact of VITO for the Flemish government, the largest part of this return comes from the personal taxation and the social security payments created by the employed due to the operations of VITO (due to direct, indirect and induced employment creation).

VIB: Scientific Impact

VIB (the Flanders Inter-university Institute for Biotechnology) was established in 1995. VIB conducts strategic basic research in the various life science domains and has a decentralised structure in which nine VIB research departments are linked with the partner universities (Ghent University, the Catholic University of Leuven, the University of Antwerp and the Free University of Brussels). Through close cooperation with these universities and a solid funding programme for strategic basic research,

VIB joins the forces of approximately 950 scientists and technologists in one single institute.

For the analysis of the evolution of the scientific output of VIB for the relevant period (2001–05) a number of indicators have been used, as listed below:

- Bibliometric data: number and evolution of publications and citations of VIB broken down by department, journals' impact factors and comparisons with international averages (through a benchmarking exercise).
- Information on participation in committees and professorships, international invited lectures and presentations that increase the opportunities for networking of VIB researchers and the international visibility of the institution. This is positively related to the transfer of knowledge and the stimulation of networking within the scientific community, which in turn can be realised in the future with new collaborations or development of project-related initiatives.
- Information on education and training opportunities for VIB researchers, mainly focusing on the number of VIB researchers pursuing a PhD. This also relates to the opportunities for participation in PhD programmes on the basis of research conducted for the project under consideration. The granting of PhDs resulting from research conducted for VIB constitutes a good indicator of the quality of the research, taking into account the scientific standards that PhD programmes entail. The organisation of seminars, workshops, invited lectures etc. is also taken into account in the evaluation of the scientific impact of VIB.

The quantitative analysis was complemented by a more qualitative analysis provided by the peers of VIB. During a three-day visit to VIB in Ghent, the scientific output of VIB was carefully screened and compared to the 'standards' used by the peers. Titles and abstracts of publications were screened and discussions with researchers took place. This allowed the 'peers' to form a good opinion on the quality of the scientific output. The complementarity is obvious (Verbeek et al., 2002).

The result of the analysis shows that the scientific quality of VIB is excellent. The annual quantitative targets in relation to scientific performance were met over the last contract period. They underline the need to provide public funds in order to support operations of organisations such as VIB. In this respect it is interesting to note that, subsequent to the evaluation, VIB managed to increase its share of public funding.

IMEC: Technological Impact

IMEC (Inter-university Microelectronics Centre) was founded in 1984. As a world-leading independent research centre in nanoelectronics and nanotechnology, its research focuses on the next generations of chips and systems, and on the enabling technologies for ambient intelligence, bridging the gap between fundamental research at universities and technology development in industry. IMEC is headquartered in Leuven, Belgium, and has representatives in the USA, China and Japan. Its staff of about 1400 people includes close to 500 industrial residents and guest researchers. In 2006, its revenues were estimated to be over €200 million.

IMEC has been actively involved in both applied and basic R&D. Part of the knowledge and technological know-how developed within IMEC spills over into the economy, improving the know-how of other agents (suppliers, competitors, customers). The impacts of this diffusion of knowledge and technology should therefore be taken into account when estimating the technological impact of IMEC on the Flemish economy. For that reason, the evaluation of the technological impact of IMEC is divided into two parts: the first analysing the technological impacts of IMEC in relation to the creation of knowledge and know-how, and the second focusing mainly on the technological impacts of IMEC realised through technology/knowledge spillovers.

The creation of knowledge and the development of new technologies require investments in R&D. Concerning the transfer of knowledge the following factors have been taken into account:

- Indicators of cooperation with other partners, mainly using information on income through contracting with other (industrial) partners.
- Information on participation of IMEC in (inter)national public research programmes, which stimulates the transfer of knowledge and know-how among the participating partners.
- Data on the number of patents applied for by IMEC. This information constitutes not only an indicator of the possibilities for commercial application of research, but also an indicator of the opportunities for public transfer of knowledge and know-how.
- Information on the operations of IMEC's spin-offs, being closely related to technology transfer. This information focuses mainly on the profitability of IMEC's spin-offs as well as on their size in terms of the number of employees.

The results of the evaluation of the technological impact of IMEC indicate that IMEC plays an important role in the Flemish economy with respect to the introduction of technological developments and transfer of knowledge. To mention one example, over the period 2000–04 there was a significant increase in the value of technology/knowledge transfer of IMEC via contract research. Moreover, IMEC transferred knowledge to both research-intensive companies and SMEs. Through these interactions and knowledge transfers to public research institutions (such as universities) and private companies, a significant technological impact is created, contributing to the innovation performance and economic growth of Flanders.

We mention in this respect that IMEC has also created a 'location' effect. Since knowledge transfers often require face-to-face cooperation among staff of firms, geographical proximity is important. A number of companies have been located around IMEC, making the region of Leuven an important geographical cluster of technology-intensive companies.

CONCLUSIONS

The objective of this chapter has been to evaluate the effectiveness of public funding of R&D institutes in relation to the Flemish centres of excellence. The presently available methods to do so have serious drawbacks.

We have developed and applied the MI²A methodology, which provides an integrated approach for the impact assessment of innovation policies. It takes into account a wide range of impacts of innovation policy measures, in particular economic, fiscal, scientific and technological impacts. We have applied the method to the impacts of the Flemish centres of excellence, which are publicly funded and specialised R&D centres.

The results indicate first the adequacy of the method. In particular, the distinction between direct, indirect and induced impacts has proved to bring deeper insights. Indeed, in some cases the impact of the indirect effects induced through the supply chain seem to be quantitatively significant in comparison with the direct effects of the intervention. The methodology also has the advantage of easy modification for applications in different sectors.

The results show next the policy relevance of the method. Using the MI²A approach, the assessment of the impacts of the institutes on the regional (or national) economy has provided information on two levels: at the level of the institute's management team to which it provides information on the effects of its operations, which permits the institute to explore new possibilities for improving its activities or expanding their scope. In addition, at the level of the government, the impact assessment provides useful evidence on the specific effects of a publicly financed institute on the economy and thus on the justification of the levels of public funding.

However, all is not yet perfect. On many points improvements can be made. The main one is the switch from *ex post* to *ex ante* assessments. The assessment studies briefly described in the previous sections indeed represent only *ex post* evaluation of the impacts of particular Flemish institutes. However, policy makers often prefer to know the likely effects of alternative policies before they are initiated (*ex ante* evaluation). To limit the uncertainty and risk inherent in the application of this approach, we need to obtain more information from *ex post* assessments so as to draw at least some general rules and preferably some quantification of cause–effect relations given certain institutional and other conditions.

NOTES

1. Idea Consult is a member of ECORYS Group.
2. When trying to evaluate the impact of particular policy interventions on the economy, differences among sectors in matters of behaviour, strategy etc. should be acknowledged and the methodology should be suitably adjusted. Indeed, the impacts on technology developments can vary significantly between sectors. So, while comparing firms or institutions in the biotechnology sector with firms in the ICT sector the measures employed to assess the different types of impacts should be adjusted according to the particular practices characterising production patterns and interactions within these sectors.
3. For more background we refer to a recent study on the behavioural additionality of the Flemish subsidies carried out by Steurs et al. (2006) and to the contribution of Steurs et al. to this volume (Chapter 6).
4. Demand as a driver of innovation – towards a more effective European innovation policy', Discussion Note to the Informal Meeting of the Competitiveness Ministers, Jyväskylä, Finland, 10–11 July, 2006.
5. At this point we should also add the need to consider the geographical scope of the impact assessment. In the cases analysed here, impacts in the Flemish economy have been assessed. However, these impacts can also be analysed in the context of a broader geographical scope, i.e. the impacts at EU level. In such cases the methodology should be adjusted accordingly.
6. The literature has mostly concentrated on the economic dimensions of the impacts of science. Research has focused on issues such as the impact of R&D on economic growth and productivity (Solow, 1957), the estimation of the rate of return of investments in R&D (Jaffe, 1996; Griliches, 1980), and the impact of science on international trade (Vernon, 1970). The analysis of other dimensions of the impact of science is as yet less developed. However, citation count has also been used for the measurement of the impact of scientific publications (see, e.g., Hall et al., 2001).
7. Clearly, the content of the terminology used depends on the scope and level of analysis. In other words, a direct effect of a specific policy measure may very well be an indirect effect of a broader set of policy actions. The same applies to the induced effects. The attraction of foreign companies can be regarded as an induced effect when looking at specific initiatives to stimulate the local science base (which then plays an important role in the attraction of R&D centres). It may however also be a direct effect of a broader socioeconomic policy aiming at attracting foreign businesses. Depending on the scope and level of analysis, the terminology will have a different content.

8. However, value added can have a broader meaning as well. For example, it can be used as a indication of the contribution of an organisation to the total performance of a programme. In this respect the EU uses the term value added to reflect the extra rewards gained by the intervention of the Structural Funds. For the purposes of this chapter, we focus on value added as the difference between sales and intermediary purchases, as mentioned above.
9. Research has underlined the importance of scientific research for technological developments (Mansfield, 1991; Rosenberg and Nelson, 1996). Studies on the impact of new technologies in the labour market have been developed (OECD, 1996). Attention has often been focused on measuring technological impacts mainly because these impacts are 'diffused in space and time' (Godin and Doré, 2004).

REFERENCES

Anderson, F., C. Lonmo, S. Schaan and I. Schenk (2006), 'New directions for understanding innovation', presentation at OECD Blue Sky II Forum, Ottawa.
Arundel, A. (2006), 'Innovation survey indicators: any progress since 1996? Or how to address the "Oslo" paradox: we see innovation surveys everywhere but where is the impact on innovation policy?', paper presented at OECD Blue Sky II Conference, Ottawa.
AWI (2006), 'Evaluation of the performance of VIB' ('Evaluatie van de werking van het Vlaams Interuniversitair Instituut voor de Biotechnologie (VIB)'), Brussels.
Bernstein, A., V. Hicks, P. Borbey and T. Campbell (2006), 'A framework to measure the impact of investments in health research', presentation at OECD Blue Sky Forum II, Ottawa.
Bond, R., J. Curran, C. Kirkpatrick, N. Lee and P. Francis (2001), 'Integrated impact assessment for sustainable development: a case study approach', *World Development*, **29** (6), 1011–24.
Buisseret, T.J., H.M. Cameron and L. Georghiou (1995), 'What difference does it make? Additionality in public support of R&D in large firms', *International Journal of Technology Management*, **10**, 587–600.
Debackere, K., A. Verbeek, M. Luwel and E. Zimmermann (2002), 'Measuring progress and evolution in science and technology: part II: the multiple uses of technometric indicators', *International Journal of Management Review*, **4** (3), 213–31
Eales, R., S. Smith, C. Twigger-Ross, W. Sheate, E. Özdemiroglu, C. Fry, P. Tomlinson and C. Foan (2005), 'Emerging approaches to integrated appraisal in the UK', *Impact Assessment and Project Appraisal*, **23** (2), 113–23.
Enqvist, R., I. Miles, P. Cunningham, A. Quevreux and L. Lengrand (2006), 'Draft terms of reference for an EC pilot initiative – supporting the monitoring and evaluation of innovation programmes', Brussels: European Commission.
Ertl, H., M. Bordt, L. Earl, A. Lacroix, C. Lonmo, C. McNiven, S. Schaan, M. Uhrbach, B. van Tol and B. Veenhof (2006), 'Towards understanding impacts in science, technology and innovation activities', Ottawa: Statistics Canada.
Georghiou, L. (1997), 'Issues in the evaluation of innovation and technology policy', *OECD Conference Report*, Paris: OECD.
Georghiou, L., J. Rigby and H. Cameron (eds) (2002), 'Assessing the socio-economic impacts of the framework programme', Brussels: European Commission.

Godin, B. and C. Doré (2004), 'Measuring the impacts of science: beyond the economic dimension', CSIIC working paper, Ottawa.

Griliches, Z. (1980), 'Returns to R&D expenditures in the private sector', in K.W. Kendrick and B. Vaccara (eds), *New Developments in Productivity Measurement*, Chicago, IL: Chicago University Press, pp. 419–62.

IMEC (2005), '*De waarde van IMEC als technologische poort - Een analyse van de impact voor Vlaanderen*', Leuven: IMEC.

Jaffe, A. (1986), 'Technological opportunities and spillovers of R&D: evidence from firms patents, profits and market value', *American Economic Review*, **76**, 984–1000.

Lee, N. and C. Kirkpatrick (2006), 'Evidence-based policy-making in Europe: an evaluation of European Commission integrated impact assessments', *Impact Assessment and Project Appraisal*, **24** (1), 23–33.

Mansfield, E. (1991), 'Academic research and industrial innovation', *Research Policy*, **20** (1), 1–12.

Marburger, J. (2006), 'What indicators for science, technology and innovation policies in the 21st century?', Keynote Address at OCED Blue Sky II Conference, Ottawa.

Miles, I. and P. Cunningham (2006), *SMART INNOVATION – Supporting the Monitoring and Evaluation of Innovation Programmes*, Brussels: European Commission.

OECD (1996), *Technology, Productivity and Job Creation*, Paris: OECD.

Papaconstantinou, G. and W. Polt (1997), 'Policy evaluation in innovation and technology: an overview', *OECD Conference Report*, Paris: OECD.

Peeters, L. (1998), 'Diffusie van belichaamde technologie in Vlaanderen: een empirisch onderzoek op basis van input/output gegevens', VTO 7, Brussels: IWT.

Rosenberg, N. and R.R. Nelson (1996), 'The roles of universities in the advance of industrial technology', in R.S. Rosenbloom and W.J. Spencer (eds), *Engines of Innovation: US Industrial Research at the end of an Era*, Boston, MA: Harvard University School Press, pp. 87–110.

Solow, R. (1957), 'Technical change and the aggregate production function', *Review of Economics and Statistics*, **39**, 312–20.

Steurs, G., A. Verbeek, H. Vermeulen and B. Clarysse (2006), 'A look into the black box: what difference do IWT grants make for their clients?', IWT Report No. 56, Brussels.

Verbeek, A. and K. Debackere (2006), 'Patent evolution in relation to public/private R&D investment and corporate profitability: evidence from the United States – a compilation of relationships based on long run time series techniques', *Scientometrics*, **66** (2), 279–94.

Verbeek, A., K. Debackere, M. Luwel and E. Zimmermann (2002), 'Measuring progress and evolution in science and technology: part I: the multiple uses of bibliometric indicators', *International Journal of Management Review*, **4** (2), 179–211.

Vernon, R. (ed.) (1970), *The Technology Factor in International Trade*, New York: Columbia University Press for NBER.

Veugelers, R. (2006), 'Developments in EU statistics on science, technology and innovation: taking stock and moving towards evidence based policy analysis', paper prepared for the OCED Blue Sky Indicator Conference, Ottawa.

VITO (2006), *Een analyse van de impact voor België*, Brussels: IDEA Consult.

4. The geography of transfer of university knowledge to firms: the case of Southern England

Adrian Healy

INTRODUCTION

Public sector interventions supporting R&D are increasingly justified by reference to the economic benefits that this can bring to the local and regional economy, rather than the more traditional justification centring on public good. New endogenous models of economic growth that allow for positive externalities and increasing returns to investment provide powerful arguments in favour of such an approach. Married to this shift in rationale is a concomitant decentralisation of responsibility for such interventions from the national to the regional scale. A new 'regional turn' is apparent, reflected in concepts such as regional systems of innovation.

Yet the emphasis on a regional dimension and the role of R&D investment in promoting regional economic development relies on many assumptions, not least the importance of geographical proximity in the appropriation of the potential economic benefits. It also makes some strong assumptions about the nature of the linkages between places and organisations, and how learning and innovation occur. This chapter examines the geographical dimension to university–business knowledge transfer relationships in the UK and considers the importance of geographical proximity in practice.[1]

The structure of the chapter is as follows. First, we give some theoretical foundations for the study and provide evidence from the empirical literature on the subject. Second, we make explicit our approach. Third, we describe the situation of the knowledge institutes in the Greater South East Area of the UK, which is our study area as far as the origin of the innovations is concerned. Fourth, we explore the spatial distribution of the knowledge transfer activity; we thereby place particular emphasis on the role of proximity. Fifth, we try to capture the factors that determine these spatial patterns of knowledge exchange over space: we look into the effects of the size of firms; the rationale of the behaviour of organisations on both the supply and demand side, and into the type of link created between the two sides of the 'market'. Finally we look into the question of whether there is a role for public intervention to enhance the effectiveness of the knowledge transfer.

SOME CONCEPTS AND THEORY

Routes of Knowledge Transfer

The transfer of knowledge and ideas between firms and individuals has long been acknowledged as an important influence on levels of innovation and economic development. As far back as 1890 Marshall identified the fact that 'if one man starts a new idea it is taken up by others and combined with suggestions of their own, and this becomes the source of yet more ideas' (Marshall, 1890/1920, p. 271). This exchange of knowledge may be formal or informal, and may not be fully compensated for by market mechanisms.

Despite the difficulties of measuring spillover effects in practice (Krugman, 1991), a raft of studies has identified the positive effects emanating from flows of knowledge and information (Audretsch and Feldmann, 1996; Feldmann, 1999; Harhoff, 1999; Lissoni, 2001; Co, 2004). Universities, as an important source of new ideas and knowledge, are perceived to have a major role to play in stimulating knowledge exchange and promoting positive spillover effects (Freel, 2003; HM Treasury, 2003) – so much so that stimulating the exchange, or transfer, of knowledge between businesses and universities is now regarded as an important component of public policy approaches to stimulating innovation.

Five primary routes for knowledge transfer are commonly identified. This list does not include the internal routes from in-house R&D activities to production although many of the routes remain pertinent.

1. Cooperation in education and training (such as academic training or, increasingly, provision of courses for employees of firms).
2. People and knowledge flows (through the exchange of staff, for example).
3. Collaborative research projects.
4. Commercialisation of R&D outputs (through licensing or spin-out enterprises, for example).
5. Publication of scientific papers and the training of scientists.

As Figure 4.1 demonstrates, it is not always the most tangible forms of knowledge transfer (KT), such as licensing and the establishment of

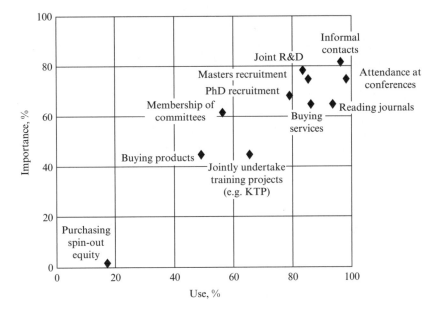

Source: Technopolis (2004).

Figure 4.1   Correlation between use and importance of KT mechanisms

start-up companies around intellectual property generated from R&D activity, that are regarded by users as the most important. Less tangible forms of knowledge exchange, particularly informal contacts and the attendance of conferences, can be as important as joint R&D activities.

Universities increasingly acknowledge the contribution that their activities can make to economic development. While training and skills top the list, it is notable that universities, particularly those with a strong research profile, attach high importance to knowledge transfer activities more generally (Figure 4.2).

The Effect of Distance

It has generally been held that the effect of knowledge spillovers declines with distance (Anselin et al., 1997). Examination of variables such as patent registrations (Jaffe, 1989), bibliographic referencing techniques (Acs et al., 1994), and patent citation rates (Jaffe et al., 1993) all demonstrate that levels of innovation tend to be higher in the vicinity of R&D activity. Such evidence, alongside powerful arguments regarding the importance of tacit knowledge in the innovation process, has provided a strong foundation for

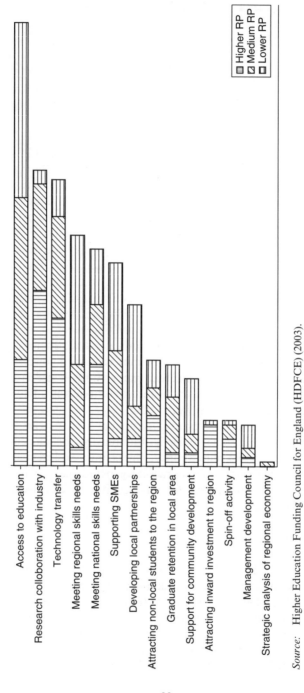

Source: Higher Education Funding Council for England (HDFCE) (2003).

Figure 4.2   Economic development priorities by university research profile (RP)

policy makers seeking to stimulate regionally focused knowledge transfer systems.

However, several studies have identified strong evidence for the existence of positive knowledge spillovers between regions (Caniëls, 2000; Verspagen and Schoenmakers, 2004; Cantwell and Piscitello, 2005), suggesting that the relationships are more complex than previously assumed. With the easing of communications and increasing levels of regular dispersed contacts it has been argued that spatial proximity is now less relevant than it was in the past (Thrift, 2000, Cairncross, 1997). Building on the work of Nonaka and Konno, among others, Amin and Cohendet (2004, p. 107) echo this view, arguing that there has been 'an explosion of virtual communities, communities that can no longer be seen as somehow less able than physically proximate communities'. Concluding that 'nodal knowledge' is not a local affair but is shaped by a range of extra-local interactions and linkages, they argue that relational proximity involves more than 'being there' in terms of physical proximity. They cite Allen (2000, p. 128), who states that 'what matters . . . is not the fact of local embeddedness but the existence of relationships in which people are able to internalise shared understandings or are able to translate particular performances of their own tacit and codified communities'. Morgan (2004, p. 8) for one does not disagree with this but argues that 'something gets lost, or degraded, when individuals or organisations communicate at a distance even when they know each other well'. Spatial proximity remains a powerful force in shaping patterns of innovation and learning, with the home base forming the heart of a knowledge network whose outer reaches might 'straddle multiple spatial scales' (ibid., p. 12).

The spatial dimension to knowledge transfer activity thus remains a contested consideration, but one that is of supreme importance considering the focus of much current public policy. This chapter explores the extent to which knowledge transfer activities reflect a geographical proximity versus relational proximity through the analysis of university knowledge transfer activities in the UK.

APPROACH

In order to examine the patterns of knowledge transfer from universities and other higher education institutions (known collectively as HEIs), this study examined patterns of activity in the Greater South East of England (GSE). The GSE is an informal grouping of three English regions: London, East of England and South East England. Throughout this chapter the terms university and HEI are used interchangeably.

A multidimensional approach combined qualitative interviews with a sample of universities and university departments, coupled with a small-scale survey of businesses linked through knowledge transfer activities to these departments, with a more quantitative assessment of secondary data sources.

The sample of university departments was created using a multistage dimensional sampling approach. In the first instance the focus was on those universities located in the GSE. Five broad subject areas were identified as being particularly related to commercial knowledge transfer activity and were selected as the focus for this study. These subject areas are:

- Business, marketing, management, enterprise
- Computer science and computing
- Engineering and technology
- Art and design (not fine art)
- Biological sciences (including biochemistry).

This provided the foundation for constructing an initial sample of universities located in the GSE that had a department, or departments, covering at least one of these subject areas. From this base a subsample of 15 universities was selected, based upon research profile, the level of formal interaction with business and the range of knowledge transfer activities, from which a total of 52 departments was contacted. Three declined to participate, leaving a final sample of 49 departments. In addition the study was extended to consider two public sector research establishments (PSREs).[2] Overall:

- 52 face-to-face interviews were carried out with heads of department or their equivalent in the PSREs;
- 16 face-to-face interviews were held with other officials responsible for liaison with the business sector. These tended to be based in central corporate or industry liaison offices;
- 89 interviews were held with individual academics;
- 12 interviews were also undertaken with a mixture of SMEs and multinationals to assess the factors that influence the use of different knowledge transfer mechanisms and why they chose to make links with the identified university.

During the pilot stage of the research it became clear that data on the spatial distribution of contacts were not available from individual departments. It was also proving difficult to access such data at a corporate level. The principal reasons for data not being available were commercial confidentiality and data not held in a format capable of spatial disaggregation. To overcome this problem a quantified assessment of the broader pattern of knowledge transfer activity in the UK was undertaken using secondary data sources published by public sector knowledge transfer programmes. Data were available for Knowledge Transfer Partnerships (KTPs), Faraday Partnerships and the LINK programme, and the spatial distribution of this activity was identified based on some 248 identified individual partnerships.

Further quantified data were obtained from the Higher Education Business Interaction Survey. This is undertaken in the UK approximately every two years. It is a survey of all HEIs in the UK and provides an indication of the nature, scope and extent of university interactions with businesses. Data from the surveys published in 2003 and 2005 were analysed to examine the overall pattern of business–university linkages in the UK. These data also provided the baseline of activity in individual universities used to undertake the sampling exercise set out above.

Finally, a series of interviews was undertaken with key individuals to assess the broader context in which knowledge transfer activities were set. Twenty semi-structured interviews with representatives from public and private sector stakeholders, at a national and regional level, were also undertaken to gain a wider perspective on innovation, university knowledge transfer and the factors influencing this.

HEIS IN THE GSE

Public Funding

There are some 169 HEIs in the UK, of which two-fifths are located in the GSE (Table 4.1).[3] Each year some 33 per cent of all graduates in the UK emanate from HEIs located in the GSE. The following section briefly details levels of research, consultancy and other knowledge transfer activities undertaken.

Public funding for the HEI sector in the UK primarily emanates from one of the four funding councils[4] (some 40 per cent) and the various research councils (some 25 per cent).[5, 6] So most of the £3.8 million received came from UK government sources. A small proportion (7 per cent) is directly funded by UK industry, although the £250 million spent by industry on research activities with HEIs constitutes a very minor part of the £16.6 billion spent annually by the UK's 700 largest private R&D investors.[7]

Table 4.1   Number of HEIs in the UK and student numbers

	No. of HEIs	% of UK	Student nos 2002–03 (000)	% of UK
GSE	67*	40	870	33
England	132*	78	2296	86
UK	169*	100	2672	100

Note: * 19 schools and institutes included together as the University of London.

Source: Adapted from HEFCE (2005) and HESA statistics.

Research Funds from Businesses

On average, HEIs in the GSE are slightly more likely to engage in research activities than universities elsewhere in the UK, receiving some £9.6 million each year in research funds from HEFCE, compared to an English average of £8.3 million per annum. However, closer inspection reveals that this is primarily due to the presence of a small number of highly research-intensive HEIs in the GSE, all of which are members of the Russell Group.[8] The research incomes of a small number of research-intensive HEIs in the GSE is some ten times as important than the income from the other institutes.

Overall, HEIs in the GSE have a similar propensity to engage in research activities with businesses as HEIs across the UK (Table 4.2), but are relatively less likely to engage in consultancy work. There is, though, strong variation between the individual regions of the GSE, demonstrating that there is little or no consistent spatial pattern in terms of the propensity of individual HEIs to engage with businesses.

There is some variation in the propensity to work with large firms compared to SMEs, particularly with respect to consultancy work. In comparison to HEIs elsewhere in the UK, HEIs in the GSE are more likely to undertake consultancy work with large firms than SMEs.

Student Exchange

A third area where HEIs may contribute to knowledge exchange is through projects in which students are engaged with non-academic partners. Two strong national schemes exist in this area. The first involves CASE studentships, whereby doctoral students are engaged on a joint research project with an academic and non-academic partner. The second involves KTPs (previously known as the Teaching Company Scheme), where businesses work with a university partner on a common project. The university

Table 4.2   Average number of contacts with business for each HEI

	Total		SMEs		Commercial non-SME	
	Consultancy	Research	Consultancy	Research	Consultancy	Research
East of England	134	97	84	19	34	78
London	76	37	23	4	40	33
South East England	66	158	14	86	44	71
GSE	81	78	29	28	40	49
UK	118	78	48	26	27	52

Source: Adapted from HEFCE (2005).

provides staff expertise plus a Knowledge Transfer Associate – normally a recent graduate – who is located within the company and dedicated to the particular project. It appears that the former are largely utilised by larger organisations and the latter by SMEs. In the East of England, HEIs held an average of 15 CASE awards per institution, of which 20 per cent were with partners in the same region. Each London HEI held an average of four CASE awards, one of which would be with a partner in the same region. HEIs in the South East held 11 CASE awards per institution, 45 per cent of which were with partners within the region. HEIs in the GSE have a higher propensity to engage with the KTPs than the UK average, although in proportionate terms partner firms tend to be based within the region.

THE SPATIAL DISTRIBUTION OF KNOWLEDGE TRANSFER ACTIVITY

Contacts between HEI and Firms

Based on the findings of the 2001–02 HEBI survey, around 60 per cent of HEI consultancy contacts are within the region in which the HEI is located, with two-fifths undertaken elsewhere in the UK or abroad. That finding is corroborated by this study, in which around half of all business contacts appear to be within the same region as the department concerned. Around one-fifth are located elsewhere in the GSE, demonstrating the strength of the proximity effect. On this basis, the proportion of business contacts located outside of the GSE lies somewhere between one-quarter and one-third of all

Table 4.3 Geographic spread of businesses linked to all South East
universities via formal research programmes (LINK, KTP,
Faraday)

Region	Total no. of businesses	%
South East	187	38.3
London	125	25.6
East of England	63	12.9
GSE	375	76.8
Rest of UK	104	21.4
Abroad	9	1.8
Total	488	100

Source: Adapted from LINK, KTP and Faraday programme data.

contacts. The remainder (some 30 per cent) is equally split over elsewhere in
the UK and overseas.

Nine out of ten departments identified links within their own region,
with two-fifths of departments identifying that such local linkages consti-
tuted more than half of all their contacts with businesses. One-third had no
links outside of the GSE and two-fifths had no overseas links, demonstrating that links within the region are the most prevalent. For less than half of
the departments interviewed did links elsewhere in the UK constitute more
than 10 per cent of their total contacts, and for only just over one-third
could the same be said for overseas contacts.

Specific Knowledge Transfer Programmes

A similar pattern emerges when the links between HEIs and businesses
funded by the three formal knowledge transfer programmes – LINK,
Faraday Partnerships and KTPs – are examined, although in this case the
proportion of overseas links is much reduced owing to the nature of the
programmes. More than three-quarters of the projects involving HEIs in
the GSE are focused on links with businesses within the area (Table 4.3),
with a half of these businesses located in the South East.

Types of Institution

One of the results of our study was to highlight the important differences in
spatial reach of different types of institution (Table 4.4). PSREs are more
likely to have links with companies based outside the GSE, both overseas
and in the UK, followed by the four universities with the highest amounts

Table 4.4   Spatial distribution by sub-group (%)

	Regional	GSE	Rest of UK	Overseas
PSREs	27	14	29	31
Leading four research universities	36	20	21	23
Remaining universities	59	18	12	11

Table 4.5   Spatial distribution of different knowledge transfer routes (%)

	Within GSE	Within rest of UK	Overseas
Contract research	58	20	22
Collaborative research	58	23	19
Undergraduate placements	86	9	5

of research funding. The remaining universities tend to have a stronger local focus.

Similarly, different knowledge transfer programmes also exhibit different spatial distributions. The KTP/TCS has the strongest regional focus: 90 per cent of businesses collaborating with universities located in the GSE are also based there themselves. The Faraday Partnerships, by contrast, appear to have the greatest geographical spread of business locations and the lowest share of businesses in the GSE, although 51 per cent of businesses collaborating with universities in the GSE are still based in this area themselves.[9] The LINK programme appears to take a middle position.

A comparison of the different knowledge transfer routes (Table 4.5) also suggests the presence of differential geographies. In the case of collaborative research and consultancy activity (contract research) there is a strong similarity, with around two-fifths of business contacts occurring within the GSE, with the balance split relatively evenly between the rest of the UK and overseas. Graduate placements, however, tend to be predominantly local, with overseas placements partly related to the prevalence of overseas students on some courses.

An important finding of the study was that the strength of the respective contacts can also vary. Intuitively this is not surprising, but it is an important consideration in any study of knowledge transfer activity. It is not just the fact that a relationship is in place; the strength of that relationship is also important. Most contacts within the region are regarded by respondents to the study as high or medium in strength. In contrast, almost two-fifths

Table 4.6   Estimated strength of links with different areas

	Region	GSE	UK	Overseas
Low (%)	24	41	59	47
Medium (%)	35	38	26	29
High (%)	40	21	15	24

Source: HEI survey.

of respondents regarded contacts elsewhere in the UK as of low strength (Table 4.6), with contacts overseas generally being regarded as stronger.

Outside of the GSE there does not appear to be any significant pattern to the geographical distribution of activity. The departmental survey suggests that the single most important region was the North West, followed by the East Midlands, although a strong proportion of respondents identified links in all regions of the UK. The result does seem to suggest, however, that there is no significant 'gravity' effect occurring whereby links with nearby regions are more prevalent.

Similarly, in the case of the KTPs identified, most partners outside of the GSE are located in the West Midlands (6.6 per cent) and the East Midlands (2.9 per cent), followed by the South West (2.5 per cent) and the North West (2.5 per cent), as well as Scotland (2.3 per cent). KTPs are most likely to be 'near local' in the sense that most of the partners outside the GSE are located in bordering regions. There are few links with businesses abroad, and these are primarily through the LINK programme. Of the 1.8 per cent of overseas businesses linked to HEIs in the GSE, most are located in the USA and Switzerland.

FACTORS INFLUENCING THE SPATIAL DISTRIBUTION OF KNOWLEDGE EXCHANGE

Pattern of Demand

Understanding the geography of knowledge transfer activity involves an appreciation of the factors that influence its spatial distribution and bring about the patterns identified above. One of the major spatial influences is, not surprisingly, the pattern of demand. Where clusters, or other con-centrations of economic activity, occur, knowledge transfer activities are pulled towards it. For example, 80 per cent of the work of the Institute of Manufacturing at the University of Cambridge is reported to be located outside the GSE owing to the location of most of the potential users of its research, whilst art and design schools reported that they had strong links with London as this was where many of the design houses they worked with were located. Similarly, some 60 per cent of all business R&D expenditure in the UK occurs in the GSE (Adams and Smith, 2005), increasing the likelihood that universities will work with companies located here.

Size of the Firm

The size of the firm can also affect the spatial distribution of knowledge exchange activities. Relationships with SMEs appear to be more likely to be localised whereas those with larger firms are less constrained by distance. As one head of department commented: 'We probably wouldn't be involved in start-ups in Birmingham or Newcastle and medium sized companies beyond a 50–60 mile radius.' In another case a university's corporate liaison unit felt that the main impacts beyond the GSE were through relationships with large global businesses. In practice, individual academics tended to work with both large firms and SMEs, as each offers benefits (Box 4.1). The general tenor was summed up by one head of department, who stated, 'You will find people here who are familiar with start-ups and you will find people who are familiar with large MNCs. We do not want to be pigeon-holed as a department dealing with a particular stage of business development or size of company.'

BOX 4.1   THE RELATIVE MERITS OF WORKING WITH SMES AND LARGE FIRMS

Few departments focus on working with just one type, or size, of firm. There are some common perceptions of the relative merits of working with SMEs or large firms.

SMEs may be preferred because:

- they represent the industrial landscape and the amount of their activity is increasing;
- they are more likely to do DTI-funded research;
- smaller research projects are very useful, and it is possible to have much more influence;
- they do not have the resources to undertake research in house;
- they offer niche research opportunities;
- it is quicker to establish relationships with SMEs than with a large 'blue-chip' company.

Large firms may be preferred because:

- they have the resources to engage in research-orientated activities;
- they are the source of the most income;
- they are more likely to get involved in course development and add value;
- they are more realistic than SMEs about operational times-cales;
- longer-term relationships can be established.

Capacity to Develop Linkages with Firms

A factor that emerges as a significant influence on the geography of knowledge transfer activity is the capacity to develop linkages with firms. Teaching loads, staff–student ratios and other commitments, particularly publishing research in academic journals, were all reported as affecting the time available to work with business, with researchers reporting that business-related knowledge transfer activity was generally undertaken in the 'spare' time left over after these commitments wcrc mct. The real effect of this is in terms of the amount of time staff have to spend on developing contacts and relationships with businesses, with financial costs to the individual or the department also playing a part in limiting the number of contacts acted upon, or the travel distance considered. As one respondent reported: there are no barriers distance-wise if you have knowledge of the latest technology; however, where there are limited resources, you need to be selective. The result of these constraints is that researchers tend to build contacts with those businesses that are the easiest to access, or where the returns are likely to be greatest. For some this will be locally based businesses; for others it will be large multinational companies met on the international conference circuit, or who have approached the academic themselves.

Initial Contacts

Making the initial contact with business recurs as one of the most important factors underpinning the number and distribution of HEI–business linkages. A lack of contacts was reported as the second most common restriction on developing links with business. In this respect, one academic pointed out, awareness of those businesses that might be interested in academic collaboration is an important factor in developing contacts.

Personal and Professional Networks

An important source of contacts is personal and professional networks. These can act as a filtering mechanism – screening out those that are not interested or do not have something to offer – and reduce the potential transaction costs of contact development. The membership of such networks clearly influences the geography of relationships. Some networks are national industry bodies – the National Composites Network, for example – others are more regional. Some, such as the London Technology Network, have started regionally but are now serving as a wider contact point and, in the words of one academic, 'help to bring in businesses from further away'. The geography of the networks of which academics are members thus plays a crucial role in determining the geography of knowledge transfer activity more widely – in some cases broadening the reach of a university, in others limiting it.

Requests for Support from Businesses

Universities and academics also respond to requests for support from businesses. Here, reputation – of either the individual or the institution[10] – is seen as a fundamental influence on the choice of whom to approach. Those with wider reputations will, all else being equal, receive a greater number of requests to collaborate. This knowledge can be transmitted in different ways. Often it is based upon publications and conference activity, at times it is held in databases, sometimes it is based on student and graduate links, sometimes it is linked to sectoral networks and at other times it is about being known in a region. Awareness of who is doing what in a field, coupled with issues of trust, can play an important part in influencing the geography of knowledge transfer activity. A great deal of effort has been expended on overcoming the knowledge deficit and bringing businesses and academics together. Formal innovation programmes, such as KTP and the Faraday Partnerships, operate alongside broader third-stream funding through the Higher Education Innovation Fund (HEIF). Yet despite all these resources businesses still reportedly find it difficult to know whom to work with. Clearly the focus of efforts to build awareness and bring potential partners together has a significant influence on the spatial distribution of knowledge transfer activities.

Strategy Adopted by a University

One clear influence on the geography of knowledge transfer can be the strategy adopted by a university towards the links that it seeks to nurture.

It is fair to say that no university or department interviewed adopts an overtly spatial focus to its activities. In nearly all cases the emphasis is on developing links with businesses, wherever these might be located. Any spatial dimension is an unintended outcome of those decisions. As one London-based commentator reported: 'the CLU [Corporate Liaison Unit] doesn't think in "geographical" terms. Although London is important and will remain so, the strategy is driven by sectoral considerations and knowledge transfer opportunities – where these are is immaterial.' However, it is also clear that for at least some universities the spatial geography of their business contacts is becoming a stronger consideration.

HEIs certainly perceive that there is strong pressure to focus on generating intraregional benefits. The decentralisation of policy and resources to the regional level and the development of stronger working links with the Regional Development Agencies (RDAs) reinforce this and are influencing behaviour. One leading HEI reported that it is not a regional HEI but it is happy to 'do' this and tick the 'regional' box. Similarly, all three universities that have identifiable spatial targets for knowledge transfer activity in their corporate plans aim to increase the proportion of activity they undertake within the region. If carried through, these effectively work against the development of a wider spatial focus. At a practical level a similar message emerges, for example one university informed this study that in terms of working outside the GSE there are no real barriers as they work mainly with manufacturing businesses; however, the increased working links with the region's economic development agency mean that they are focusing more on the region itself and therefore have reduced capacity to work elsewhere.

There is as yet no countervailing pressure to adopt an interregional approach, although there are signs that, for some, this is becoming a stronger consideration. There is also hesitation among some universities as to where the regional turn is leading. As one university interviewee reported, geography is irrelevant as the university just wants to work with the best, wherever they are, so pushing the regional agenda does not necessarily sit well with this.

HOW IMPORTANT IS PROXIMITY?

One of the great debates in the field of knowledge transfer activity is the importance of co-location, or geographical proximity. As noted previously, much research highlights the fact that knowledge spillovers tend to decline with distance, with other research stressing the importance of a rich local 'learning' environment. However, whether this remains valid in the context of new communications technologies is a moot point.

The data derived through this study appear to support the suggestion that proximity is an important factor influencing the spatial distribution of knowledge exchange and innovation. Yet academics repeatedly report that proximity is not an important factor influencing the spatial geography of their linkages with business (Box 4.2). This view is supported by R&D-intensive firms themselves. For multinational corporations, relationships are forged on the basis of expertise rather than the geographic location of the HEI. For one firm, based in the North East, Southampton University was its favoured partner because – in this case – it was 'where the science is at its best'. Finally, one PSRE noted that they do world-class research and that local and regional networks have not been good in terms of business for them, but have been good for the businesses themselves because they allow them to stay up to date with the latest developments.

BOX 4.2   PROXIMITY IS NOT SEEN AS A KEY DRIVER

In general, proximity was not seen as a critical factor influencing the spatial pattern of university–business linkages. Typical comments included:

'Strategy is driven by industry needs/sectoral opportunities – it doesn't matter where they are.'

'Geography is not the point–it's industry. Certain areas are better for certain industries.'

'Spatial location is irrelevant to academics. [The HEI] undertakes research in locations where there are research units.'

'Communications are such nowadays that distance is not as important after initial contact.'

Where proximity does have an influence is in terms of initiating contacts, as hinted at in the last comment in Box 4.2. Universities and academics can have a better awareness of their local market, and travel costs (in terms of money and time) tend to be lower. As one academic reported, it is more difficult to gain access to businesses outside the GSE as they are further away. This makes it more difficult to engage with them. These two factors appear to favour the development of local links, all other things being equal. Where geographical proximity is important is in terms of the place-ment of students with firms, such as in the case of KTPs. The vast majority of placements are proximate to the university. In these instances depth and frequency of contact, coupled with residential preferences, appear to be important influencing factors. In some cases this is due to the requirements of the university; for example, for some courses it is a requirement that the student lives locally, thus restricting the opportunities to undertake place-ments further afield. In others it is due to the preference of the students, and in others it is due to the contacts base of the HEI/academic arranging the placements. Where placements are more widely distributed they tend to be with companies with which the department has a long-standing arrange-ment. It appears that the tendency for placements is for more localised ones in the UK and a greater proportion of overseas placements, reflecting the increasing numbers of overseas students.

This pattern of near and far links, with relatively fewer connections in between, appears to be quite strong for all knowledge transfer linkages, at least in the UK, and particularly with respect to the intensity of the connections made. There is a preference for local/regional linkages, with links beyond the region bearing few signs of prevalent gravity effects, in that universities are as likely to engage with collaborators elsewhere in the world as they are with those located elsewhere in the UK.

A ROLE FOR PUBLIC SECTOR INTERVENTION?

There has been much consideration by the public sector as to how to promote greater levels of knowledge transfer activity. In the UK this has focused, at a national level, around building capacity within HEIs to engage with businesses; stimulating spin-outs and licensing, and making direct connections with individual businesses through collaborative research and through placement and sponsorship schemes. These policies are, broadly, aspatial. The spatial effects of their implementation rely upon the focus of participating universities, PSREs and businesses, as well as the nature of the activity itself; for example, spin-outs tend to have strong local impacts, at least in the short term, while licensing effects tend to be more global. As we have seen, this is presently leading to a mixed geography of knowledge transfer activity.

At a regional level there is an equal, and increasing, interest in stimulating knowledge transfer within the region, particularly in terms of capitalising on a region's knowledge base of universities and research centres. In part this relies upon a regionalisation of national policy initiatives, but commonly also includes brokering contacts and fostering networks of business people and academics. Here there is a much stronger, albeit often implicit, emphasis on the spatial dimension to knowledge transfer activities. This is certainly the perception of the HEIs involved in this study and of many of the public bodies interviewed. Where spatial targets exist they tend to be regional rather than interregional. This chapter does not question whether this increasingly regional turn to knowledge transfer policies is appropriate. Rather, it offers some pointers to effective mechanisms for stimulating regional knowledge transfer activities, based upon the lessons of the research undertaken.

First, public policy makers can support awareness of available skills and knowledge as well as interest in engaging in knowledge transfer activities. A recurring criticism of efforts to bring academics and businesses together is the current lack of knowledge of what expertise resides where. The costs of acquiring this knowledge are a barrier for many companies and academics. Efforts to make such knowledge acquisition simpler and more straightforward, such as mapping of key areas of expertise and knowledge strengths within a region, can go some way towards improving levels of information here. This is already occurring within regions; for example, i10 in the East of England now has a database of more than 10 000 academics. At a national level a basic framework is also in place, for example on the UK INVEST website.

Whilst effective databases can be an important start, they are not enough on their own. Evidence taken by the UK's Small Business Service suggests that businesses are looking for a 'human face'. Stimulating effective relationships between businesses and HEIs requires a more active brokerage role, by facilitators that have strong specialist knowledge of where expertise lies. Networks, such as the London Technology Network and Jumpstart, also in London, can play an important role in this regard. One of the success factors behind networks is that they improve the participants' knowledge of what expertise exists where and which businesses are potentially interested in academic expertise. Specialist business advisers, acting in a trans-regional capacity, can also prove valuable brokers.

However, stimulating demand for business–HEI collaborations may be missing a key dimension of knowledge exchange. The greatest contribution that HEIs make to knowledge transfer tends to be through the contributions made to published papers, conference presentations and informal advice. Whilst collaborative research and consultancy activity can benefit individual companies or organisations, the development and publication of new knowledge has the ability to reach a wider audience. How to help

SMEs access and digest new knowledge is a key question for public policy. The challenge facing public agencies is, then, how to assist the dissemination and assimilation of knowledge. At one level this may involve generating a stronger innovation culture among firms more generally, reaching out to both managers and employees. At another level public agencies, such as the Manufacturing Advisory Service in the UK, can provide a valuable service informing companies of new developments. Strengthening linkages of bodies such as these with new developments emanating from academia is an important dimension to spreading the knowledge generated in HEIs more widely. It can also ensure that publicly funded research benefits companies and organisations across the UK by helping to draw externally generated knowledge into a region to the benefit of the firms located there that do not necessarily wish to undertaken collaborative work with HEIs on an individual basis.

CONCLUSIONS

Knowledge transfer activity has both near and far horizons. The dominant form is local contacts – hence the near horizons. Between a half and two-fifths of all activities are undertaken within the respective region. However, this is not a consistent picture. More research-active organisations tend to have fewer local links, while different types of knowledge transfer activity also have differential spatial geographies, with those relating to student placements tending to be the most localised.

The strength of the contacts also varies by location. Local contacts tend to be the strongest, followed by those that are overseas. Contacts with organisations located elsewhere in the UK – the medium horizon – were, in this study, the least strong. There is also no consistent 'distance–decay' pattern observable in terms of research contacts within different regions elsewhere in the UK.

A range of factors, both external to and internal to individual universities and departments, influences the geography of knowledge transfer activity revealed in this study. One of the recurring messages, however, is that geographical proximity is not regarded as a key criterion by most academics, despite the finding that local contacts dominate knowledge transfer activity patterns. Rather, the revealed geography is a function of the complex interplay of many different factors.

The study has provided further support to the contention that strong local spillovers emanate from universities located within a region, but it has also highlighted the importance of interregional spillovers. The latter do not appear to have an observable spatial geography. This supports

Morgan's observation, mentioned earlier in this chapter, that the home base forms the heart of a knowledge network that straddles multiple spatial scales.

This finding has important ramifications for those interested in the development of regional innovation systems. While the local remains important, the relationship between the local and wider scales must also be considered. In practice, many of these relationships are mediated by individuals operating in different networks or communities of practice. In this respect it is the relational geography that is critical to the geography of knowledge transfer activities. The choice, it appears, is not between spatial proximity and relational proximity, but rather concerns the mix between the two.

An important message is that simply enhancing the capacity of universities to engage in knowledge transfer activities will not necessarily lead to any change in the geography of these activities. It is a well-known truism that not all knowledge transfer routes are the same. Different types of route, whether contract relationships, collaborative research or student placements, exhibit a different geography. This is an important message for public policy makers seeking to build stronger regional knowledge transfer networks. The focus to date has been on developing HEI–business interactions *per se*, regardless of geography. As a stronger regional turn to this policy emerges, a more nuanced approach will be needed. In some cases this should focus on strengthening intraregional knowledge transfer activities but in others policy makers will do well to consider how to encourage interregional knowledge exchange to the benefit of local firms and universities.

NOTES

1. This chapter is based on research undertaken in 2005 for a consortium of clients led by the South East England Development Agency. We thank them for permission to publish extracts of this work. Of course, the opinions expressed throughout are those of the author, and I remain responsible for any inaccuracies that remain. The full report is available at http://www.seeda.co.uk/Publications/Policy_&_Economics/Docs/ECOTEC_ReportMay05.pdf.
2. CCLRC (South East) and the Institute for Food Research (East of England).
3. *HEFCE 2005 Guide: Higher Education in the United Kingdom*, February.
4. The Higher Education Funding Councils for England, Wales, Scotland and Northern Ireland.
5. There are seven research councils in the UK responsible for investing public money in science and research.
6. *HEFCE 2005 Guide*.
7. DTI R&D scorecard.
8. In the UK the most research-intensive universities form a group known as the Russell

Group. Seven of the 19 members of the Russell Group (37 per cent) are located in the GSE.
9. This analysis is based on a sample of seven current Faraday Partnerships.
10. This might be the university or the PSRE as a whole or a particular department, school or college.

REFERENCES

Acs, Z., F. Fitzroy and I. Smith (1994), 'High technology employment and university R&D spillovers: evidence from US cities', paper presented at the 41st North American Meetings of the Regional Science Association International, Niagara Falls.

Adams, J. and D. Smith (2005), *Research and Regions: An Overview of the Distribution of Research in UK Regions, Regional Research Capacity and Links between Strategic Research Partners*, Oxford: Higher Education Policy Institute.

Allen, J. (2000) 'Power/economic knowledges: symbolic and spatial formations', in Bryson, J. Roy, P.W. Daniels, N.D. Henry and J.S. Pollard (eds), *Knowledge, Space, Economy*, London: Routledge, pp. 15–33.

Amin, A. and P. Cohendet (2004), *Architectures of Knowledge: Firms, Capabilities, and Communities*, Oxford: Oxford University Press.

Anselin, L., A. Varga and Z. Acs (1997), 'Local geographic spillovers between university research and high technology innovations', *Journal of Urban Economics*, **42** (3), 422–7.

Audretsch, D. and M. Feldman (1996), 'R&D spillovers and the geography of innovation and production', *American Economic Review*, **86**, 630–40.

Cairncross, F. (1997), *The Death of Distance*, Boston, MA: HBS Press.

Caniëls, M. (2000) *Knowledge Spillovers and Economic Growth: Regional Growth Differentials across Europe*, Cheltenham, UK and Northampton, MA, USA: Edward Elgar.

Cantwell, J. and L. Piscitello (2005), 'Recent location of foreign-owned research and development activities by large multinational corporations in the European regions: the role of spillovers and externalities', *Regional Studies*, **39** (1), 1–16.

Co, C. (2004), 'Evolution of the geography of innovation: evidence from patent data', *Growth and Change*, **33** (4), 393–423.

Feldman, M. (1999), 'The new economics of innovation, spillovers and agglomeration: a review of empirical studies', *Economic Innovation and New Technology*, **8**, 5–25.

Freel, M.S. (2003), 'Sectoral patterns of small firm innovation, networking and proximity', *Research Policy*, **32** (5), 751–70.

Harhoff, D. (1999) 'Firm formation and regional spillovers – evidence from Germany', *Economics of Innovation & New Technology*, **8**, 27–55.

HEFCE (2003), Higher Education Business Interaction Survey 2000–01.

HEFCE (2005), Higher Education Business Interaction Survey 2002–03.

HM Treasury (2003), Lambert Review of Business–University Collaboration.

Jaffe, A.B. (1989), 'Real effects of academic research', *American Economic Review*, **79** (5), 957–70.

Jaffe, A., M. Trajtenberg and R. Henderson (1993), 'Geographical localization of knowledge spillovers, as Evidenced by Patent Citations', *Quarterly Journal of Economics*, **58**, 577–98.

Krugman, P. (1991), *Geography and Trade*, Cambridge, MA: MIT Press.

Lissoni, F. (2001), 'Knowledge codification and the geography of innovation: the case of Breshia Mechanical Cluster', *Research Policy*, **30** (9), 1479–550.

Marshall, A. (1920), *Industry and Trade*, London: Macmillan.

Morgan, K. (2004), 'The exaggerated death of geography: learning, proximity and territorial innovation systems', *Journal of Economic Geography*, **4** (1), 3–21.

Technopolis (2004), 'Survey of knowledge transfer between NERC-funded researchers and the users of their outputs: a report to the NERC Director of Knowledge Transfer and the NERC Knowledge Transfer Advisory Group (KTAG)', Brighton: Technopolis Ltd, 8 July.

Thrift, N. (2000), 'Everyday life in the city', in G. Bridge and S. Watson (eds), *A Companion to the City*, Oxford: Blackwell, pp. 398–409.

Verspagen, B. and W. Schoenmakers (2004), 'The spatial dimension of patenting by multinational firms in Europe', *Journal of Economic Geography*, **4** (1), 23–42.

PART II

Firms

5. ICT and firm innovation in European 'catching-up' countries

Jacob Dencik and Julia Djarova[1]

INTRODUCTION

Many economists consider the development, application and utilisation of ICT as a critical factor for economic performance and competitiveness in general, and for productivity, efficiency and innovation in particular. At the firm level, increased use of ICT leads to greater efficiency, lower costs and access to larger and new markets. At the national level, the enhanced application and use of ICT generates higher national productivity, job creation and competitiveness.

We have seen in the introductory chapter that there are considerable differences between countries and regions as to their levels of innovation and their degree of inclusion in the knowledge economy. The new EU member countries score in general rather low on the relevant indicators. In order to catch up with the EU medium, these countries have to speed up the application of ICT by firms. As this will not happen by itself, the governments of these countries must adopt policies that facilitate and stimulate the use of ICT by firms.

However, there is a general lack of understanding of the relation between ICT and firms that have to work under the conditions that prevail in most new member states. As a consequence there is also a lack of clarity as to the best way for the public authorities at all levels (EU, nation, region) to intervene. The objective of this chapter is to shed some light on these two issues.

To that end we have made an investigation at the firm level into the dynamics of their adoption of ICT in a number of countries in Central and Eastern Europe (see InfoDev 2008).

The structure of the present chapter is as follows. In the next section we present some preliminary pieces of information on the scale of ICT usage and its business applications. In the core of the chapter we address successively the following four questions:

1. What is the contribution of ICT utilisation to the economic performance of firms?
2. What is the contribution of ICT utilisation to innovation among firms?[2]
3. What are the enablers, barriers and constraints for ICT utilisation at firm level?
4. What are the actions that the public authorities can take in order to encourage the use of ICT by the business sector?

We summarise the findings and list recommendations in a concluding section.

SOME PRELIMINARY REMARKS ON THE APPROACH FOLLOWED

Many existing studies on the impact of ICT have looked at national, regional or sectoral impacts as their unit of analysis.[3] The findings of these studies suggest that ICT has contributed greatly to productivity growth and competitiveness. However, they have serious limitations. They mostly look at the role of ICT at a fairly aggregate level, and fail to capture the critical role and complexity of the utilisation of ICT as a determining factor in shaping at the firm level enhanced innovation and economic performance.

Studies that focus on the processes of application and use of ICT within firms have been carried out for different countries. The OECD has reviewed a number of them,[4] concluding that at the firm level 'ICT use is beneficial – though under certain conditions – to firm performance in all countries for which micro level studies have been conducted' (OECD, 2003, p. 76). However, the benefits of ICT emerge only over time, as they need to be accompanied by a number of innovations on the level of the organisation of the firm[5] and the development of new skills by the staff of the firm. Moreover, they are dependent on the simultaneous development of ICT use in other firms (upstream and downstream) and in government, notably through computer networks. In this respect it is interesting to note that the E-commerce Business Impacts Project[6] (EBIP) of the OECD came to the conclusion that there is a need to reassess the notion of e-commerce or e-business. Hence the evolution of ICT usage comes closer to electronic business networking – the use of ICT to forge closer and more interactive links between business processes within the firm and commercial processes in the market place.

Methodology of the Study

For the countries that are not in the premier league of ICT use, very few studies on the influence of ICT on the firm level have been made.[7] Past surveys on ICT at the firm level in such (catching-up) countries have often been of the 'e-readiness' variety.[8] These surveys gather data on firm-level ICT investments and construct profiles of the technological evolution in various sectors and industries. This evolution is then tied to assumptions and estimates about use patterns and probable effects on performance and productivity. Industry-wide impacts are then produced by means of aggregations and projections based upon these assumptions and estimations.

This type of approach does not sufficiently serve the purpose of analysing the effects of ICT on the economic performance of firms, and on their position in the marketplace. Nor does it provide a solid foundation for linking the ICT take-up by firms with key enablers, barriers and constraints in conditions prevailing in the less developed countries of Europe.

To overcome some of the weaknesses of existing approaches we have designed a survey methodology that permits us to identify the impact of ICT at the firm level. Central to this is an Electronic Business Survey (EBS),[9] which collects data at firm level so as to allow us to place the application and utilisation of ICT within its proper context. The EBS methodology explores productivity and performance impacts of technical change – ICT for this case – from the general perspective of how businesses and industries evolve relative to their specific product and/or service groups and markets. EBS therefore does not impose any *a priori* assumptions about how any particular technology investment and any particular productivity or performance outcome are linked. Instead, the survey question routine is set up such that firms enumerate the impacts of ICT within the business dynamics and within their own firm–supplier–customer context. (See Box 5.1.)

BOX 5.1   SUMMARY OF THE EBS
             METHODOLOGY AND ITS APPLICATION
             TO THE STUDY

In order to be able to answer the question of how ICT take-up and usage relate to competitiveness and economic performance, six sub-questions are addressed in the different modules of the survey:

Module A serves to identify a number of basic characteristics of the enterprise and its position in the market. These 'calibration data' are important to assess the enterprise's capacity to adopt and use ICT business applications and/or their capacity to influence the ICT usage of other enterprises in their market. (This module relates to research question 1.)

Module B, about which technologies are available in the enterprise, is similar to that of most ICT diffusion studies. This part of the survey questionnaire is based largely on existing procedures used by the European Commission and/or the OECD in order to allow international comparison. (This module relates to research questions 1 and 2.)

Module C examines how these applications are being used in distinct business processes. It looks into the effects of ICT usage as well as other factors on productivity, competitiveness and innovation. In addition it investigates how ICT usage and other factors relate to each other in increasing or reducing the firm's performance, and in this context provides an indication of the additionality of ICT. (This module relates to research question 2.)

Module D, on effects, assesses the contribution of ICT to the enterprise's performance. The aim of this question is to establish the causal relation between the usage of certain technologies in certain business processes and their effects, including negative effects. Unlike most surveys, the EBS methodology produces these estimations in a quantified and comparative way. (This module relates to research question 1.)

Module E, on the relation between the enterprise and its environment, aims at identifying so-called strategic issues, which are not easily quantified. Questions refer to the relation between the enterprise and its business environment, in particular the value chain(s) in which the enterprise is active.

Finally, *Module F* relates to the policy and regulatory environment in which firms operate. A specific approach, tested in the Electronic Business Survey (EBS), is used to weigh the relative importance of incentives and obstacles to the usage of ICT applications. (This module relates to research questions 3 and 4.)

The methodology has allowed us to take account of the context specificity of the utilisation of ICT within different sectors and firms. The survey findings have been complemented with eight case studies of firms that have allowed us to ascertain in greater detail the factors shaping ICT take-up and use.

The Problem of 'Additionality'

A principal problem with all impact measurement is how to separate the effects of the key variable (ICT in our case) from all the other factors and forces that affect productivity – in other words to show the additionality of ICT. In quantitative analysis the solution to the problem is often sought in the use of long data time series, but these are unavailable in our case. We have used a specific protocol during the data-gathering process to check for additionality. Respondents were asked to:

- identify normally expected performance parameters for specific business segments or product areas (e.g. expected growth rates, cost reductions, etc.);
- benchmark themselves against these parameters during the period in which ICT applications were made;
- estimate the degree to which positive or negative outcomes could be attributed to ICT investments.

In other words, rather than benchmarking with a control group of firms with no or low-level ICT, additionality effects have been determined at the firm level by comparison over time – before and after the ICT take-up. This method is more efficient and more effective than using control groups, in terms of both resources used and results obtained.

Geographic Coverage, Selection of Regions and Sectors

The focus of the study is on firms that are confronted with deficiencies as to their environment in terms of infrastructure, institutions etc. The study was conducted in Estonia, Latvia, Lithuania, Poland and Russia. These countries share a number of features as they have all been subject to significant transformations associated with their transition process from a command to a market economy. Moreover, the first four have been integrated into the EU, which gave them access to the EU Structural Funds. However, there are also a number of differences between the countries. For example, Estonia is at the forefront of ICT and innovation, while Russia has yet to establish a solid ICT infrastructure that can serve as a foundation for economic growth. Accordingly, the selection of countries offers the opportunity to study the role of ICT and innovation in different settings and contexts. The three Baltic countries are fairly small, while in contrast Poland is large and Russia is even larger. Thus we have concentrated the area of analysis in the latter two on a small number of regions that are of significant economic importance to the two countries (e.g. Pomorskie, Mazowieckie and Slaskie regions in Poland, and Moscow and St Petersburg in Russia).

We selected a set of key sectors (finance, food processing, furniture, heavy machinery, ICT services and retail & wholesale) on the basis of the following criteria:

- growth potential and/or strategic importance for economic development of the country concerned;
- potential for cross-country comparisons and extrapolation of findings to other sectors;
- ICT and innovation content.

The target group for the study was companies at the forefront in ICT usage. They have been using ICT comparatively (to other firms in the same sector) intensely, successfully and for a period of at least three years. Covering the forerunners rather than being a representative sample of the sector, the study is representative of trends that are likely to affect the industry or sector in the foreseeable future.

In total, 620 firms participated in the survey. The survey was based on face-to-face interviews and run in two iterations in order to ensure a clean dataset for all 620 companies.

Performance and innovation are analysed across the whole sample as well as across large, medium and micro and small companies, and sectors.

CONTRIBUTION OF ICT UTILISATION TO THE ECONOMIC PERFORMANCE OF FIRMS

Level of ICT Usage

The first major question we have to answer is: what is the contribution of ICT utilisation to the economic performance of firms? To answer that question a set of analyses have been made. The first is to establish the present situation as to ICT usage. The results of this part of the study show that the picture is different for different dimensions of ICT. Access to the Internet and the use of email are almost universal among the firms surveyed. Local area networks were also found to be rather popular. However, it is mainly less advanced ICT that is used, rather than its latest generations.

While almost all companies surveyed had made use of the Internet during the last three years, the means of connecting to the Internet differed greatly. For example, almost 22 per cent of the surveyed firms were making use of fast connections with download speeds of more than 2 Mbps, while almost 18 per cent of the firms were still using an analogue connection.

The use of the advanced forms was found to depend heavily on the technical infrastructure available within the individual countries, which varied greatly from country to country in the sample. While Estonia was moving fast towards broadband connections, the other countries were lagging behind. Nevertheless, perhaps contrary to expectations, companies did not find that the technical infrastructure (defined as network reliability, network flexibility and range of available services or geographic coverage) disturbed or hampered their activities. Neither did they find that telecommunication prices inhibited their use of ICT.

ICT usage was found to be geared towards serving customers and markets. About half of the companies in the survey placed a high priority on two interrelated business areas: purchasing and procurement, and marketing and sales. Selling via the Internet was less popular than buying: more than 47 per cent of firms placed orders, while less than 40 per cent received and processed orders using the Internet.

Firms actively use computer networks for these activities, and almost all of them were using the Internet to buy and sell goods and services. The Internet is a common means for servicing customers, providing them with information on products and services, contact facilities and often after-sales support. Market/customer-related activities were found to be automated within half of the firms. This seemed to be the primary driving force for automation and ICT use in other business areas such as procurement and purchasing, finance (especially invoicing), delivery and stock control.

ICT Utilisation and Economic Performance

ICT utilisation had a clear impact on the economic performance of firms in the survey countries. ICT was a substantial contributor to productivity, to profitability and to growth (see first two columns of Table 5.1). The fact that 30 per cent of the firms said that ICT usage itself generates increases in ICT investment indicates that engagement in ICT usage is to a certain extent a self-sustaining process that requires cumulative investment.

However, while the use of ICT is resulting in improved economic performance of firms, it is important to note that ICT utilisation does not

Firms

Table 5.1   ICT and economic performance of firms

Performance indicators	% of firms with reported increase	ICT contribution (%)	ICT in combination with other factors (%)
Labour productivity	50	13	47
Operational cost	41	5	28
Revenue from sales	55	7	43
Profitability	44	11	48
Capital investment in innovation	52	16	58
ICT investment	45	30	46
Competition in price	57	5	29
Competition in quality	64	10	40
	% of firms with reported decrease		
Operational costs	19	16	52

automatically translate into economic impacts, but requires a range of complementary factors (see third column of Table 5.1). Three factors were found to be most critical for successfully translating the adoption and utilisation of ICT into positive economic outcomes. These are: new marketing strategy; capital investment in equipment; and organisational change. Moreover, these factors affect different dimensions of the economic performance of firms.

A new marketing strategy is particularly relevant for translating the introduction and use of ICT into the improvement of profitability. This is mainly because the use of ICT together with new marketing initiatives enables firms to strengthen their position in existing markets, or enter new markets, and thereby improve profitability.

Investment in equipment is particularly important for lowering operational costs and increasing revenues. This is perhaps unsurprising as ICT is said to allow for new and more efficient production processes, which in turn require investment in new equipment. The impact of ICT on production processes thus does not primarily arise from ICT in itself. Rather, ICT is a means by which new and more efficient production processes can be achieved when combined with new equipment.

Organisational change is particularly important for achieving greater labour productivity, lower operational costs and increased revenues. The close correlation between these dimensions of improved economic performance from ICT and organisational change identified in this study corresponds well with findings from other studies on the impact of ICT on firm performance (e.g. Room et al., 2004). It has thus often been argued that the effective utilisation of ICT requires more horizontal organisational structures, with greater levels of responsibility for the overall coordination of work placed on the individual employee. It also requires the implementation of clearer functional descriptions of tasks. All this often needs a complete reshaping of the organisational structure of the firm where all aspects of organisational development are consequently addressed. This view is further supported by the case studies conducted as part of this project, which highlighted the importance of changes in organisational structures and in ensuring that all employees have a sense of responsibility for their work.

The findings also show that ICT contributes to firms' efforts to compete on quality rather than on price. This finding should be placed in the wider context of ICT as a decisive factor in generating efficiency gains, but is not generally considered a distinguishing factor in effectively attaining a competitive advantage over competitors that are equally investing in ICT.

All findings should be seen in the light of the transition process that shaped the context in which the firms operated at the time of the survey. It forced the firms towards rapid modernisation, emphasising improved production processes and flexible organisations that address the needs of the market. This may in part explain why ICT is combined with other factors, such as new marketing strategies and organisational change, for improved economic performance.

The size of the firm appears to matter for the effect of ICT on performance. About two-thirds of large firms reported a positive effect of ICT on productivity and profitability; this figure was about halved for small enterprises, which score relatively better for revenue increases and cost reductions.

Sectoral and Spatial Differences in ICT Use and Economic Impacts

By sorting data on the basis of positive effects of ICT ('mainly ICT' and 'ICT and other factors' taken together), the contribution of ICT to economic performance of the sectors can be defined (see Table 5.2). On the basis of the analysis, the most revealing and/or inclusive indicators were selected. For performance these are productivity, profitability, operational costs and revenues from sales.

For both productivity and profitability heavy machinery is the lead sector in terms of attribution of positive effects to ICT usage, with almost

Table 5.2   Sector-related key findings on ICT and economic performance

Sector	Contribution of ICT to economic performance
Finance	High
Food processing	Low
Furniture	Low
Heavy machinery	High
ICT services	High
Retail & wholesale	Medium

75 per cent of firms attributing positive effects to either ICT alone or ICT and other factors. The direct attribution of effects to ICT, however, is much higher for productivity (31 per cent) than for profitability (17 per cent). ICT services, finance and retail & wholesale form a trio, with around 70 per cent of the firms attributing positive effects to ICT alone or ICT and other factors.

The financial sector by far exceeds the other sectors in terms of positive attribution to ICT of both cost reductions for 100 per cent of firms and revenue increases for 82 per cent of firms. The difference between the categories is accentuated by a very high direct attribution to ICT of 57 per cent for cost reduction. For heavy machinery the positive attribution of effects to ICT is higher for cost reduction (67 per cent of firms) than for revenue increases (58 per cent). Most significantly, the direct attribution of effect to ICT for revenue increased is nil (compared with 17 per cent for cost reduction). Furniture is the only sector where the positive rate of attribution to ICT is higher for revenue increases (46 per cent of firms) than for cost reductions (33 per cent of firms).

The figures confirm that the distinctions between tangibles and intangibles, or services and goods, are rudimentary when it comes to predicting the potential of ICT to enhance economic performance. The number one ranking of heavy machinery for both productivity and profitability increases, wholly or partially attributable to ICT, confirms this. We may confidently assume that the explanation for this high ranking is to be found in the product characteristics of heavy machinery.

We feel that it is more accurate to posit that the potential effect of ICT on the firm's performance will be determined by the information intensity of the product. This involves both product and transaction characteristics. For example, the products of finance and ICT services sectors have a high informational component and can be traded electronically as well. Financial products have an even higher informational nature than

ICT services, which is expressed in the higher average ranking of finance and in particular a higher attribution for revenue increases. The latter subject will be touched on again in the section on relational innovation below.

Furniture manufacturing and food processing are undoubtedly the sectors with the lowest information intensity, in both the product and transaction areas. Logically, both close the ranks in all categories under scrutiny: productivity, profitability, cost and revenues. However, furniture scores relatively better for revenue increases. This result, as will be demonstrated in the following sections, can be related to the usage of ICT for customisation and the effect this has on customer relations.

Finally, retail & wholesale hold a middle position in general, but score significantly above average on the cost reduction category. Contrary to heavy machinery, finance and ICT services, the information intensity of these products generally does not provide much potential for spectacular performance improvements through ICT usage. The gains of ICT usage are found in the area of transactions, and can be due either to the high frequency of transactions and/or the amount of customers and suppliers involved.

Due to data limitations a comprehensive comparative analysis of the five countries included in this study is not possible. However, at a general level we see that Estonia holds the first place at some distance from the others; the situation varies according to the specific aspect taken into consideration. We shall come back to this point in a later section, where we relate scores to barriers and enablers.

At a general level, when comparing productivity effects, a ranking is obtained in which Estonia holds the first place, followed by Russia and Poland, but with only marginal differences between the latter two. Note that these figures are not a static ranking, but an indication of the dynamism displayed by the industry in the last three years (2002–05). It may well be, for example, that the rate of adoption of ICT in a given country is higher in absolute terms, but the pace of adoption has recently been higher in another country.

Among the firms that reported an increase in productivity, Russia and Estonia both show a significant contribution from ICT, while the role of ICT in generating productivity gains is much more limited in Poland.[10] Similarly, the role of ICT in delivering cost reductions, revenue increases and improved profitability is far more limited in Poland compared to Estonia and Russia. It is thus evident that the overall role and impact of ICT in the transition countries differ significantly between countries. This should perhaps not surprise us, as the diverse overall socioeconomic and political contexts of the different countries will create varied environments for ICT adoption and utilisation. We explore these issues further when discussing barriers and enablers.

CONTRIBUTION OF ICT UTILISATION TO INNOVATION AMONG FIRMS

Effects on Different Types of Innovation

The second major question that we would like to answer is: 'How do firms use ICT to improve innovation, a major determinant of their future performance?' The study found that the role of ICT is different for different types of innovation. ICT utilisation has substantial effects on process innovation,[11] a moderate effect on product innovation,[12] and only a limited effect on relational innovation.[13] In other words, the use of ICT is mainly for changes in production processes within the organisation, rather than the development of new products or the furthering of relationships, especially with suppliers.

The study found that ICT in itself is only a minor facilitator of innovation; it becomes powerful only in combination with a number of other complementary factors. Paramount among these was a new marketing strategy. Also important were operational change and capital investment in equipment.

Table 5.3 summarises our key findings on ICT and innovation looking at three aspects: (1) the effect of ICT; (2) the main determining factors; and (3) the main ways in which this outcome has been realised.

In a comparable study of Western European firms (Verhoest et al., 2004) the contribution of ICT to product innovation was higher than in our sample. Even more significant was the difference between the two samples in the contribution of ICT to relational innovation, in particular its contribution to increasing customer loyalty and consolidating preferential relations with suppliers. This comparison confirms the picture of the Eastern European sample as composed of firms that are rapidly modernising their organisational structures.

Sector Differences in ICT Use and Innovation

As with ICT and the economic performance of firms, there appear to be sectoral differences in the role of ICT for innovation. Again, the degree of information intensity correlates positively with the impact of ICT on innovation. Table 5.4 summarises the impact of ICT on the different types of innovation for the respective sectors.

Table 5.3   Key findings of the study related to ICT and innovation

Type of innovation	Findings
Process innovation	ICT contributes positively to speed and reliability of business processes and a reduction of business process costs. Key factors of importance for process innovation, beyond ICT, are organisational change, a new marketing strategy and capital investment in equipment. Main outcomes: processes improved mainly through automation, information management, and wider processes of organisational change.
Product innovation	ICT contributes only to a limited extent to product innovation. Key factors of importance for product innovation are new marketing strategies, investment in equipment, training of staff and organisational change. Main outcomes: customisation of products and new bundled offerings.
Relational innovation	ICT contributes in only a minor role in facilitating relational innovation with customers, but is more important for the relationships with suppliers. Key factors of importance for relational innovation are, perhaps unsurprisingly, a new marketing strategy, organisational change and capital investment in equipment. Main outcomes towards customers: changes in sales value per customer, a greater share of retained customers and changes in the sales value per retained customer. Main outcomes towards suppliers: changes in the number of suppliers, changes in value of purchases per supplier, changes in the number of repeat suppliers and the value of purchases by repeat suppliers.

Apart from sector characteristics, product characteristics seem to influence heavily the performance in terms of innovation. They relate to the information intensity of a product (service or good) and associated transactions (inter- and intra-firm). The informational nature of the product is an important variable because it determines the extent to which production can be ICT supported or even entirely ICT based, as well as the extent to which inter- and intra-firm transactions can be performed entirely electronically or not. On the basis of our observations, four additional main important characteristics can be specified:

Table 5.4   Sector-related key findings on ICT and innovation

Sector	Contribution of ICT to process innovation	Contribution of ICT to product innovation	Contribution of ICT to relational innovation
Finance	High	High	Medium
Food processing	Low	Low	Low
Furniture	Medium	Medium	Medium
Heavy machinery	High	High	High
ICT services	High	High	High
Retail & wholesale	Medium	Medium	Medium

1. *Product complexity* Complex products require more information processing than simple products. This very complexity may form an obstacle to implementing ICT solutions, but the potential for performance improvements through informatisation is larger for complex than for simple products.
2. *Product standardisation* Standardised products require less information handling than products that are produced on a one-off basis, which require additional information handling before the actual production process can be started. The obvious example of this is product customisation.
3. *Frequency of transactions*   The higher the frequency of transactions, the higher the potential for cost reduction through ICT usage compared to occasional transactions and increased economies of scale.
4. *Number of transactions* This factor equally determines whether transaction costs can be reduced through scale effects. Mass transactions will yield more cost reductions than dedicated ones.

The above characteristics may or may not occur simultaneously but will tend to be mutually reinforcing when they do.

FACILITATING ENVIRONMENT FOR ICT UTILISATION IN FIRMS

Major Factors

From the previous sections it has become evident that ICT is playing an increasingly important role in shaping economic progress in the Central and Eastern European countries surveyed. For these processes of transformation to continue and to ensure that the changes translate into economic growth, there should be an appropriate regulatory and policy environment. Indeed, the transformations associated with the introduction of ICT and innovative activity are by no means an automatic process, but require an appropriate facilitative environment shaped by appropriate policies and regulations.

So, the third question we want to answer is: 'What factors external to the firm influence ICT use?' And, following from this: 'How do they affect innovation and economic growth?' To answer that question the study analysed to what extent the existing policy and regulatory environments facilitate or inhibit the take-up and use of ICT among firms.

A central finding of this part of our study is that there are significant policy areas in need of improvement, if firms in the countries included in the study are to benefit fully from the opportunities offered by ICT. The surveyed firms found that the most constraining elements were inadequate education and training, and inappropriate taxation. The provision of online government services was also considered an area to improve upon. In contrast, commercial law, intellectual property and security policy were generally evaluated relatively positively, while telecommunication prices and quality of service were seen most positively.

In interpreting these findings, it should also be taken into account that even though they have been positively evaluated on average, many of these external factors have also been obstacles for firms to engage in or to intensify ICT usage. Surmountable obstacles for proactive players may be insurmountable for the lesser players. Our findings therefore indicate an order of priority (established by experienced users) but do not allow conclusions about levels of satisfaction in general.

Wider socioeconomic factors, and the regulatory and policy context in particular, have been shown to be of significance for the extent to which firms can and will make use of ICT as a means for enhancing innovation and hence for improving their competitiveness. Countries that have established an appropriate policy and regulatory environment will thus stimulate firm growth and hence national GDP growth.

In addition to these general findings on enabling and inhibiting policy and regulatory environments, a number of results pertaining to the specific circumstances of the individual countries were also identified. Hence it is important to emphasise that the five countries included in the study face a range of very different policy challenges that require different approaches and prioritisation. For example, in Estonia the introduction of appropriate legislative, regulatory and policy initiatives has played a significant positive role in the development of the information society in the country. Indeed, all the Baltic States and Poland have introduced a range of reforms, as part of their accession to the EU, that have acted as a catalyst for improved take-up and use of ICT. However, Estonia has been by far the quickest in adapting existing legislative and regulatory frameworks, resulting in a more advanced position with respect to ICT adoption and use compared to the other four countries included in the study.

Russia has been slower in taking steps to establish a policy and regulatory environment conducive to greater ICT adoption and utilisation by firms.[14] However, at the beginning of this decade more significant efforts were made to improve ICT dissemination and use in Russia. Notably, the 'Electronic Russia 2002–2010' programme was initiated in January 2002 with the aim 'to increase the efficiency of the economy both in the public and private sectors, to make wider use of information technology in government departments, and transfer much of the state's work online'.[15]

The main results as to external environment of firms in the countries surveyed are given in Table 5.5. We distinguish here three criteria: (1) the quality of the ICT infrastructure; (2) the level of satisfaction of firms with their regulatory environment; and (3) the key areas of concern.

POLICY ACTIONS TO ENHANCE ICT USE BY FIRMS

In the previous sections we highlighted the importance of the improvement of many external conditions for the increase in ICT use by firms. We also discussed the findings in relation to policy implications. That brings us to the fourth and final question we have to answer in this chapter: 'What are the actions public authorities can take in order to improve these conditions and thereby enhance the pro-growth use of ICT by the business sector?'

The Need for Sector-specific Policies

Our data have shown that generic measures with an indirect effect on businesses' performance such as telecommunication regulation, education etc. make a difference (see our findings on the Baltic States). Second, the data show a direct relation between investment levels in ICT and performance increase (see our findings on the differences in average performance increases in Russia and Poland). Such investments may be enhanced by generic measures such as competition law and taxation measures.

With regard to investment, however, our data also suggest that policies should take into account sectoral variations. Indeed, the effect of ICT investment may vary per sector and per industry (some sectors will benefit more than others). Moreover, within a given sector or industry, investment will yield more or fewer results depending on the application area (business processes that benefit the most from ICT in terms of performance vary).

Table 5.5   Country-related key findings of the study

Country	Key findings
Estonia	*ICT*: Estonia is at the forefront with respect to ICT among the five countries. *Satisfaction* with the policy and regulatory environment was generally high. *Key areas of concern* are the lack of sufficient government training programmes and somewhat inadequate protection of intellectual property rights and public financial support for R&D, diffusion or uptake.
Latvia	*ICT*: Latvia has a fast-growing ICT sector, but is generally worse placed in terms of ICT infrastructure compared to its Northern Baltic neighbour. *Satisfaction* with the policy and regulatory environment was moderate. *Key areas of concern* are the insufficient public financial support for R&D and the inadequate government training programmes. In addition, Latvia needs more public and private awareness-raising activities and an improved education system for ICT usage.
Lithuania	*ICT*: Lithuania has had greater difficulties than Estonia or Latvia with respect to the establishment of an ICT infrastructure. *Satisfaction* with the policy and regulatory environment was at a reasonable level. *The key areas of concern* are the inadequate government training programmes and the insufficient public financial support for R&D, diffusion or uptake.
Poland	*ICT*: The overall infrastructure for ICT and innovation in Poland is relatively poor. *Satisfaction* with the policy and regulatory environment was considered moderate to poor. *The key areas of concern* are the inappropriate taxation measures and public financial support for R&D, diffusion or uptake that act as critical barriers for further ICT development and innovation. In addition, the government training programmes are viewed as inadequate.
Russia	*ICT*: Russia has a comparatively weak ICT and innovation infrastructure, and according to some assessments, the development of ICT in Russia is lagging behind that of the leading Western countries by some 5–10 years. *Satisfaction* with the policy and regulatory environment is generally poor. *The key areas of concern* are the inappropriate taxation measures and lack of public financial support for R&D, diffusion or uptake. In addition, the inadequate commercial law is a cause for concern, while public and private awareness-raising measures and government training programmes will also need to be improved.

In light of the findings of the study, a set of recommendations for policy makers can be outlined.

The first is that policies should be designed to have more direct effects on specific industries, such as science and technology and support to innovation. Our findings suggest that, given public financial resources (tax revenue), such policies can be inspired by two types of choices. First, what are the types of industry that are of strategic importance to a country and, once identified, should these industries therefore receive preferential treatment? Second, given the nature of the sectors, what kind of application areas are likely to yield the most effect and should therefore be targeted by innovation and ICT programmes?

In many cases it will not be possible to answer questions of this kind on a nationwide scale due to the existence of regional clusters of economic activity. But this observation actually amounts to saying that sectoral differences matter to industrial policies.

The more concrete recommendations (ordered by six main policy priorities) that follow should be read with this in mind. Accordingly, while the recommendations are of a fairly general nature, their implementation requires consideration of how they are best tailored to sectoral differences.

Six General Policy Priorities

Encourage greater take-up and utilisation of ICT in the private sector

While ICT is already making its mark on the economic fabric in the transition economies, there are still significant unexploited opportunities. A high priority for governments in the transition countries should therefore be the further adoption and utilisation of ICT among companies within the countries. This will involve highlighting the benefits to companies of using the new technologies and promoting good practice in how to introduce and utilise ICT within organisations. In addition, policy makers must provide a tax and fiscal system that encourages investment in ICT products. This includes addressing issues such as the types of goods included as investment (e.g. software) and their deductibility and depreciation rates. It can also involve tax credits for investments by firms in ICT skills for employees.

Encourage greater adoption of ICT in the public sector

The public sector has a critical role to play in the development of a wider ICT infrastructure within the transition countries. The more public services are available online, the greater is the incentive for private enterprises and individuals to adopt the new technologies. Accordingly, the use of ICT for the provision of public services (e.g. taxation and registration) can lead to significant efficiency gains from ICT to private enterprises.

Indeed, the more 'networked' the society and economy become, the more gains can accrue from the new technologies (as noted by Metcalfe's law[16]). Furthermore, the public sector can act as an example to the private sector on how to introduce and use ICT. An example of good practice is outlined in Box 5.2.

BOX 5.2   GOOD PRACTICE EXAMPLE: ELECTRONIC INTEGRATED CUSTOMS DUTY AND TAX SYSTEM (POLAND)

The electronic Integrated Customs Duty and Tax System in Poland is well established, operates on a nationwide scale and offers extensive functionality in supporting all customs procedures and documents as well as the financial processes relating to the collection, settlement and justification of customs duties and tax due. In addition, it supports the budgeting and account functions of all the customs department's activities and provides a well-used means for electronic data interchange with traders, thus bringing significant benefits to all its users and Poland as a whole.

Promoting Internet security and trust

In order to promote greater use of ICT, enterprises and individuals must trust the technologies and security of the information they provide and receive via the Internet. Consequently, improving the overall security of Internet use (e-security) should be considered a key priority for the development of the ICT infrastructure. It is, for example, of interest to note that this study found only limited use of ICT for selling goods and services among the companies surveyed. This may in part be due to inadequate security, or at least a perception of risk, associated with the use of ICT for consumption. Improving Internet security can therefore be a catalyst for increasing the opportunities for firms to make more extensive use of ICT for improving sales. A further example of good practice is given in Box 5.3.

BOX 5.3   GOOD-PRACTICE EXAMPLE: ESTONIA'S ID PROGRAMME

The purpose of the Estonian ID programme is to use nationwide electronic identity and develop a new personal identification card that would be a generally acceptable identification document

and contain both visually and electronically accessible information. On 28 January 2002 the first ID cards were issued to
Estonian citizens.

The output of the ID programme is the ID card, which functions on
an electronic crypto-processor, based on smart-card technology. It
includes personal certificates and private keys of the card-owner.

Supporting research and innovation

Both economic theory and empirical analysis underline the key role of
research and innovation in economic growth and progress. Yet market failures (in the form of spillovers and externalities) generally cause enterprises
to under-invest in research and innovation. This is generally referred to as
the 'appropriability' issue, where key knowledge and the return of being the
first to develop are only partly appropriable. Accordingly, there is a need to
design and implement tailor-made policy instruments and funding in order
to stimulate R&D spending and innovation. This involves an approach that
begins with the identification of the needs on the level where innovation,
growth and job creation take place: industry, sectors and companies. By
identifying specific needs or drivers instrumental to an increase in research
and innovation, specific policy measures can be designed.

In addition, the transition countries that have obtained, or are about
to obtain, membership of the EU have a range of new opportunities and
funds available for supporting research and innovation (see Chapter 7
of this book). Successfully exploiting the opportunities offered by EU
membership is critical for successfully advancing the knowledge economy.
Good-practice examples are outlined in Box 5.4.

BOX 5.4   GOOD-PRACTICE EXAMPLES: ESTONIA AND LITHUANIA

Tallinn Technical University Innovation Centre (Estonia)
A number of specific initiatives have been taken in Estonia to encourage the development of new knowledge-based businesses, including the Tallinn Technical University Innovation Centre (TUIC). The
TUIC seeks to promote linkages between the R&D base of Tallinn
Technical University and businesses. Its activities include active
marketing of R&D projects that have market potential, providing
assistance to university staff seeking to cooperate with industry,
managing the spin-off programme and developing incubation services for knowledge-based start-up companies.

Use of EU Structural Funds (Lithuania)

Membership of the EU has given several transition countries access to significant EU funds for supporting research and innovation. Lithuania provides an illustrative example of how EU membership gives rise to new opportunities to support research and innovation. EU accession in May 2004 was followed by a first round of implementation of the EU's Structural Funds, which allowed Lithuania to double the amount of funding available for innovation. Several measures directly addressing innovation have been implemented in order to strengthen the innovation support infrastructure and develop its institutional capacities, to improve R&D and business cooperation in innovation development, to improve the quality of human resources for R&D and innovation, and to strengthen the public and private R&D base. Direct support for innovation in firms was also offered.

Stimulate fair competition

Ensuring that the ICT markets are competitive is critical for lowering connectivity prices and increasing take-up. The liberalisation of the telecommunication market is therefore a critical priority for the successful furthering of the information society. A more open and competitive telecommunication market will also ensure that new technologies are rolled out quickly, as competitive pressures provide the incentive to develop better and more efficient telecommunication products and services. In addition, it is important to ensure a regulatory framework that protects intellectual property rights, such that markets remain open to new products and services. See Box 5.5 for an example of good practice in this area.

BOX 5.5   GOOD-PRACTICE EXAMPLE: ESTONIA'S LIBERALISATION OF THE TELECOMMUNICATIONS MARKET

Estonia has been among the first CEE countries to open the telecommunications market for liberalisation, providing a basis for the development of the Estonian information society. The telecommunications market in Estonia was fully liberalised from 1 January 2001. Increased competition in the telecommunications market since 1991 has resulted in a 50–80 per cent reduction in the price of international long-distance calls, lower prices on national long-distance calls and price reductions of 50 per cent for Internet connections.

Underpin developments in skills and the labour market
It is widely recognised that success in the era of the knowledge economy is dependent upon the availability of appropriate skills, so that the workforce can deal effectively with technological innovation in ICT and organisational change. Meanwhile, the opportunities for learning are also enhanced by the emergence of ICT, with the new technologies enabling learning in a range of new ways and environments. ICT is thus said to offer a host of new e-learning opportunities. In order to exploit the new education and training possibilities offered and necessitated by ICT, governments need to increase levels of investment in human capital in general, and in ICT-related skills in particular. Moreover, the policy and regulatory environment should encourage firms and private individuals to invest in their human capital. A good-practice example is detailed in Box 5.6.

BOX 5.6   GOOD-PRACTICE EXAMPLE: ESTONIA'S TIGER LEAP

The Estonian 'Tiger Leap' is a national target programme launched by the Ministry of Education of Estonia, with the objective to modernise the educational system in the country by introducing ICT. Initiated by Estonia's President and sponsored in part by the UNDP, Tiger Leap is based on cooperation between schools, universities, private enterprises and public institutions. The programme builds up structures for distance and continuous learning for teachers and students, and Estonian teachers are given training in computer skills and the use of educational software. The programme has ensured that 98 per cent of Estonia's schools have access to the Internet, with more than one computer per 20 students, and has created a national learning network for teachers and trained 40 per cent of Estonian teachers in 'advanced computer skills'.

CONCLUSIONS AND RECOMMENDATIONS

The study has explored whether and how ICT is being used by firms in transition countries and the impact of introducing ICT on innovation and economic growth. The findings emerging from the study reveal a number of issues surrounding the development, application and utilisation of ICT and its implications for innovation and economic growth. The main conclusions can be summarised as follows:

- ICT plays an important role in facilitating the modernisation and improved economic performance of firms in transition countries.
- ICT in itself is often insufficient for improving economic performance. Rather, a range of complementary factors is required such as organisational change and new marketing strategies.
- ICT use among firms in transition countries is primarily geared towards improved production and transaction processes, e.g. organisational change and improved marketing, rather than the development of new or improved products.
- There are significant sectoral differences in the role, scope and impact of ICT use. The potential effect of ICT on the firm's performance is strongly determined by the information intensity of the product. The greater the information intensity of production and transaction processes, the greater the scope for applying and using ICT.
- Promoting the application and use of ICT for improved economic performance requires tailored policies to the individual sector as well to the individual country.

From a policy-making perspective, it is thus necessary to identify how ICT fits within the overall socioeconomic fabric and the sectors relevant for the country's comparative advantage, rather than how the socioeconomic fabric needs dramatic restructuring in order to realise some preconceived notion of an optimal and uniform knowledge economy. The emphasis should therefore be on how ICT can be used to increase value added and improve performance within the prevailing socioeconomic context, and thus explore opportunities for using ICT as a vehicle for moving up the value chain within existing sectors.

Notwithstanding the differences between countries, the findings of this study have highlighted that a suitable policy and regulatory environment is needed in order to provide firms with an incentive to use ICT to improve their competitiveness. It is important to stress that differences in the wider institutional and socioeconomic context do not mean that there are no opportunities for countries to learn from each other's experiences and engage in active policy learning (Djarova, 2004). Rather, such policy learning has to take account of the different contexts in which the policies are implemented. Finally, it is important to note that the activities and processes of the emerging knowledge economy (or economies) are increasingly taking place across a global terrain. From this conclusion it does not necessarily follow that national policy makers are powerless. On the contrary, the more the world becomes a single marketplace, the more significant it may become that the actions of national authorities provide a supportive regulatory and policy regime.

NOTES

1. We thank InfoDev (The World Bank) for the opportunity to carry out this study and for permission to publish the summary results of the study. Full information is contained in InfoDev (2008). We acknowledge the contributions of many experts to this collective work. The distribution of the roles has been as follows: Dr Julia Djarova (ECORYS) for overall project management and final editing; Pascal Verhoest (TNO) for design of questionnaire and analysis of survey results; Dr Jacob Dencik (ECORYS) for overall editing and analysis of project results; Dr Valentijn Bilsen (IDEA) for organisation of data and analysis of the dataset; Dr Frans van der Zee (ECORYS/TNO) for design of study and analysis of the survey results; Jay Wissema (ECORYS) for data processing. The organisation of the surveys in the five countries, the supply of countries' overal information and the organisation of the case studies were coordinated by Diederik Rietveldt (ECORYS) and managed by three local consultancy bureaux: ECORYS Polska (Warsaw) – responsible for the survey in Poland; Cycleplan (Tallinn) – responsible for the survey in the three Baltic States; International Management Institute of St Petersburg (MISP) (St Petersburg) – responsible for the surveys in Russia. Professor Dr Andrey Medvedev (IMISP) managed the data collection process in Russia with the support of Ekkona Consulting Group.

   Ando Lipp (Cycleplan) managed the data collection process in the three Baltic States with the support of Saar Poll Ltd – Estonia, InMind – Latvia, Spinter – Lithuania.

   Rado Piontek (ECORYS Polska) managed the data surveys in Poland with the support of PP-consulting.
2. Note that innovation is the main determinant of future competitiveness and thus of future performance.
3. See, e.g., Jorgensen (2001) for the USA, van Ark et al. (2003) for the EU and Inklaar et al. (2005) for a comparison between the EU and the USA on a sectoral level.
4. An illustrative example is the study by Crepon and Heckel (2002) for France and Scarpetta et al. (2002) for a number of OECD countries. Relevant also are the more recent studies such as Brynjolfsson and Hitt (2003).
5. See, e.g., Read (2000) for a review of the literature on innovation and organisation.
6. The Electronic Commerce Business Impacts Project (EBIP) was carried out by the OECD in 2001 and 2002.
7. There is increasing interest in the role of ICT for development: see, e.g., OECD (2005).
8. E.g. the EBIP carried out by the OECD in 2001 and 2002.
9. The EBS methodology was first applied in a mainly qualitative form by the OECD in 2001 and formed the basis for the Electronic Commerce Business Impacts Project (EBIP). This study included 217 case studies covering 20 industry sectors spread among 11 participating countries (Canada, France, Italy, Korea, Mexico, the Netherlands, Norway, Spain, Sweden and the UK). A fully quantitative iteration of the EBS meth-

odology was then applied to a sample of 220 enterprises in four different sectors of the Belgian economy (for a summary see Verhoest et al., 2003, 2004a, 2004b).

10. It should be noted that the starting points of the countries are also different, which may explain some of the differences in the results.

11. Process innovation covers: speed and reliability of business processes; automation; information management; organisational change.

12. Product innovation considers: new products and services; customisation; new bundling offerings.

13. Relational innovation looks at a number of indicators describing innovation in the customer's relationship and innovation in the supplier's relationship: number of customers and suppliers; change in sales value per customer; value of purchases per supplier; share of retained customers; number of repeat suppliers; changes in sales value per retained customer; value of purchases per repeat supplier.

14. For example, weak enforcement of intellectual property rights and regulation has been a major inhibitor for the development of the ICT market. In the 1990s, it was common for most Russian businesses to use pirated copies of the Windows Operating System and, while the piracy rate is falling, the Business Software Alliance reported a piracy rate of 87 per cent in 2002 (http://www.american.edu/initeb/sw5840a/analysis.htm).

15. In part motivated by the objective of gaining WTO (World Trade Organization) membership, the programme targets four key areas of ICT: regulatory environment and institutional framework; Internet infrastructure; e-government and e-education. The policy and regulatory environment for ICT adoption and use is thus expected to improve significantly in Russia in the near future. However, the current weaknesses manifest themselves in the relatively low productivity impact of ICT identified in this study.

16. Metcalfe's law states that the value of a telecommunications network is proportional to the square of the number of users of the system. First formulated by Robert Metcalfe, Metcalfe's law explains many of the network effects of communication technologies and networks such as the Internet, social networking, and the World Wide Web (source: Wikipedia).

REFERENCES

Ark, B. van, J. Melka, N. Mulder, M. Timmer and G. Ypma (2003), 'ICT Investments and Growth account for the European Union, 1980–2000', Research memorandum GD 56, University of Groningen, the Netherlands.

Brynjolfsson, E. and L. Hitt (2003), 'Computing productivity: firm level evidence', *The Review of Economics and Statistics*, **85** (4), 793–808.

Crepon, B. and T. Heckel (2002), 'Computerization in France: an evaluation based on individual company data', *The Review of Income and Wealth*, **48** (1), 77–98.

Djarova, J. (2004), 'Executive Summary' in White Paper: How to develop SME innovation business in Russia, Recommendations to Federal and Regional authorities, ECORYS publication within the frame of the project 'Promotion of Innovative SMEs in the Baltic Region of the Russian Federation'.

EC (2006a), 'Policy brief: Latvia', available at http://europa.eu.int/information_society/activities/ gothenburg_conference/doc/pdf/brief_latvia.pdf.

EC (2006b), 'Policy brief: Lithuania', available at http://europa.eu.int/comm/regional_policy/ sources/docconf/gothenburg/doc/briefl_lithuania.pdf.

EC (2006c), 'Policy brief: Poland', available at http://europa.eu.int/information_society/activities/ gothenburg_conference/doc/pdf/brief_poland.pdf.

InfoDev (2008), *ICT, Innovation and Economic Growth in Transition Economies: A Multi-country Study on Poland, Russia and the Baltic Countries*, Washington, DC: The World Bank, August.

Inklaar, R., M. O'Mahoney and M. Timmer (2005), 'ICT and Europe's productivity performance: industry level growth account comparisons with the United States', *Review of Income and Wealth*, **51** (4), 505–36.

Jorgenson, D.W. (2001), 'Information technology and the US economy', *The American Economic Review*, **91** (1), 1–32.

OECD (2003), 'ICT and economic growth, evidence from OECD countries, industries and firms', Series Information and Communication Technologies, Paris: OECD.

OECD (2005), *Good practice paper on ICTs for economic growth and poverty reduction*, Paris: OECD.

Polish Council of Ministers (2002), *Improving Innovation of the Economy in Poland by 2006*.

Read, A. (2000), 'Determinants of successful organisational innovation: a review of current research', *Journal of Management Practice*, **3** (1), 95–119.

Room, G., J. Dencik et al. (2004), *Final report on conceptualisation and analysis of the New Information Economy*, Bath: University of Bath.

Scarpetta, S., P. Hemmings, T. Tressel and J. Woo (2002), 'The role of policy and institutions for productivity and firm dynamics: evidence from micro and industry data', Economics Department Working Paper, no 329, OECD, Paris.

Verhoest, P., R. Hawkins, P. Desruelle, et al. (2003), 'Electronic business networks: an assessment of the dynamics of business-to-business electronic commerce in eleven OECD countries: a summary report of the e-Business Impacts Project (EBIS)', Brussels: European Commission, available at http://www.jrc.es/home/publications/publication.cfm?pub=1122. Also available in print (Report Eur 20776).

Verhoest, P., C. Huveneers and R. Hawkins (2004), 'E-business and entreprise's performances', paper for the eChallenges e-2004 conference sponsored by the European Commission, Vienna, 27–29 October 2004 (http://www.echallenges.org/2004/). Preliminary findings presented at the OECD's Working Party on the Information Economy, Paris, 5–6 May 2003. Main findings discussed at an OECD Workshop on 3 December 2003.

6. The behavioural additionality of business R&D subsidies: theoretical considerations and empirical results for Flanders

Geert Steurs, Arnold Verbeek and Elissavet Lykogianni

INTRODUCTION

The objectives of the Lisbon Agenda have underlined the importance of innovation in making Europe 'the most dynamic and competitive knowledge-based economy in the world' by 2010. In order to fulfil the target of achieving a 3 per cent average economic growth and the creation of 20 million jobs by 2010, a range of policy measures has been proposed. One of the main policy areas that has been targeted by these measures is that of innovation. As a consequence, many countries in Europe have increased their public support for R&D and innovation activities by the business sector. This support, by means of subsidies, beneficial tax treatment of R&D investments and many other kinds of policy measures, should increase the competitiveness of the business sector as well as the productivity and growth of the overall economy.

Within this context of increased public support for R&D and innovation, the analysis of the efficiency and effectiveness of such policies has become very important due to public accountability issues and the scarcity of public funds (OECD, 2006; Barberis, 1988). Governments are therefore increasingly interested in assessing the 'additionality' of public support for business R&D. In other words, they often seek to answer the question 'What difference does public support make?'

Until recently, the analysis of the 'additionalities' of public support focused on either the calculation of the additional amount spent on R&D due to government support (input additionality) or on the additional outputs that resulted from the R&D process (output additionality). Both input and output additionality raise measurement issues.

Other disadvantages relate to the policy conclusions one can draw from these types of analyses. Evaluations of R&D programmes that focus on input additionality as a criterion are based, at least implicitly, on the assumption that higher R&D inputs will automatically result in more innovative outputs. This assumption is based on a too simple linear view of innovation. Evaluations that focus on output additionality may induce attitudes that prefer low-risk, short-term-oriented projects.

But the most important drawback relates to the fact that the analysis of these two types of additionality (input and output) leaves the possible impact of public intervention on the firms' R&D behaviour in the dark (a 'black box'). In order to open this box (and bring some light in the dark), another type of additionality has recently been introduced: 'behavioural additionality' refers to the effects on firms' behaviour and strategy as a result of a government intervention, looking therefore inside the 'black box'. This approach aims at assessing the changes in the ways that firms conduct R&D, caused by government support measures.

Some of the questions that this approach intends to address are the following: do public interventions encourage firms to pursue different types of R&D or to strive for more collaboration in the R&D process? Is there an effect on the duration or the speed of the projects? Do firms develop improved R&D management capabilities while carrying out publicly funded R&D projects?

The research into the behavioural additionality of business R&D support has received more attention during recent years because, among other reasons, the OECD Working Party on Innovation and Technology Policy (TIP) has undertaken the initiative of coordinating a multinational effort to develop ways of measuring it. The project involved researchers and policy makers from 11 OECD countries who developed a common conceptual framework for behavioural additionality and experimented with different approaches for measuring it. The resulting country studies reveal a number of qualitative changes in the types of R&D conducted by firms and the way in which they carry out R&D as a result of their participation in government R&D funding programmes.

This chapter has the objective to provide a theoretical background to the issue of behavioural additionality and to present the results of the assessment of behavioural additionality for firms participating in R&D support programmes of the IWT (Institute for the Promotion of Innovation through Science and Technology in Flanders).

It is structured as follows. The next section gives some background on the concepts underlying the assessment of (behavioural) additionality of public policies supporting R&D. The following section summarises the main results of the study analysing the behavioural additionality of IWT funding to support business R&D in Flanders.[1] The final section provides some concluding remarks and a brief discussion on further research possibilities.

THEORETICAL BACKGROUND

Input, Output and Behavioural Additionality

Traditionally, the analysis of additionality (which results from public policy measures supporting business R&D) has focused on the determination of the additional R&D spending from businesses supported by the government (input additionality) or on the additional outputs produced by the R&D process (output additionality).

More specifically, input additionality checks to what extent firms spend an additional amount on R&D for every sum of public money spent to support business R&D. In other words, it examines whether government funding crowds out private R&D investment. The aim is of course to finance only R&D projects that would not have taken place anyway (that is, without public support). However, the use of input measurements is beset with difficulties. Attempts to overcome them have led to the measurement of additionality in terms of outputs. Output additionality therefore focuses on the proportion of outputs that would not have been achieved without public support. However, in practice this entails even more problems than input additionality given the difficulties of identifying accurately the outputs of the R&D process. These can be measured in terms of patents obtained, papers published, but also in terms of downstream effects on sales, new product development, know-how improvements etc.

Testing on crowding-out effects is often used as a way to empirically test for the existence of additionality effects. However, a rejection of crowding-out effects does not necessarily mean that there are additionalities (Aerts and Czarnitzki, 2006). Here are two examples.

First, where subsidies just increase the wages of R&D employees without being supplemented by increases of their productivity, crowding-out effects would be rejected but the innovation output would not have increased.

Second, where the risk of subsidised projects is significantly higher than that of privately financed projects, the subsidy can result in a higher investment in R&D but not necessarily in higher output. These considerations imply that input and output additionalities should both be considered when analysing the additionalities of publicly funded R&D.

However, this is not sufficient as none of these types of additionalities looks into the effects of public funding for R&D on the behaviour and strategy of firms. To fill this gap, the concept of behavioural additionality has been proposed. This concept (Buisseret, 1995) focuses on the difference in firm behaviour reported as a result of the R&D process due to public support.

The Dimensions of Behavioural Additionality

The literature shows that behavioural additionality is a multidimensional concept. Different types of behavioural additionality are distinguished. Falk (2006), for instance, mentions the following types:

- *Scale additionality* is said to occur if public funding allows the project to be conducted on a larger scale.
- *Scope additionality* refers to cases where the coverage of an activity is expanded to a wider range of markets, applications or players than would have been possible without public assistance.
- *Cognitive capacity additionality* refers to the positive impact on competencies and expertise.
- *Acceleration additionality* is present if participation in innovation schemes speeds up the course of the project.
- *Impact additionality* refers to improvements in productivity or competitive position.

In the summary of country studies mentioned above, the OECD (2006) considers four more types of behavioural additionality:

- *Challenge additionality*: when government support helps to take more risk in projects.
- *Network additionality*: when government support helps to create networks.
- *Follow-up additionality*: when government support helps to establish follow-up projects.
- *Management additionality*: when government support improves company management routines.

A number of authors have tried to fit these dimensions into a conceptual framework. Here we briefly summarise three such approaches.

The first (by Clarysse et al., 2006) is based on three dimensions. The idea behind the first dimension is that the effect on the behaviour can vary according to the organisational level where it is initiated. The authors distinguish two main organisational levels. The strategic level is related to the overall direction of the firm. The operational level refers to management capabilities for implementing a strategy. The second dimension is based on the idea that the behavioural effect varies according to the duration and timing of the effects. Short-term effects are normally manifested during the lifetime

Table 6.1   Levels and sustainability of behavioural effects

	Project-level effect (example)	Company-level effect (example)
Strategy	ST: project in new business area for firm	ST: developing capabilities in new business/market
	LT: new market alliance	LT: joint venture or supply chain arrangement, SME shift from contract research to manufacturing
Operation	ST: new project reporting procedures to comply with monitoring requirements	LT: Acquisition of management capability for collaborative projects

Notes: ST: short term; LT: long term.

Source: Clarysse et al. (2006).

of a project. Long-term or sustainable/persistent effects refer to acquired competencies. The third dimension refers to scope. Here one can distinguish between the project level and the company level. Table 6.1 provides some examples of behavioural effects according to these three dimensions.

An alternative framework has been proposed, mainly in view of the need for a self-assessment approach for R&D funding agencies (Närfelt and Wildeberger, 2006). It makes a distinction between system, organisational and project effects.

Among the system effects, the authors make a further distinction between two sub-classes. Resource allocation effects refer to all economic, human capital, technology and other allocations/acquisitions that are influenced by the activities of the agency and involve several actors in a given innovation system. Networking effects cover the networks or relations created directly or indirectly by agency activities.

The class of organisational effects covers value-adding outcomes that are confined to a certain actor. The actor or organisation could be a funded client, a rejected client or any organisation that is influenced by the activities of the agency. The effects classified under this dimension are capability effects such as access to new technologies, new competencies, capital, management skills, as well as range-of-activity effects, which cover the kind of R&D activities of the organisation as a whole, such as more risky, new market, new technology domain etc.

Finally, project effects refer to the effects on the projects that the agency selects, such as acceleration, scale, scope and result effects, the last referring to new or additional results that the project produces due to the support by the agency.

A third conceptual framework (Falk, 2007) integrates input and output additionality with the different dimensions of behavioural additionality by classifying all different types of additionalities under three headings:

1. resource-based concepts (such as input additionality);
2. process-based concepts that measure the success of the policy intervention by examining desirable changes in the process of the innovation (i.e. behavioural additionality effects); and
3. result-based concepts (such as output additionality).

The presentation of the results on the additionality of the IWT grants provided to companies located in Flanders will be structured according to this framework (see next section).

When one reflects on these three different approaches to (behavioural) additionality, it becomes clear that a great deal of conceptual fuzziness remains. The distinctions between the different types of behavioural additionality are not always clear cut. For instance, if scope additionality includes the expansion of an activity to a wider range of players, then the difference with network additionality becomes very small. There also seems to be only a minor difference between cognitive capacity additionality and management additionality. And the case of assisted firms advancing into new research areas could be reflected in a greater risk profile of the innovation projects, since activities in areas beyond the firm's key competencies entail greater technical difficulty (hence an increase in technical risk) and bring about less predictable business success (hence an increase in commercial risk). Therefore scope and challenge additionality are also closely connected.

Moreover, the difference between behavioural additionality and input and output additionality is not always very sharp. Some authors, such as Shin (2005), consider changes in R&D investments over time also as a behavioural change. But this would imply that the difference between input and behavioural additionality becomes very subtle.

Besides the conceptual fuzziness, many of the different dimensions of behavioural additionality have never been empirically tested. The study whose results we present in the following sections is an attempt to do so.

RESEARCH DESIGN

Introduction

In this section we discuss the methodological approach of the study: the combination of a telephone survey with in-depth interviews and the use of two control groups besides the experimental group that received government support.

We first provide some background information on the type of projects the study focuses on. Subsequently, we present the classification of the different (behavioural) additionality concepts we used. Thereafter, we describe the set-up of the telephone survey as well as of the approach followed for the in-depth interviews. We conclude with some methodological remarks on the proof of additionality.

Background Information on Type of Projects

We concentrate on the assessment of behavioural additionality for firms participating in R&D support programmes of the IWT (Institute for the Promotion of Innovation through Science and Technology in Flanders). IWT is a Flemish organisation stimulating and supporting innovation through two instruments: financial support and services.

The study focused on the additionality of the financial support given to companies, in particular the support given to R&D projects for industrial basic research activities and for industrial development activities. The first type of project receives a subsidy of 50 per cent of the overall project costs (with an additional 10 per cent for SMEs), the second type of project a subsidy of 25 per cent (with an additional 10 per cent for SMEs).

The rules for IWT support are quite simple. Projects can be submitted by industrial enterprises (bottom-up projects) in all scientific or technological disciplines. Applications for R&D support can be introduced continuously. Cooperation with universities or other research institutes is not mandatory. Companies have the opportunity to discuss their ideas for a project with IWT before they submit their proposal. When submitted, the project proposals are evaluated by independent experts, who prepare a report. It is on the basis of this report that the decision to award a grant is taken by IWT's board of directors.

Additionality Concepts Covered

We aim to analyse whether there is a 'difference in firm behaviour resulting from the intervention' (Georghiou, 1997). As we indicated in the second section, the literature shows that behavioural additionality is a multi-dimensional concept. The different types of additionalities that are covered in the study are shown in Figure 6.1. They are classified using the framework proposed by Falk (2006). Under the resource-based concepts we rank input as well as project additionality. Under the process-based concepts we investigated scope and scale additionality, network additionality, competence

Firms

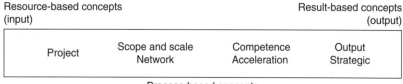

Resource-based concepts (input)			Result-based concepts (output)
Project	Scope and scale Network	Competence Acceleration	Output Strategic

Process-based concepts
(behavioural)

Source: Based on Falk (2006).

Figure 6.1   Additionalities in resources, processes and results

additionality[2] and acceleration additionality of IWT subsidies. Under the result-based concepts, we opted for output and strategic additionality. We defined strategic additionality as referring to the strategic impacts on the company's (innovative) behaviour as a consequence of public support for R&D.

The key question is to what extent these different types of additionality occur within the sample of companies involved in the survey and whether conclusions can be drawn regarding the population of IWT clients. The information we used to address this main research question came from two sources: a telephone survey and in-depth interviews.

The Telephone Survey

The telephone survey was set up among three different samples: an experimental group and two control groups.

- The experimental group consists of companies that received IWT support for one or more projects in the period 2001–04.[3] The analysis of the experimental group was based on a total number of 194 projects of as many companies.
- Control group A consists of companies that applied for IWT support but were rejected. We were able to contact 88 of these companies. We consider them as the 'treated' control group. Their contacts with IWT when preparing the proposal, at the moment of submission and maybe also when they were informed about the negative decision of IWT, may have had an impact on their behaviour. For instance, the way they had to prepare their proposal for the project that was not finally selected may have had an influence on the way they subsequently organised R&D projects in the company.
- Control group B contained companies that are known to be innovative, but that never applied for IWT support. We received

responses from 100 companies. Because they have not been in touch with IWT, we consider this control group as the 'pure' control group. They were selected from two different databases. The first was a database with companies that participated in the Community Innovation Survey and on the basis of their responses can be considered as innovative firms. The second was a database composed by innovation advisers who visit companies to draw up their innovation profile and to eventually support them in setting up innovation activities.

The use of control groups, and particularly of a control group that has never been in contact with the public agency (i.e. control group B), is one of the innovations of this research.

The Questionnaire

The questionnaire for the experimental group was largely based on the survey model that was elaborated and refined during the pilot project.[4] The unit of observation is the project level. In the case of the experimental group, the questionnaire focused on a specific project supported by IWT. In the case of control group A, the project discussed during the interview was the one that was refused IWT support. The participants of control group B were asked at the beginning of the telephone interview to define an R&D project that had taken place in the last five years. Thirty respondents were able to identify such a project.

Representativity

Table 6.2 provides information on the representativity of the samples.

The population of the experimental group consisted of 712 companies that submitted 1312 projects in the period considered. A total of 1090 projects were granted a subsidy. The sample of the experimental group represents more than one out of four companies in the population.[5] In the selection of companies, quota had to be respected in terms of company size. Due to the overall limited size of the sample, we used no other quota restrictions. Nevertheless, when comparing the sector distribution between the population and the sample, the biases are limited.

When comparing the populations of control group A and the experimental group in terms of company size, we observe that the starters are more strongly represented in the control group, while the large companies are less present. The representativity of the sample of firms in control group A is very high, with nearly one out of three companies included. Because of

Firms

Table 6.2   Representativity of the samples

No. of companies by size	Population	%	Sample	%	Representativity
Experimental group					
Large companies	130	18	36	19	28
SMEs	403	57	111	57	28
Starters	179	25	47	24	26
Total	*712*	*100*	*194*	*100*	27
Control group A					
Large companies	35	*12*	9	*10*	26
SMEs	162	*55*	53	*60*	33
Starters	96	*33*	26	*30*	27
Total	*293*	*100*	*88*	*100*	30
Control group B					
Large companies	76	*14*	13	*13*	17
SMEs	400	*76*	81	*81*	20
Starters	51	*10*	6	*6*	12
Total	*527*	*100*	*100*	*100*	19

Source: IDEA Consult on the basis of data provided by IWT.

the limited size of the population (293 companies), the quotas in terms of size could not be perfectly respected.

The population of control group B consisted of 527 companies, of which more than three out of four are SMEs. We obtained valid responses from nearly 20 per cent of them.

In-depth Interviews

In addition to the telephone survey, 49 IWT clients were interviewed in order to get a deeper, more qualitative insight into the behavioural additionality of the IWT subsidies for these companies. The approach was different for the 'occasional' versus the 'regular' IWT clients.

The occasional clients were defined as the companies having a maximum of two projects approved in the period 2001–04. Twenty companies were selected from the list of companies already involved in the telephone survey, where the selection was based on the outliers, the 'extreme' answers given by the project leaders during the telephone survey. These answers to the particular questions formed the basis for the interviews, again with the project leaders. The objective was to get the background to these answers.

The regular clients were defined as the companies having at least three projects approved in the period 2001–04. In order to get a picture of the impact on the company as a whole, the R&D managers were interviewed in these cases instead of the project leaders. Before these interviews (29 in total) took place, the interviewers were briefed by the IWT adviser responsible for the follow-up of the projects of the respective companies.

In Search of Additionality

How can we 'prove' the behavioural additionality of IWT subsidies? It is hard if not impossible to apply standard econometric methods and techniques. The variables that capture 'behaviour' would have to be regressed on the incidence or even the size of public assistance. But many unobserved variables can simply not be taken into account. Also, it is not clear how to treat the potential time lag between intervention and change in behaviour. Therefore most of the empirical analyses of behavioural additionality use one of the following frameworks (Falk, 2006).

In the first, supported firms are compared to unsupported ones on any of the dimensions of behavioural additionality. This is also the approach used in this study, since we included two control groups in our survey approach. We have the strongest proof of additionality when we have a statistically significant difference between the experimental (i.e. companies with funded projects) and the control groups, in particular control group B (i.e. companies that never applied for IWT subsidies). When the differences are not statistically significant, we speak instead about 'effects'. For example, a scale item having a high score for the experimental group without any significant difference with the control group has a strong scale effect but no scale additionality.

However, the challenge would be to compare on a 'matched' basis, particularly with control group B, which never applied for IWT funding. The problem with this is that the control groups were not explicitly set up as matched samples in the sense that the companies in both groups are similar, except that the experimental group received IWT subsidies while the control groups did not. Nevertheless, it turned out that the differences in terms of sector and size distribution between the experimental and control group A are not statistically significant. So control group A is comparable in these respects to the experimental group. However, the sample of respondents of control group B differs significantly from the experimental group. This may imply that in cases where we have a significant difference between the groups on certain questions or items, this may be due to the different underlying sector or size distribution. This limits the potential use of control group B as a control group. It should not be a surprise that control group B differs significantly from the experimental group. This reflects the different profile between IWT clients and non-IWT clients. If we were to look for a perfect match between the experimental group and control group B, the latter would very likely not be representative of the non-IWT clients.

In the second approach one directly 'asks' the supported companies how their innovation-related behaviour has changed. Some of the questions ask explicitly about the impact of the IWT project under investigation on the innovative behaviour and strategy of the company. Another type of question asks the respondents of the experimental group to compare the outcome with IWT support with the situation in which they received no IWT support. It may be difficult for the respondents to reflect on this hypothetical and counterfactual situation. Maybe they also have an incentive to answer in a strategic way and to be more positive towards IWT and the impact of its subsidies. But we also addressed these questions to the respondents of control group A that were denied IWT support but where the project took place anyway. This allows us to compare the 'hypothetical' answers of the experimental group with what happened in 'reality' (control group A).

To sum up, the proof of 'additionality' as opposed to merely 'effects' remains a challenging problem in the research into the behavioural additionality of public R&D support.

RESULTS ON THE ADDITIONALITY OF IWT SUBSIDIES[6]

Introduction

This section presents a descriptive analysis of the telephone survey results, complemented with the results from the additional interviews. First, we present some descriptive statistics on the company and R&D profiles of the respondents, as well as on the competitive position of the experimental group versus the control groups. The following section briefly describes the profile of the companies in the dataset concerning their investments in R&D and their export intensity. Later subsections give more details on the additionality effects of public funding on several aspects of firm behaviour.

Profile of Companies

Table 6.3 provides information on the trend in the total R&D outlays of the firms surveyed, their sales outside Belgium and the degree of competition they face in the markets in which they are active for the different samples.

Table 6.3   Average trend total R&D outlays and sales outside Belgium

	Large companies	SMEs	Starters	Total
Total R&D outlays[1]				
Experimental group	3.42	3.75	3.66	3.66
Control group A	2.71	3.46	3.09*	3.26**
Control group B	3.40	3.41**	3.4[a]	3.40*
% sales outside Belgium[2]				
Experimental group	75	51	50	55
Control group A	69	45	26**	41**
Control group B	54	29***	15***	32**
Degree of competition[3]				
Experimental group	3.44	3.19	2.72	3.12
Control group A	3.38	2.7***	2.77	2.78***
Control group B	2.60	3.22	2.33	3.03

Notes:
1. 'What has been the trend in the total R&D outlays of your company, expressed as a % of sales, in the last five years ?' Mean score 1 to 5, with 1 = strongly decreasing and 5 = strongly increasing.
2. 'What per cent share of total turnover (last year) did you realise in the following geographical regions?' The percentages refer to the share of the turnover that is exported.
3. 'How would you describe the competition on the product market?' Mean score with 1 = no competition and 5 = strong competition.
Significant difference with experimental group at * = 10 % level, ** = 5 % level, *** = 1 % level.
a.   Sample too small to test significance of difference.

On the question 'What has been the trend in the total R&D outlays of your company, expressed as a percentage of sales?', respondents of the control groups as a whole responded significantly differently from the experimental group. On average, budgets are stable to slightly increasing for all groups, but control groups A and B are characterised as having a significantly lower average trend compared to the answers of the experimental group.

Concerning the percentage share of total turnover of sales outside Belgium, Table 6.3 shows an average export percentage for the experimental group of 55 per cent. The export share is significantly lower for the respondents of the control groups, in particular for the subsample of starters.

Table 6.3 also deals with the degree of competition on the product market most closely related to the project subject of the survey.[7] On average, respondents of the experimental group indicate that competition is moderate to strong on this product market. The experimental group (IWT-funded clients) turns out to be significantly more present in the more competitive markets than control group A (IWT clients without IWT funding). For respondents who never submitted an IWT proposal (control group B), there is no significant difference in degree of competition from those of the IWT-funded clients, except for the subsample of large companies.

Project Additionality

The most obvious way to evaluate the effectiveness of public support is to determine whether it has resulted in so-called project additionalities (Falk, 2006). These are in place if the project is cancelled, due to the fact that support from public funds was not forthcoming. Therefore we asked the respondents of the experimental group what would have happened to the project if it had not received IWT support. For the experimental group, this is a hypothetical situation. It raises the question of whether the respondents are indeed able to reflect on their behaviour in hypothetical, counterfactual situations. Respondents may have an interest in the continuation of public support, which may affect the kind of answers they provide. Therefore it is interesting to be able to compare the answers with those of the respondents in control group A that did not receive the IWT grant. Their answers refer to the actual situation.

Table 6.4 summarises the results of the telephone survey on the go–no go decision. When we consider the results for the experimental group separately, only about 11 per cent of the respondents replied that the project would have taken place with the same budget, which would imply no project additionality at all. On the other hand, 41 per cent of these respondents indicated that the project would not have taken place at all, which would imply full project additionality. But the decision is not a yes–no decision. About half of the projects would have taken place but with a smaller budget, implying partial project additionality.[8] We found no statistically significant relation between company size and project additionality.

If we compare these hypothetical answers of the experimental group with the 'actual' answers of the respondents in control group A, the percentage of projects that would have been cancelled according to the respondents of the experimental group (41 per cent) is nearly the same as the percentage of projects that have not taken place according to the respondents of control group A (43 per cent). However, the percentage of projects that have taken place, but with a smaller budget, is in reality lower (for control group A) than hypothetically estimated by the experimental group: 25 per cent compared to 48 per cent. On the other hand, 33 per cent of the respondents of

Table 6.4   Project additionality (%)

	Experimental group (hypothetical)[a]	Control group A (actual)[b]
No project additionality (The project would have/has taken place with the same budget)	11	32
Partial project additionality (The project would have/has taken place with a smaller budget)	48	25
Full project additionality (The project would not have/has not taken place at all)	41	43
n	191	80
Response rate (%)	98	89

Notes:
a.   What would have happened if the project had not received IWT R&D support?
b.   What happened after you did not receive the IWT grant?

control group A indicate that the project has taken place with the same budget, compared to 11 per cent for the experimental group.

The interview results provide some additional information on the conditions under which a project would be cancelled or not, completely or partially. Four different types of companies can be distinguished:

1. In these companies, the projects will always take place, independently of whether they receive an IWT subsidy or not. In these very innovative companies the innovation process is organised as a funnel with a number of gates where a go–no go decision is taken on the basis of business cases. For the projects that underwent a business case, their continuation will not depend on IWT support. Nevertheless, if these companies receive IWT support, this sometimes allows them to do more, especially to involve more partners, because IWT support very often serves to pay such partners.
2. For these companies, the project will also take place, but with a limited scope and budget. The project may also be reoriented with less fundamental and more applied research.
3. In these companies, continuation will depend on the characteristics of the project. Projects still far from valorisation will in most cases be cancelled. Another reason for cancellation is the fact that the project does not fall within current business lines. If the project takes place, the budget will typically be reduced by eliminating the extras, or

the stages are dealt with in sequential order instead of taking place simultaneously.

4.   In these companies, typically SMEs in industrial sectors, innovation is too risky and the projects depend on external public funding, i.e. IWT support. Internal financing will not be possible without disrupting the daily business, and non-public external financing is mostly not available. Several interviewees also mentioned that the support helps to persuade management to take the risk. So if the support is denied, the project is cancelled. In a sense, the IWT subsidy thus serves as an insurance for these companies and is therefore important for the go–no go decision. Within these companies, the only innovation projects that take place are IWT-supported projects.

Scope and Scale Additionality

The results of the analysis for scope and scale are given at the top of Table 6.5. It can be seen that, on average, the respondents of the experimental group indicate that there is a positive, but not large, impact of IWT support on the goals (more ambitious) and the scale (larger scale) of the project. The opinion of the experimental group is more or less confirmed by the respondents of control group A. The projects that took place (and therefore were not cancelled) after IWT support was rejected had less ambitious goals and a smaller scale than if they had received an IWT subsidy. However, the positive impact of IWT support on the level of ambition of the project seems to be overestimated by the experimental group, in particular by the large companies.

In general, the telephone survey results give limited support to the scope and scale additionality of the IWT subsidies. For instance, we also found that about 90 per cent of the respondents within the experimental group were already active in the product market most closely related to the IWT-funded project. So these IWT projects do not seem to expand companies' scope to new product markets. This percentage is also about the same when compared with control groups A and B. A lower percentage for the experimental group would have been an indication of scope additionality.

Also, the percentage of projects described as additional to ongoing R&D is higher among the experimental group, while relatively more of the control groups' projects are described as entirely new. This is a surprising result (contradicting scope additionality) that is not, however, supported by the qualitative evidence we collected during the interviews.

The interview results indeed seem to be more affirmative about the occurrence of these types of additionalities. It remains true that a number of large

Table 6.5   Results on scope, scale, network and acceleration additionality

	Large companies	SMEs	Starters	Total
Scope additionality				
Experimental group	4.00	3.66	3.83	3.77
Control group A	3.20***	3.47	3.60	3.48**
Scale additionality				
Experimental group	3.90	3.58	3.90	3.73
Control group A	3.60	3.83	3.86	3.82
Network additionality				
Experimental group	3.58	3.21	2.88	3.20
Control group A	3.60	3.33	3.53**	3.43
Acceleration additionality				
Experimental group	3.86	3.72	4.10	3.85
Control group A	3.67	3.68	3.40*	3.59

Notes:
The respondents of both the experimental group and control group A were asked to compare the project with and without IWT support in terms of the goals ($\approx$ scope), the scale, the number of external collaborators and the speed of the project. For the experimental group, this again refers to a hypothetical situation. For the respondents of control group A, it refers to the actual situation.
   We compare the situation with IWT support with the situation without IWT support. Question: 'Has/would receiving IWT grant enable(d) you to undertake the project . . . than what would be/has been possible without IWT support?' Mean scores 1 to 5.
1.   . . . with much less ambitious goals = 1; with much more ambitious goals = 5;
2.   . . . on a much smaller scale = 1; on a much bigger scale = 5;
3.   . . . with many fewer external collaborators = 1; with many more external collaborators = 5;
4.   . . . much slower = 1; much faster = 5.
Significant difference with experimental group at * 10% level, ** 5 % level, *** 1 % level.

companies with a strongly formalised innovation decision process do not fundamentally adapt their strategy to make projects fundable by IWT. But the IWT subsidies nevertheless allow for additional work of a more explorative nature. Most other interviewees agreed that the projects they submit for IWT support are of a different nature from those that they do internally. The IWT projects are typically larger projects that the companies could not do on their own (scale additionality). Similarly, several companies mentioned that IWT support allows them to do more fundamental research that is not 100 per cent linked to commercial potential, so that the projects done with IWT support have a more fundamental research character compared to the internal projects. It was also emphasised that more fundamental research may not be necessary in the short run. However, it allows the development of new and more generic knowledge that results in broader applicable outcomes important to remain competitive in the long run. IWT grants also seem to allow companies to undertake more high risk-projects.

Network Additionality

According to the respondents in the experimental group, IWT support has a limited positive effect (on average) on the number of external collaborators when compared to the situation in which they would not have received the IWT subsidy. The respondents of control group A confirm the positive, although limited, impact of IWT support on the number of external partners. In other words, as a consequence of not receiving the IWT subsidy, they (marginally) reduced the extent of collaboration in the project.

Project leaders of projects completed with partners were also asked about the continuation of the partnership after finishing the project. Eighty-three per cent of the respondents of the experimental group indicated that the partnership continued after the project was finished, in most cases with the same intensity (42 per cent). Only in 17 per cent of the cases was the partnership stopped. What we do not know, however, is whether the partners in the project were new to the company or whether they had worked together before.

What we do know is that more than two out of three companies within the experimental group (69 per cent) are involved in non-subsidised R&D cooperation. There is no significant relationship with company size. The companies in the control groups are less involved in non-subsidised R&D cooperation. This is true in particular for the respondents in control group B, where the difference with the experimental group is highly significant for all size categories.

Based on the interviews, we can conclude that the group of companies that indicated no project additionality, nor scale or scope additionality, seems also to experience no network additionality. However, many interviewees, especially among the SMEs but also among the large companies, indicated that the IWT subsidies are very often used to pay the partners. IWT financing also allows them to pay partners with specific knowledge that they do not have. There seems to be more network additionality when the firms cooperate with partners that are more oriented towards basic research (universities, research centres), since there are often opportunities for collaboration with partners that are more oriented towards applied research outside the IWT projects. This does not mean that IWT influences the selection of the partners. In most cases, it seems that (potential) partners are known to the company and so there is no influence of IWT.

Acceleration Additionality

According to the respondents of the experimental group, the IWT grant enabled them to undertake the project faster (on average) than would have been possible without IWT support. There is a significant relationship between company size and impact in terms of speed of the project, indicating that the impact is largest for the starters' group. The 'hypothetical' impact in terms of speed is confirmed by the answers of control group A. However, the impact seems on average to be significantly lower for the starters (see bottom part of Table 6.5).

During the interviews, it was mentioned in several cases that if projects need to go fast (i.e. when time to market is important), companies will not submit them for IWT support because they must first write a proposal and then wait for the decision on the funding. If a project is submitted, the IWT support may help to start a project earlier. As a result, products that come out will also be earlier on the market. For instance, it was mentioned a few times that funding may allow the project to start earlier because without funding it would be postponed due to lack of internal financing.

Several companies also confirmed that projects can be realised faster, resulting in a better competitive position. One reason mentioned is that the support allows including external partners that can do certain tasks more efficiently and therefore faster. Another reason mentioned is that if one is forced to write reports and to respect delivery periods because of the funding, there is more pressure behind the projects. This reason seems to be especially relevant for SMEs, where time spent on innovation must compete with day-to-day production activities. A third reason is that due to the support, more research paths can be developed in parallel, while without the subsidies companies would be able to invest in only one project at a time.

Competence Additionality

Competence additionality refers to the positive impact on competencies and expertise. This section explores the main results on a number of questions that deal with the impact of the projects on different kinds of abilities and capabilities, such as the ability to network or innovation management capabilities. All items were on average situated below the 'agreement' score by the respondents of the experimental group. Comparing results with control group A, no significant differences on the exception of the networking with universities or knowledge centres are observed: the non-IWT-funded clients agree to a lesser extent with the impact on networking with universities. Compared with the results of control group

B, the experimental group seems to have an additionality for HR (human resources) upgrading; respondents of control group B disagree on this statement. Surprisingly, respondents of control group B agree significantly more with the statement that the project increased their innovation management capabilities. However, the number of observations for both control groups on these questions is very limited.

Based on the interviews, it seems that the impact on the competencies of the companies receiving IWT subsidies depends on the degree of formalisation of R&D activities within the companies. If this formalisation degree is high, IWT will have little influence on project management organisation or innovation management capabilities. Some of these companies spoke about fine-tuning their R&D process monitoring: there is more thorough evaluation in the process follow-up or more structuring in the process, but no radical changes or implications on the internal project organisation occur due to IWT support. In one case there was an influence of the IWT reporting on own reporting principles, resulting in the adoption of a reporting scheme coming closer to IWT requirements. The same company also mentioned that the partnerships allowed the company to develop its critical sense in looking at the technologies of third parties. In addition, there was one example of a very innovative consumer goods company where the IWT project proposals are used internally as didactic material.

Among the companies with a less formalised R&D and innovation process, the impact of IWT funding on their competencies seems to be more tangible. For instance, it was mentioned on several occasions that writing a proposal helps to define the research questions more clearly. Some companies also learned to work in a more project-oriented way, with a more formalised R&D process as a consequence. One company indicated that it learned how to draw up a schedule and to put in place milestones that contributed to acquiring more discipline, something also important for clients. Some companies mentioned an impact on their network competencies because many companies use the IWT funding to pay their (scientific) partners. One company gave the example of the high-level contacts it developed (not simply on the business line level) with high-tech companies. That would not have been possible without the IWT grant.

Output Additionality

Output additionality of public R&D support refers to the additional 'output' resulting from the projects that receive public R&D support when compared to the output that would result without such support. For the evaluation of the output additionality of IWT support the questionnaire

Table 6.6   Output additionality (%)

Projects that resulted in the introduction of . . .	Large companies	SMEs	Starters	Total
a new or improved product	54	71	77	69
and that would have been cancelled without IWT support	14	38	23	30
a new or improved process	60	55	71	58
and that would have been cancelled without IWT support	33	39	40	38

included a series of questions related to the output of the projects, such as the introduction of new products or production processes.

On average, nearly 70 per cent of the product innovation projects of the experimental group resulted in the introduction of a new or improved product (see Table 6.6). Large companies seem to have been less successful, while the reverse is true for the starters, but there is no statistically significant relationship. In addition, of those projects that have not as yet resulted in the introduction of a new product, 18 per cent (total average) will very probably or certainly be successful in the next two to five years, according to the respondents of the telephone survey.

Analogously, nearly 60 per cent of the process innovation projects resulted in the introduction of a new or improved production process. Again, there is no significant relationship between success of process-oriented projects and company size. Of those projects that have not yet resulted in the introduction of a new process, 21 per cent (total average) will very probably or certainly be successful in the next two to five years.

We compared the 'success' of the projects between the experimental group and control group A.[9] The projects in control group A have been less successful; in particular the projects with a focus on process innovation.

During the interviews, we collected several nice examples of projects that resulted in new products that have been successfully commercialised. A small enterprise, for instance, developing and producing machinery for the food industry, developed with the aid of IWT an oven using gas instead of electricity that is successfully commercialised in several countries, even in the USA. These commercial successes on some occasions led to an increase in employment.

Sometimes the output of the project was considered to be very positive because the results could be used in follow-up projects. One company said it was using the experiences and calculations from the preliminary IWT-granted study in new research projects. Based on the initial research and the resulting prototype, the company did some further research and developed another product that became very successful. For another company, the project was unsuccessful in terms of new product development, but the knowledge it acquired was very useful in the context of new projects that resulted in a derived product that is actually very successful.

New products or processes are not the only kind of outputs that can be considered as a measure of success of the projects. Some companies patented the knowledge they developed and now have revenues from these patents, such as royalties and licences. Yet other companies stressed the fact that IWT support is important for long-term development, so that in the short run one should not expect important outputs in terms of new products.

We also investigated whether the projects that were successful in terms of product or process innovation would have been cancelled without IWT support. If that is the case, then output additionality seems to be present since these new or improved products or processes would not have been introduced without IWT support. Table 6.6 indicates that, on average, 30 per cent of the product innovations and 38 per cent of the process innovations resulted from projects that would have been cancelled without IWT support.

Strategic (Innovation) Additionality

In this last section we consider the impacts of the (IWT) projects that are of a more strategic nature. When this impact is considered to be greater by the respondents of the experimental group in comparison with the respondents of the control groups, we consider this as strategic additionality, i.e. a difference in strategic behaviour that is the consequence of public intervention.

Table 6.7 describes the impact of specific projects on the (innovation) strategy of the company. All statements refer to company-level effects. The statements are ranked by the mean score for the respondents of the experimental group.

The experimental group agreed most with the statement that the project let the firm enter into a new enabling technology. In fact, three out of four respondents (completely) agreed with this statement. They also (mostly) agreed with the statement 'The project allowed my company to undertake research in areas beyond our short-term business needs'. Large companies agreed more with the latter statement compared to the SMEs, but the differences by company size are not statistically significant.

Table 6.7   *Strategic (innovation) additionality*

	Experimental group				Control group A	Control group B
	Large companies	SMEs	Starters	Total	Total	Total
The project let my firm enter into a new enabling technology	3.2	2.9	2.9	3.0 (n = 182)	2.9 (n = 34)	2.8 (n = 20)
The project allowed my company to undertake research in areas beyond our short-term business needs	3.1	2.7	2.9	2.8 (n = 180)	2.6 (n = 34)	2.6 (n = 20)
The project resulted in a more formalised innovation process within the firm	2.4	2.7	2.7	2.6 (n = 179)	2.4 (n = 34)	2.5 (n = 20)
The project caused my company to undertake higher-risk research than would otherwise be the case	2.6	2.6	2.7	2.6 (n = 181)	1.7*** (n = 33)	2.5 (n = 20)
The project eventually led to a change in business strategy	1.9	2.2	2.2	2.1 (n = 181)	2.4 (n = 33)	2.1 (n = 20)
The project affected our choice of location for our R&D facilities	1.9	1.5	1.5	1.6 (n = 180)	1.8** (n = 34)	1.5 (n = 20)
The project affected our choice of location for manufacturing facilities	1.6	1.4	1.3	1.4 (n = 174)	1.8*** (n = 34)	1.5 (n = 20)

Notes:
Question: 'Do you agree with the following statements?' Mean value with 1 = completely disagree; 2 = disagree; 3 = agree; 4 = completely agree.
Significant difference with experimental group at * = 10 % level, ** = 5 % level, *** = 1 % level.

There is no strong support among the experimental group for the statement 'The project resulted in a more formalised innovation process within the firm'. Not surprisingly, one of four respondents from large companies completely disagreed with this statement. The opposite is true for the SMEs, with one out of five respondents completely agreeing with this statement. There is also no strong impact of the projects on the risk behaviour of the company since the statement that 'The project caused my company to undertake higher-risk research than would otherwise be the case' gets a total mean score of 2.6.

Subsequently, we get a number of statements where the respondents of the experimental group tend to disagree. For instance, respondents tend to disagree with the statement that the project eventually led to a change in business strategy. This would of course be a very strong impact. Among the SMEs and starters, but not among the large companies, there are nevertheless a number of respondents who completely agreed with this statement.

The results for the last two statements indicate that the projects, on average, do not seem to affect the location of the R&D or production facilities of the companies within the experimental group. However, the interviews with the R&D managers of regular IWT clients resulted in some nice examples of these strategic impacts (see below). Maybe that is because they have a better view on the strategic impact of the IWT projects on the company compared to the project leaders questioned during the telephone survey.

When we compare the strategic impact of the IWT projects with the projects of the control groups, we cannot draw strong conclusions.[10] The mean values are not significantly higher (sometimes they are even lower) for the experimental group. The exception is the statement 'The project caused my company to undertake higher-risk research than would otherwise be the case', for which the mean value is significantly higher for the experimental group when compared to control group A, but not when compared to control group B.

During the interviews with the (R&D) managers of the regular clients, we collected some nice examples of strategic additionality, or at least strategic effects. One large company entered a new technology and product domain resulting in an investment of over €50 million to set up the most modern production line in Europe. Another, but small, company indicated that IWT support allows them to take the lead in the market, while otherwise they would be a follower.

Contrary to what the telephone survey results indicate, we collected some qualitative evidence of the impact of IWT subsidies on the R&D and even production location decisions of the supported companies. This was in particular the case among the large foreign-owned companies we interviewed.

One of these companies explained that when the company was taken over, the idea was to centralise the R&D activities. In the context of internal competition for scarce R&D budgets, IWT support was important to keep and even further invest in R&D activities in Flanders. Another company indicated that the IWT subsidies that support the research centre allow them to keep the expertise in stainless steel in Flanders. Without support, foreign decision makers could take different decisions. This was confirmed by another company, which explained that the optimisation of R&D decisions happens at group level where they will check whether a project can be subsidised by IWT and therefore be undertaken in Flanders. Yet another company put it another way: without subsidies, the company can do the research where it wants. In this way the subsidies function as an insurance against risks for the research in Flanders, with the effect that the research remains there. A final example is that of a company that indicated that IWT projects are important to support the competitiveness of its location in Flanders. This has a positive impact on the attitude of the foreign mother company towards an R&D organisation model that is based on local needs and organised on site.

The fact that the IWT subsidies allow some companies to keep certain activities in Flanders also translates into employment that can be kept stable. Lack of IWT support would result in less R&D capacity in Flanders, a more limited research portfolio and fewer new products, according to a large telecom company.

A number of other companies also stressed the employment effects, both direct and indirect. One company indicated that there was no impact of IWT subsidies on the R&D location, but on the location of production facilities. The more complex designs in close relationship with the R&D activities are first produced in Flanders, while the more standard products are produced in the proximity of the clients, located elsewhere in Europe. So without IWT support, these production activities in Flanders would be in danger.

Another strategic effect mentioned by a number of companies is that IWT subsidies allow companies to continue their research activities during economic recessions. When budgets are tight and savings need to be realised, IWT projects can still continue. IWT support can be used as an important internal argument to continue the project, since R&D should be a long-term story, not affected by short-term problems.

Finally, we spoke with a number of starters who indicated that they would simply not exist (or not survive) without IWT subsidies. The public support they receive is crucial for them to bridge the gap until they become viable on their own or can attract alternative financial means from the private market.

CONCLUSIONS AND FURTHER RESEARCH

Traditionally, input and output additionalities are the main dimensions of impact considered when analysing the impact of public funding on business R&D. This view has focused on input and output measures in business R&D, treating the firm as a 'black box'. This chapter has attempted to provide insights into this black box by analysing the effects of public interventions on firms' attitudes towards R&D and overall behaviour. It therefore looked into the behavioural additionalities of publicly funded R&D, complementing the traditional methodologies of input and output additionalities.

We found evidence for different types of behavioural additionality. The IWT-supported clients indicated that the support had a positive impact on the goals, the scale, the number of partners and the speed of the project, but in general this impact was not large. Their answers, reflecting on a hypothetical situation by comparing the project with and without support, are in general confirmed by the respondents of control group A whose application for IWT support was rejected.

The in-depth interviews resulted in additional insights into the black box. For instance, projects still far 'away' from valorisation or not within the current business lines have a high chance of being cancelled if not supported by IWT. Similarly, several companies mentioned that IWT support allows them to perform more basic research projects with a higher risk profile. Many interviewees, especially among the SMEs but also among the larger companies, indicated that the IWT funds are often used to pay their partners. These partners are typically oriented towards basic research, while those with whom they cooperate outside IWT projects are oriented towards applied research. Many of the interviewed companies confirmed that IWT support might help to start a project earlier because the funding gives it a higher priority within the company. Projects may also be realised faster because, among other reasons, the subsidised companies have to submit progress reports and respect deadlines.

The innovative character and, more particularly, the formalisation of the R&D process are more important than merely the size of the company to explain the observed behavioural additionality effects. IWT support will on average have only a marginal impact on the R&D behaviour of companies where the innovation process is highly formalised, for instance in companies where decisions on R&D projects are taken on the basis of business cases. For this type of company, fiscal measures may be more cost-efficient from a government's perspective compared to providing subsidies. By contrast, IWT support is more likely to have an impact on the behaviour of companies in more traditional sectors that are much less innovative. In some of these companies, the IWT-supported project is the only R&D project, and would be cancelled without such support.

However, an issue that remains to be explored concerns the policy implications of behavioural additionality. The assessment of the impacts of R&D programmes using the input-additionality approach is based on the assumption of a linear relation between inputs and outputs, i.e. more R&D inputs lead to more innovation outputs. On the other hand, evaluation of public interventions based on output additionality can favour low-risk, short-term-oriented projects.

It would therefore be interesting to develop indicators that allow for a more continuous monitoring of the impact on the R&D behaviour of the supported companies, and hence yield a deeper insight into the drivers of additionality of IWT support for R&D, and R&D or innovation support in general. A subsequent step could be to adapt the selection criteria used to screen the project proposals or even the R&D policy mix in order to obtain more behavioural additionality on different levels of the innovation proces within a company. However, before we can do so, further research is needed on the factors or drivers that stimulate different types of additionality as well as on the relationship between input, output and behavioural additionality. Even the proof of additionality remains a challenging problem in terms of methodology.

ACKNOWLEDGEMENTS

This chapter is based on the outcome of two studies that the authors made for IWT (Institute for the Promotion of Innovation through Science and Technology in Flanders). We would like to thank IWT for the financial support provided in the context of these studies and for permission to use the results to write this chapter. We are also grateful to Professor Dr Bart Clarysse and Dr Valentijn Bilsen for their valuable comments on an earlier version of this chapter.

NOTES

1. The complete study, undertaken by IDEA Consult in cooperation with Professor Dr Bart Clarysse, can be found at www.iwt.be.
2. We prefer the term 'competence additionality' rather than 'cognitive capacity additionality'.
3. The year 2004 was selected in order to maximise the chance of having projects that are finished today so that it is possible for the respondents to say something about the impact. On the other hand, we didn't go back further than 2001, so that respondents could remember the project sufficiently well.

4. The full questionnaire is available in the overall evaluation report at www.iwt.be.
5. The representativeness in terms of (positive) projects is lower, 18 per cent, because some companies have more than one project under way while companies were questioned about only one project.
6. Convention: n = number of observations, i.e. number of respondents that effectively answered the question, so not taking into account 'no answer/don't know'; response rate = number of companies that effectively answered the question (n) divided by the number of respondents to whom the question was addressed.
7. Note that for the experimental group this was the IWT project that was approved, for control group A it was the IWT project that did not receive a subsidy and for control group B it was a project that was defined together with the respondent at the beginning of the telephone interview.
8. If we assume that a smaller budget also implies a smaller scale, then this implies that the IWT funding results in a larger scale of the projects, which indicates scale additionality (see below).
9. A comparison with control group B was not possible because of the too small number of respondents on these questions.
10. Note again that the number of observations for the control groups is very small so that we cannot distinguish by company size.

REFERENCES

Aerts, K. and D. Czarnitzki (2006), 'The impact of public R&D-funding in Flanders', IWT report no. 54.

Barberis, P. (1998) 'The new public management and a new accountability', *Public Administration*, **76**, 451–70.

Buisseret, T.J., H. Cameron and L. Georghiou (1995), 'What difference does it make? Additionality in the public support of R&D in large firms', *International Journal of Technology Management*, **10** (4–6), 587–600.

Clarysse, B., V. Bilsen and G. Steurs (2006), 'Behavoural additionality of the R&D-subsidies programme of IWT-Flanders (Belgium)', in OECD, *Government R&D Funding and Company Behaviour: Measuring Behavioural additionality*, Paris: OECD, ch. 5.

Falk, R. (2006), 'Behavioural additionality of Austria's industrial research promotion fund (FFF)', in OECD, *Government R&D Funding and Company Behaviour: Measuring Behavioural Additionality*, Paris: OECD, ch. 3.

Falk, R. (2007), 'Measuring the effects of public support schemes on firms' innovation activities: survey evidence from Austria', *Research Policy*, **36** (5), 665–79.

Georghiou, L. (1997), 'Issues in the evaluation of innovation and technology policy', in OECD (ed.), *Policy Evaluation in Innovation and Technology: Towards Best Practice*, Paris: OECD, Chapter 3.

OECD (2006), *Government R&D Funding and Company Behaviour: Measuring Behavioural Additionality*, Paris: OECD.

Närfeld, K.-H. and A. Wildberger (2006), 'The white box approach to agency effectiveness', *Plattform Forchungs- und Technologieevaluierung*, **29**, 3–15.

Shin, T. (2005), 'The effect of public R&D expenditure on private R&D investment: behavioural additionality at the aggregate level', in OECD (ed.), *Evaluating Government Financing of Business R&D: Measuring Behavioural Additionality*, Paris: OECD, Chapter 9.

PART III

Public Sector

7. European innovation policy: increased effectiveness through coordination with cohesion policy

Willem Molle

INTRODUCTION

The EU is confronted with a series of important problems. The two that are of most interest in the present chapter are lack of competitiveness on international markets and the considerable internal imbalances. For quite some time the EU has put in place policies to address these problems. But these policies have been evolving rather independently. Our objective in this chapter is to see to what extent further dovetailing of a key part of EU competitiveness policy, i.e. innovation, and the EU policy to reduce imbalances, i.e. cohesion policy, can improve their effectiveness.[1]

In order to tackle this question we have structured the chapter as follows. In the next section we briefly describe the overall policy framework of the innovation policy, i.e. the Lisbon Strategy. We mention its objectives, instruments and governance, and also its inadequacies. The main inadequacy is the lack of funds. The solution that has been found to this problem is to use the funds originally designed to address imbalances (Structural and Cohesion Funds) with the aim to improve innovation and competitiveness.

Next we describe in some detail the problem of the EU regarding the spatial distribution of its innovation activity. We indicate that innovation within the EU is largely concentrated in a limited number of countries in the North West and within each member state in the more central regions.

The two sections that follow go into the intricacies of the EU policies set up to deal with the two main problem areas that this chapter addresses. One is devoted to innovation policy; the other to cohesion policy. In both sections we follow the same structure. We describe in a succinct way the emergence and gradual development of the policy, the main ways in which it is delivered (through financial support to programmes and coordination of national regulation), and the effect these have on each other (innovation policy on cohesion policy and vice versa).

We complement the chapter with a section that gives a synopsis of the solution that has been found for the coordination problem and conclude it with a section that gives some recommendations for a further increase in effectiveness.

THE LISBON STRATEGY: INCREASING COMPETITIVENESS THROUGH INNOVATION

Objectives: A Hierarchy of Primary and Subsidiary Goals

The EU faces a lack of competitiveness that can partly be attributed to a lack of innovation. The EU has for decades tried to get to grips with this problem and has experimented with different policy solutions.[2]

At the turn of the century the EU decided that a bolder initiative was needed to realise success. So it set itself the objective of becoming the most competitive and dynamic knowledge-based economy in the world, capable of sustainable economic growth with more and better jobs, and greater social cohesion. To realise this objective the so-called Lisbon Strategy was formulated, later complemented by the so-called Gothenburg Strategy, which has the objective of realising environmental sustainability (EC, 2003a, 2003b). The original Lisbon Strategy refers only obliquely to the objective of cohesion (see EC, 2000). In 2003 the Brussels European Council introduced a somewhat more explicit reference in the sense that it specified as an additional objective the reduction in employment disparities. All in all, however, the cohesion objective is not central to the Lisbon/Gothenburg Strategy.

To realise the ambitious objectives of the Lisbon Strategy a range of intermediate policy goals has been defined. They fall essentially in the following three categories:[3]

1. *Enhance the transition to a knowledge-based economy and society*   This category comprises: (1) an information society for all; (2) a European area of research and innovation; and (3) a friendly environment for starting up and developing innovative SMEs.
2. *Sustain a healthy economic outlook and favourable growth prospects*   This comprises the completion of the internal market; the creation of good macro economic and monetary conditions, and the pursuit of an open external policy.
3. *Modernise the European social model*   This comprises the stimulation of education and training (notably for the knowledge society),

the modernisation of social protection systems and the promotion of social inclusion.

In this chapter we address in particular the subjects described under (1). They relate to the positive influence that innovation has on growth.[4] The objectives of the part of the strategy that deals mainly with innovation policy (IP)[5] are the following:[6]

- Improve IT infrastructure.
- Promote e-commerce; e-governance and e-learning.
- Adapt legislation, e.g. to increase competition of network providers; introduce a European patent.
- Develop R&D networks; develop electronic scientific communications, and improve the accessibility of research results throughout the EU.
- Increase competitive funding and focus in public research.
- Stimulate the diffusion of innovation and technology by promoting interaction between universities, firms and public laboratories.
- Promote entrepreneurship, access to finance; facilitate firm entry and exit; encourage an entrepreneurial spirit in society.
- Promote the dissemination of technology in SMEs and improve the capacity of SMEs to identify, select and adopt technologies.

The Main Instrument: Coordination

The Lisbon Strategy leaves implementation to a soft form of coordination. The actual delivery of the Lisbon Strategy is very complicated due to the width of policy areas addressed and the range of mechanisms for its implementation. What complicates it even more is the fact that most of the instruments are in the domain of the member states. So the delivery of the strategy hinges on vertical coordination.

The EU has decided to use the so-called 'open method of coordination' to align EU and member states' targets and instruments. In order to avoid the situation that Brussels would be perceived as telling the member states what to do, the idea of benchmarking was adopted. The best national practices would then be selected for adoption in other countries. In a sort of open market of competing policies, the best solutions would be selected by each member state. In practice this means:

- Setting of EU Guidelines and their translation into policy targets and actions (benchmarks) on the national and regional levels.

- Setting up of monitoring systems to allow progress to be measured and 'best practices' to be identified. To facilitate monitoring, a system of indicators has been introduced (EC, 2000).[7] In matters of innovation these include on one hand indicators on spending (on R&D, human resources, ICT etc.) and on the other hand indicators on the level of scientific and innovative activity (e.g. number of researchers, patents etc.).
- Evaluating the progress made and subsequent adapting of the policy.

As an illustration of the practice of the open method of coordination we mention the eEurope Action Plans. These aim to provide a framework that guides the adoption of new legislation by member states and the refocusing of national public expenditure on specific goals. The first eEurope Action Plan was agreed in 2002 and focused on the potential of the Internet and hence on stimulating connectivity. The second one, agreed in 2005, focused on exploiting broadband technologies to deliver online services. Both specified very detailed targets as to the number of households to be reached by the Internet etc.

It appeared, however, that it is very difficult to identify which policy instrument could be called 'best practice'. Due to the context dependency of many innovation policy issues, the mere copying of policies that have proven to be successful in one country may not be the best solution for another. In order to stimulate country-specific solutions the accent is now put on national reform programmes (NRPs). The open method of coordination allows member states to adopt an approach to implementation that best suits their administrative and policy contexts. This certainly has the advantage of flexibility. However, it also has some disadvantages: it can lead to a lack of effectiveness and can undermine EU-wide consistency.

Realisation: What are the Reasons for the Lack of Results?

The realisation of the Libson Strategy is not easy to sum up in one or two words or figures; its complexity precludes that. So we need to look in detail at its various aspects. In 2005 a study into the Libson Strategy found that it had had a clear impact in the sense that a number of member states had increased their efforts devoted to R&D, IT infrastructure and the promotion of skills for the information society (DTI, 2005, p. 9). For instance, Italy had decided to increase spending on R&D in the period 2003–06 from 0.6 per cent of GDP to 1.0 per cent; Denmark created a new high-technology research fund of significant size; while Austria introduced tax schemes to boost private R&D.

Notwithstanding these encouraging signs, the general criticism was that progress towards the higher objectives was too slow and that more should be done to reach to the target results.

The reason for the lack of progress was generally seen in the poor match between ways and means. Indeed, the EU has set very ambitious goals without providing adequate instruments to realise them. The open method of coordination as a voluntary coordination of member states' policies is dependent for its effectiveness on the degree to which member states agree with the objectives and are prepared to change their priorities accordingly. Up until 2006 the EU had not provided any additional incentives in the form of funds for supporting the compliance with the Lisbon Strategy goals. It tried to redirect the budgets of the member states towards the common goals by peer pressure. The EU has also tried to mobilise more funds for its own budget items that are particularly relevant for the Lisbon Strategy, such as its innovation and research policy. For quite some time this has not been particularly successful, but recently the 2006–13 budgetary framework did open some new opportunities in this respect.

The Solution: Use the Structural Funds for the Lisbon Objectives, especially Innovation

As substantial new financial resources on the EU level were politically not feasible, the suggestion was made to use existing EU Funds and redirect them to Lisbon Strategy targets. The most important financial resources of the EU that come into consideration are the Structural Funds and the Cohesion Fund (SCF). The main objective of these funds is to improve cohesion: in other words to reduce the disparities that exist between the 'well to do' areas and the 'backward' areas in the EU (Molle, 2007). In other words, cohesion policy aims at improving the structural features of the lagging regions and social groups, which should permit them to improve their performance and catch up with the EU average.

In order to find out whether this solution can work, one needs to analyse whether the objectives, means and governance systems of the two major policy fields (innovation and cohesion) are congruent.[8]

A comparison of the fundamentals of both policies shows that there does not seem to be much of a consistency problem.

- On the cohesion policy side, it can be noted that innovation has long been part of the promotion of regional competitiveness. At present it is a very important element in the toolbox of regional policy (see, e.g., Landabaso et al., 1997; Molle, 2007).
- On the innovation policy side, it has become increasingly obvious in the past decade that the effectiveness of innovation is enhanced

where it is implemented in a regional context (e.g. Cooke et al., 2000). So, for an effective policy in matters of innovation, the European, national and regional dimensions need to be integrated into one multi-level governance system.

Given this convergence of targets, the EU decided during the last major reform of the SCF to orient its resources more to targets that are in line with those of the Lisbon Strategy; in other words it has decided to use the SCF as instruments for the Lisbon Strategy.[9] In order to improve consistency, it has been decided to make the time horizons identical (2006–13), to clarify the orientation of each project to one of the available sources of funding and to build bridges of coordination between the institutions that are responsible for the operational aspects of both policies.[10]

Increasing Effectiveness through Stronger Coordination

On closer inspection it appears, however, that everything is not as well adjusted as one might hope. Indeed, there remain quite a few issues to be tackled to come to a consistent system in which the processes of intervention of the cohesion and innovation policies become complementary and mutually reinforcing. For example:

- The two policies have a different treaty basis. R&D and innovation policies target specific themes, while cohesion policies target specific areas. This means that the first uses a set of instruments that results in thematic specialisation, while the second results in an integrated approach.
- There are considerable differences in implementation methods. Innovation policy essentially uses EU-wide competition for funds that can be gained on the basis of proofs of excellence. Cohesion policy is implemented in a multi-layered partnership approach searching for consistency on the level of a specific region.
- The Lisbon Strategy, if not properly implemented, could aggravate interregional disparities rather than reduce them. Arguably regions that are already endowed with the factors that stimulate competitiveness (e.g. a dynamic SME and corporate business base, a highly educated workforce, state-of-the-art ICT infrastructure, modern service economy, developed research sector) are better placed to benefit from the strategy's implementation. So, to preclude such negative effects a constant assessment of technology policies with a regional (cohesion) impact is needed. The more the innovation (including research and technological development) policies are

geared towards equity, the less need there is for compensatory cohesion policies.[11]

- For the Lisbon Strategy to be delivered successfully at the regional level, the heterogeneous nature of regions must be recognised. All regions are different, and the mixture of factors that determine competitiveness and innovation vary across regional types (CE/ECORYS et al., 2003). Therefore a clear understanding is needed of the interventions that can best be implemented and funded in differing kinds of objective 1 regions (convergence) notably in the accession countries and in objective 2 (competitiveness) regions in order to use best their available specific factors of competitiveness.
- This flexible approach is dependent on having the appropriate regional administrative and governance systems that can deliver Lisbon-aligned innovation and regional development policy measures, and interact with appropriate institutions and policies at the national and European levels. The appropriate administrative capacity will be a key factor in its successful implementation in the European regions.

NATIONAL AND REGIONAL DIFFERENCES IN INNOVATION

Concepts and Data

In order to track the progress of the strategy in matters of innovation, the European Commission developed the European Innovation Scoreboard. This focuses on high-tech innovation and provides national data on some 20 indicators. Similar data have been assembled for regions. These indicators refer to the creation of new knowledge (e.g. R&D expenditure, patents); the transmission and application of existing knowledge (e.g. investment); and the marketing of products in which innovation has been materialised.[12] These data permit us to depict the differences between national and regional levels of innovation in the EU.

The theoretical discussion in the previous section suggests a chain relation between the determinants of innovation, the level of innovation and economic performance. This is indeed what the data reveal: a close correlation between the indicators of the knowledge society and those on wealth, economic structure and human resources.[13] However, this (cor)relation is far from perfect and hence it is interesting to see how the detailed picture for countries and regions presents itself.

The National Picture

In Table 7.1 we present for five basic indicators the performance of the member countries of the EU in terms of innovativeness. This information is limited to the recent situation; lack of comparable data for the past prohibits the analysis of developments over time. The basic data have been rearranged in several ways. First, all indicators have been recalculated so as to produce a maximum of 100 and a minimum of 0.[14] Moreover, a synthetic index has been constructed in order to attain a simplified picture. Finally, the EU member countries have been grouped[15] according to a combination of geography (North, South and East) and date of EU membership (old and new).

A clear split in the EU can be seen. The countries of the North West show the highest values, followed by the South West and finally the East. There is a real problem for the countries of the South. For the moment their wealth levels are higher than those of the East but their innovation potential seems to be lower than that of the East. Moreover, the countries of the East also perform better with respect to human resources and investment in equipment (Molle, 2007, chs 2–5).

Two countries are top performers in innovation, i.e. Sweden and Finland. Both are high-income countries but neither is part of the North West European metropolitan core area. The position of Sweden and Finland is due to very deliberate policy choices to step up innovation in order to stay abreast of the competition. To support these policies the two countries have adopted a new governance model whereby government science policy, university research and industry innovation operate with a great degree of synchronisation.[16]

National Typologies

The situation in the EU as depicted in Table 7.1 suggests a three-tier Europe. This suggestion is, however, the result of a superposition on the data of a certain set of characteristics. What would happen if we let the data speak first and see what categories emerged?

Most interesting would be the use of datasets concerning the different factors that determine performance as distinguished in the literature on national and regional innovation systems (see Chapter 1). These factors are somewhat more varied than the ones included in Table 7.1. The factors and a selection of their relevant indicators include:

- knowledge creation (indicated by, e.g., the share of R&D in GDP; patents);

Table 7.1   Innovation indicators by country (100 is best) (around 2003)

Country*	Public R&D expenditure	Business R&D expenditure	EPO high-tech patent applications (per million population)	Innovation expenditures (% of total turnover)	Internet access (composite indicator)	Summary innovation index
Germany	70	51	38	29	72	56
France	77	40	26	26	34	46
Italy	47	15	6	19	43	31
Netherlands	74	30	77	13	77	45
Belgium	49	48	23	28	67	47
Luxemburg	0	48	6	10	61	29
UK	53	37	26	17	69	49
Denmark	70	52	37	0	89	54
Ireland	25	23	22	n.a.	51	44
Spain	37	15	3	9	37	30
Portugal	53	8	0	28	27	30
Greece	34	5	1	20	28	20
Austria	57	36	19	n.a.	53	39
Sweden	92	100	62	n.a.	100	76
Finland	100	71	100	26	69	75
EU-15	62	38	26	22	57	44
Poland	36	2	0	17	27	14
Czech Rep.	37	21	0	7	n.a.	27
Hungary	58	9	3	11	n.a.	25
Slovakia	14	8	0	10	n.a.	24
Slovenia	54	26	3	10	45	32

Table 7.1 (continued)

Country	Public R&D expenditure	Business R&D expenditure	EPO high-tech patent applications (per million population)	Innovation expenditures (% of total turnover)	Internet access (composite indicator)	Summary innovation index
Lithuania	45	2	1	16	7	26
Cyprus	14	0	0	n.a.	44	17
Latvia	13	3	0	27	0	18
Estonia	46	5	2	12	n.a.	34
Malta	–	1	0	n.a.	n.a.	25
Romania	2	5	0	10	15	15
Bulgaria	30	1	0	n.a.	n.a.	28
EU-27	**60**	**36**	**20**	**21**	**52**	**42**
North	67	45	36	23	63	51
South	43	14	4	16	38	29
East	35	8	0	15	25	21

Note: *Ranked by date of accession and within each group by size of population.

Source: EC European Innovation Scoreboard (2004).

- absorptive capacity (indicated, e.g., by level of education, integration in information society);
- diffusion capacity (indicated, e.g., by technology diffusion infrastructure);
- demand (indicated, e.g., by GDP per capita GDP per person growth);
- government capacity (indicated, e.g., by participation in EU initiatives, e-government, websites of regional governments).

In a regression and cluster analysis on 25 such indicators for the 27 EU countries, Radosevic (2004)[17] showed different groups for each of the five dimensions given in the bullet points above. The analysis generally confirmed the existence of the group of developed EU countries (the North West). It did, however, come up with different groupings than the one used in Table 7.1 for the other countries. Indeed, among the remaining countries two more groups emerged that are both composed of South Western and Eastern countries. The most recent data (Eurostat, 2007) show again a split of the EU in two groups: above average North West and below average South East.

The Regional Picture

On the regional level the database is less complete than on the national level. It means that we are constrained in terms of time period, area coverage and type of indicator. A study made in the early 1990s described the situation in the EU-12 as Archipelago Europe, because most R&D activities were found to be located in a limited number of islands of innovation that seemed to have strong internal links, but weak links among each other and with other regions (FAST, 1992). The basic situation as to concentration has not changed much since; however, the interconnections have been improved under the impetus of various EU programmes (see later sections).

There is even now some lack of consistency between the data for the old member states and the new member states. For example, until recently the indicator on patents (which was heavily used in scoreboards) was neither relevant nor available for the new member states. The patchy information for specific indicators tends to produce fairly disparate results. Therefore we first present a comprehensive picture for the EU-15. It is based on an aggregate index (being the average of a set of indices of the type given in Table 7.1). The regions that perform best on this index are given in Table 7.2. Three salient features seem to determine performance:

- *EU centrality* Half of the regions in the top 40 and six out of the top 10 are located in the 'Pentagon', the metropolitan North Western part of the EU. Not a single region from the periphery shows up in this top group.[18]

- *National centrality*   A large number of national capital cities show up in the list (in total 11, of which six are among the 12 regions with the highest score). Moreover, many regions in the list are traditionally the most dynamic, such as Rhone–Alps in France, Catalonia in Spain, Prague in the Czech Republic etc.[19]
- *National choices*   Many of the best-performing regions are in Sweden and Finland, two countries that have over several decades not only pursued a very deliberate national innovation policy (see previous section), but have also added a regional dimension to it.

Table 7.2 conveys two important messages. First, the regional differences in innovation are to a large extent determined by centrality. Second, this is no reason for despair on the part of regions outside the central areas: a long-term policy can bring such regions up to top levels of innovation performance. Indeed, EU centralisation tendencies do not seem to be dominant forces (Cuervo-Cazurra and Un, 2007).

Additional recent information about the new member states in respect of related indicators[20] shows that none of their regions (expect Prague) shows up in the top 40 of the EU-27.[21]

Regional Typologies

The type of data used in the previous section for the establishment of the relative position of countries and regions can also be used for defining types of regions. This helps to identify their deficiencies and potentials. Aggregate figures for such groups may also be used to define policy priorities, and on that basis to attribute financial resources to each group of regions. Detailed figures can be used for specifying priorities for intervention. This applies equally to innovation policy (e.g. for the funds concerning the European Research Area) and to regional policy (e.g. the share of innovation in support under the Structural Funds).

Several (groups of) authors have produced such typologies. In the past, due to lack of data, such typologies were often based on a limited sample and a qualitative judgement (e.g. Cooke et al., 2000; ECORYS, 2004). Recently better data have become available that have allowed for the establishment of typologies based on quantitative data. We refer here to one for the old member states, one for the new member states and one for the whole of the EU-27.

For the old member states two clusters of urban regions in the North West of the EU were found (Clarysse and Muldur, 2001) that showed the

Table 7.2   Top 40 regions (above EU average) ranked by their score on the innovation index (EU-15 = 100)

Rank	Region		Index	Rank	Region		Index
1	Stockholm	S	225	21	Vlaams Gewest	BE	112
2	Uusimaa (Helsinki)	SF	208	21	Lombardia	I	112
3	Noord-Brabant	NL	191	23	Kärnten	A	111
4	Pohjois-Suomi	SF	161	23	Région Bruxelles	BE	111
4	Eastern	UK	161	23	Rhône–Alpes (Lyon)	F	111
6	Ile de France	F	160	26	Lazio	I	110
7	Bayern (Munich)	D	151	27	Piemonte (Turin)	I	109
8	South East	UK	150	27	Zuid-Holland (Rotterdam)	NL	109
9	Comunidad de Madrid	E	149	29	Hessen	D	108
10	Baden Württemberg (Stuttgart)	D	146	29	Southern and Eastern	IRE	108
11	Sydsverige	S	143	29	West Midlands (Birmingham)	UK	108
12	Berlin	D	140	32	Groningen	NL	107
12	Östra Mellansverige	S	140	33	Comunidad Foral de Navarra	E	105
14	South West (Bristol)	UK	137	33	Noord-Holland	NL	105
15	Västsverige	S	136	33	Limburg	NL	105
16	Midi-Pyrénées (Toulouse)	F	131	36	North West (Manchester/ Liverpool)	UK	104
17	Wien	A	126	37	Hamburg	D	103
18	Etelä-Suomi	SF	124	38	Scotland	UK	102
19	Utrecht	NL	123	39	Cataluña (Barcelona)	E	101
20	Flevoland	NL	114	39	Gelderland	NL	101

Sources: EC European Innovation Scoreboard (2002); Parkinson et al. (2004).

highest scores on both innovation and economic performance. Next to these a category of regions was found that were average (notably in Spain, southern France and Italy), another category of catchers up and finally a category of laggers (notably in Greece, Spain and Portugal). This typology largely confirms on the regional level the notions that we earlier found on the national level.[22]

In a statistical analysis for regions of the new member states (using a database that bears much resemblance to the one used for countries, Muller et al. (2006) identified five different groups:

1. Capital regions (high scores). These include all regions comprising the capital cities of the new member states.
2. Tertiary growth-potential regions (medium scores). In this group we find the Baltic States but also a region such as Wielkopolski.
3. Skilled manufacturing platform regions (medium scores).
4. Industrially challenged regions (weak scores). This is the largest group of the set.
5. Lagging behind agricultural regions (very low scores). Here we find many of the Romanian regions.

For the EU-27 a typology was constructed by the evaluators of the contribution of the EU funds to innovation and knowledge (EC, 2005a). They used four sets of criteria: public knowledge; urban services, private technology; and learning families. Three strategic groups were derived.

1. On the top rung of the ladder appear global consolidation regions. They are well above average on all four sets of criteria. Regions in this group include the capital cities of the countries of the North West (and Prague).
2. On the bottom rungs appear many regions in Southern and Eastern Europe that have low scores. The group is largely identical to the convergence regions of the EU (see section on cohesion policy later in this chapter) and includes most of Greece, Southern Spain and most of the regions of the new member states. These regions are broadly speaking users, not producers, of technology and knowledge.
3. The intermediate group is divided into two subgroups. One of them is strong in private technology (e.g. Baden Württemberg), while the other is strong in public technology (e.g. Midi-Pyrénées, Bratislava).

A much more detailed view of the EU-27 (provided by Dunnewijk et al., 2008) shows the large variety (ten clusters or types) in regional innovation potentials. It identifies on that basis equally detailed and varied sets of benchmarks and sets of suggestions for policy. The importance of these analyses of the regional innovation potential is highlighted by the results of a study that traces the origins of regional growth in the EU to the intricate combination of the innovation efforts of actors in the region and local and external socioeconomic and institutional conditions (Rodriguez-Pose and Crescenzi, 2008).

INNOVATION POLICY

Development of EU Policy[23]

The EU has from its outset been involved in R&D policy. Central to the beginnings were the big European R&D centres that were set up in the 1950s by one of the predecessors of the present EU (Euratom) to support nuclear energy at the European level. However, the EU role stayed relatively limited until the 1980s, when European integration got a new boost. This was evident in the strengthening of the internal market programme and in the increased accent on the motors of growth, notably innovation.

The EU recognises that certain types of R&D generate macroeconomic benefits (positive externalities) that cannot be appropriated by those who have put in the investment. This leads to underinvestment by private sector agents (e.g. because they find that their patents provide insufficient protection against imitators). So R&D is a public good that justifies public intervention.[24] Moreover there are significant economies of scale and spillovers that justify the involvement of the EU in some segments of R&D and technology policy. However, R&D by itself does not create competitive positions for new products from EU firms. So a more comprehensive policy was needed, focusing on the stimulation of innovation.

In the 1980s a start was made with framework programmes for innovation. The Single European Act (1987) provided the new institutional framework for this change and defined clearly the role of the EU in matters of R&D and innovation. It set the broad objectives and defined the type of interventions and the mechanisms for delivery (framework programmes). Since then six framework programmes (FPs) have been executed (Peterson and Sharp, 1998). The new 7th Framework Programme (FP7) covers the period 2007–13, in line with the medium-term EU financial (budget) perspectives.

Financial Support to Innovation

The total size of the budget for innovation has continuously been stepped up;[25] for the present FP7 the total size of the financial resources amounts to €53 billion for the seven-year period from 2006 to 2013. The content of the FPs has changed over time in function of the gradual interactive development of theoretical renewal and policy experimentation (Mytelka and Smith, 2002). We cannot deal with all aspects of the FPs and the EU innovation policy (EC, 2003a) here, so the following are only a few selected activities.

Support EU policy objectives
The EU traditionally finances some R&D that is executed in EU centres. These were initially limited to nuclear energy research but now cover a much wider array of subjects. This EU activity now falls under the heading of Joint Research Centre.

Support to R&D programmes of national and private institutes
These institutes apply for subsidies for projects that fall in one of the EU priority areas. Excellence is the main criterion for allotment.

Improve strategic sector R&D by stimulating cooperation
At the beginning of the century the EU has defined the European Research Area (Edler et al., 2003). This stimulated the collaboration in R&D between firms in different parts of the EU and enhanced the effectiveness of their efforts (Caloghirou et al., 2004).

Support investigator-driven research (Ideas programme)
The FP7 introduced the European Research Council, a pan-EU agency for funding research at the frontiers of science.

Improve the performance of the private sector on innovation
One bottleneck for development is the inadequate structure of finance provision for innovative firms, notably SMEs.[26] The EU facilitates networks that bring together demanders and suppliers of early-stage financing (mostly fast-growing SMEs). Examples are the EU initiatives such as Europe INNOVA or Pro INNO. The FP7 adds to that a new EU risk-sharing facility to back private investors in research projects and to improve access to loans from the European Investment Bank.

Improve exchange of R&D results
Ultimate success in the marketplace is not determined by the quality of the basic research but by the take-up of knowledge by commercial firms. This take-up is positively influenced by the quality of the institutions for innovation and technology diffusion by promoting interaction between universities, firms and public R&D institutes (OECD, 2001). The EC has encouraged the development of so-called European technology platforms (EC, 2005b) that stimulate exchange in key technology domains. It also encourages the establishment of networks of institutions and firms that work on related technologies in different member countries. The FP7 has followed up these earlier actions in the form of Joint Technology Initiatives that specifically address those areas of research activity where enhanced collaboration and considerable investment are essential to long-term success.

Coordination of National Policies

For large segments of innovation policy the instruments are in the hands of players other than the EU. Thus there is an important role for the EU in matters of coordination of national policies. This covers a number of aspects, for example:

- *Finances* Under the Lisbon Strategy, member states have agreed to increase expenditure on R&D to 3 per cent of GDP by 2010. One third must be financed from their own budgets, two-thirds is to be private sector expenditure, to be stimulated by the public sector. The FP7 has defined in this context the ERA/NET, which brings European, national and regional programmes closer together.
- *Regulation* To stimulate private sector R&D, member states have agreed to reform the elements of their regulatory frameworks that have been found to hamper private R&D. In step therewith, the EU has revised certain segments of its regulation too. In 2005, for example, the EU changed its regime for state aid in order to facilitate innovation and R&D in firms (EC, 2005c). The new rules increase the scope of allowable state aid to cover most relevant aspects of the innovation process (of course still subject to the usual safeguards).

Consistency with Cohesion

The main channel of transmission of the innovation policies to cohesion is through the EU budget. EU support is given in the framework of FPs, of which the detailed projects and programmes come up for public tendering.

The selection of projects and the allocation of EU financial support to the selected innovation projects is made on criteria that are internal to innovation policy. The search for excellence means that programmes are entrusted to those organisations that are best qualified to make them into a success. These organisations are often located in the wealthy core areas of the EU. Existing regional strengths are thus a key factor in determining a region's propensity to benefit from this type of funding (ECOTEC, 2004). So the direct impact of the EU support to R&D is not favourable to cohesion (Sharp and Pereira, 2001). Only a limited number of catching-up (dynamic) regions seemed to be capable of making use of the advantages of participation in the FPs (Clarysse and Muldur, 2001).[27]

Some form of attenuation of this anti-cohesion tendency comes from the introduction into the allotment criteria of the obligation on the winning contractor to cooperate with organisations in less developed regions. This seems to have been effective as the share of the least developed areas (objective 1; convergence regions in the jargon of the EU cohesion policy) in funding was higher than their share in R&D capabilities (ECOTEC, 2004; Sharp and Pereira, 2001). However, it was mainly the more central regions of the least wealthy EU member countries who realised this effect, which means that all other areas were left pretty much in the cold (EC, 2004). Another point of concern was that in the 'cohesion' countries and regions the participation of the private sector, in particular of SMEs, was almost non-existent, which implies that the chances of direct regional economic effects were limited.[28]

A new initiative that needs to be mentioned in this respect is the support that the FP7 gives to capacity building. It has introduced the 'regions of knowledge' programme, which brings together the various research partners within a region. Under this programme, universities, R&D centres, multinational firms, SMEs and regional authorities are invited to link up with partners in their own region and in other regions (among them leading ones) to strengthen their innovation abilities and potential. Eligible actions here comprise the organisation of conferences and networks, the exchange of staff, the mentoring of R&D activities by experts from other countries etc.

Another initiative is the capacities programme, which provides finance for projects that aim to improve the research potential of convergence regions, for which some €340 million has been set aside for the period of the FP7. Eligible projects comprise for instance the acquisition of research equipment, the evaluation of R&D facilities in matters of quality and infrastructure, and transnational secondments of research staff.

Regulation is another channel through which innovation policy can influence cohesion. For instance, EU regulation that is intended to improve the quality of the environment leads to innovation in terms of the technologies used both for products and for production. An example of a possible positive effect on cohesion is that high standards set by the EU for the quality of air may induce the relocation of industries from developed regions (that are already under heavy pressure) to regions where there is still a margin between the actual situation and the standard. An example of a negative effect is that the new standard may trigger new technologies that are best mastered by industries in wealthy regions. Unfortunately these ramifications of the effects of policy are so diverse and so uncertain that they rarely permit specific conclusions and never overall conclusions.

COHESION POLICY[29]

Development of the EU Policy

The EU has from its start been confronted with considerable disparities in wealth and employment between different parts of its territory. These disparities have been increased by the different enlargements. Such disparities lead to economic inefficiencies (unused resources) and social tension (political unrest over redistributional issues). In the EU jargon, the lack of cohesion goes with a lack of productivity (and thus competitiveness).

Cohesion has no authorised definition but is often understood as the degree to which economic, social and territorial disparities are politically and socially tolerable. The EU cohesion policy has developed over the past half a century mainly under the influence of two challenges. The first is a real increase in disparities due to enlargement. The second is the risk of increased disparities due to deeper integration (e.g. EMU – European Monetary Union). The main events that marked the evolution of the policy were the following:

- In the 1950s and 1960s there did not seem to be a need for an EU regional (cohesion) policy; the market integration process did not seem to have much negative impact.
- The 1970s saw the first enlargement of the EU, which brought with it fear about increased imbalances. To counteract such problems the European Regional Development Fund was established, which co-financed development projects in disadvantaged regions.
- The 1980s saw the second round of enlargements with the three Mediterranean countries, which greatly increased internal EU disparities. Moreover, the simultaneous programme for the completion of the internal market increased fear about negative effects of increased competition on the weaker countries. In view of these challenges the EU changed its position fundamentally. With the Single European Act of 1985 the objective of economic and social cohesion became a 'constitutional' task. In step therewith, the size of the funds was considerably increased and the rules governing their use profoundly altered. The reform introduced new principles of governance such as programming, partnership, additionality etc.
- In the present century the latest round of enlargement with the new member states of Central and Eastern Europe increased the disparities more than ever before. Moreover, globalisation, the setting of the Lisbon targets and the introduction of the euro introduced big new challenges. Consequently the scope of the cohesion policy

(funds available, areas of intervention, strictness of regulation etc.) was considerably increased again.

The objectives of cohesion policy have remained largely constant over time. The first objective is real convergence – in other words the catching up of the less well to do regions with the EU average. To that end, income, employment and economic opportunities in the weaker regions need to grow faster than those in the richer areas. Other objectives (than real convergence) have also been formulated and these have changed quite a bit over time. The most important secondary objective is now the improvement of competitiveness in the stronger regions (with a clear reference to the Lisbon Strategy; see, e.g., EC, 2003b).

Financial Instruments

The major instruments of cohesion policy are the Structural Funds and the Cohesion Fund (SCFs). Essential in their operations is the rule of co-financing, which means that the EU subsidises projects from regions and countries. EU support is higher, the lower the level of wealth in the area in question. Projects that strengthen the competitive basis ('structure') of the region in question are eligible. Most of the resources are devoted to projects in countries with levels of wealth considerably below the EU average.

Every six to seven years the SFs are evaluated and adapted to new needs. The latest changes were made in 2006. They comprised the re-allotment of the available money over the various objectives. New guidelines were issued as to the set-up of programmes and the priority areas of interventions. These imply the putting of a major part of the resources of the SCFs at the service of the Lisbon Strategy in general and of innovation policy in particular. Under the new rules the main goal is convergence, which implies support to projects that are instrumental in the catching up of the least favoured areas to the EU average. Most expenditure (more than three-quarters) is concentrated on this goal. The second objective is competitiveness of the whole EU. All non-'convergence' areas in the EU can apply for SCF support for projects that stimulate their competitiveness.

The six main sectors of expenditure are: productive; structure; infrastructure; environment; R&D; and human resources. These cover to a large extent the various primary objectives and subsidiary goals of the Lisbon Strategy. Examples are support of the European Social Fund for retraining of workers to make them better adapted to the knowledge society. In the past a major part of the SCF resources was devoted to infrastructure. As in the major beneficiary countries (notably the new member states) there is still a great need for improvement of infrastructure, this category is still important. Consequently a relatively modest part of the total resources of the SCF directed to these countries is directly relevant to innovation and knowledge.

For the present programming period the resources earmarked for priority action 1, 'Investing more in Knowledge and Innovation', amount to some €83 billion (out of total resources for cohesion of about €350 billion). Some half of this amount is devoted to innovative capacity in business; the other half is shared by support to the diffusion and use of ICT by business and citizens, and the development of skills. These figures represent a very considerable increase on the previous planning period: a doubling for the convergence objective and a tripling for the competitiveness objective.

Regulation: Coordination with National and Regional Policies

The second important instrument of cohesion policy is regulation and coordination. In the past much of the cohesion policy has been carried out through fairly light forms of coordination. However, the EU has gradually had recourse to ever-stricter forms of regulation. We give here some practical examples.

In order to preserve the effectiveness of financial support to projects in convergence regions, the EU has set limits to national state aids. Indeed, the financial capacity of the strong regions is so large that they could easily outbid any offer in the convergence regions. Moreover, the EU sets standards, for instance for the maintenance of the environmental quality. This may put an extra burden on convergence regions for which extra support may be granted.

The EU also coordinates the regional policies of the member states. It has set up very detailed regulations that govern the following three aspects.

1. *Choice of priorities* National choices are systematically aligned with EU objectives in matters of cohesion. The scope of the cohesion policy means that it often also takes on board the coordination of other policy fields, e.g. the improvement of the environment, of the social fabric etc.
2. *Multi-annual programming* This approach brings predictability in the availability of resources and stability as to their destination.
3. *Establishment of partnership* The involvement of different layers of multi-level government and third (private) parties brings commitment of all parties involved to the efforts needed to reach common goals.

Consistency with Innovation

With the reform of the Structural Funds in 1988, innovation became one of the main areas of activity of the EU cohesion policy.[30] In the period up to 1999 the share of these activities in total SCFs was about 4 per cent, so very limited. However, when added to the FPs the sums are significant for many of the beneficiary countries. In the previous and present frameworks the share of the innovation projects in total funding has increased gradually. In the 2000–06 period the SCFs made a significant contribution to achieving the Lisbon objectives (DTI, 2005). Notably programmes with a strong focus on regional competitiveness and innovation were strongly aligned with the Lisbon Strategy; much less so were programmes focusing on physical infrastructure.

Based on the 2005 Growth and Jobs Agenda, the member states have been encouraged to concentrate their efforts under the cohesion policy on Lisbon Strategy priorities. The Community Strategic Guidelines prepared by the Commission as a guiding document for the new programming period 2007–13 fully recognised the importance of the Lisbon Agenda and set high ambitions concerning the contribution that the Structural Funds are expected to play – especially so in the context of the Objective 2 Regional Competitiveness programmes. The earmarking of Structural Funds actions – formally introduced in the Implementation Guidelines issued in 2006 – is a potentially powerful instrument to check conformity with the Lisbon goals. On the basis of a preliminary analysis of the national programmes, one sees that some 65 per cent (Objective 1 convergence) to 80 per cent (Objective 2 competitiveness) of the Structural Funds interventions are now expected to directly contribute to the Lisbon targets. Innovation expenditure has been much enhanced; it will triple in the period 2007–13 compared to the previous period. This increase is even more pronounced in the new member states (EC, 2007d).

HOW MUCH CONSISTENCY?

General

Each of the two main policy domains under scrutiny here has its own rationale, set of objectives, toolbox of instruments and way of governance. These specificities are often strongly entrenched and are defended by communities of directly interested parties, lobbyists etc. The pursuit of such independent policies may lead to conflicts (e.g. between infrastructural development and the environment). The persistence of such conflicts will lead to a loss of effectiveness and efficiency, and thus a waste of resources.

Such conflicts are in general solved by coordination. Part of the coordination problem is horizontal. The EU has recognised that its policies are often conflicting (see the example given above). The EU has set itself the task of realising a strong alignment of its different policies. This has even been cast as a constitutional obligation.[31]

In the early years of the EU the coordination problem was fairly simple. Over time it has gradually become more complicated as a consequence of several factors. First, the number of competencies has greatly increased. Second, the targets have become more detailed. Third, the instruments have become stricter (as far as regulation is concerned and as far as financial support is concerned; see Molle, 2006).

In step with this, the coordination of the EU has increased, mostly through meetings between representatives of different Directorates General. These face two challenges:

1. Optimise the horizontal system of coordination on the EU level (i.e. between different European policy areas).[32]
2. Match the vertical systems of coordination that coexist for innovation and cohesion (and that comprise on the national and regional level horizontal coordination tasks).

Greater coordination is supposed to bring higher effectiveness as resources are put to work in a synergetic manner. In clear terms, it avoids unnecessary efforts and hence the waste of resources. However, it comes at a cost: more coordination brings with it higher transactions costs and thus a potential loss of efficiency. It can even entail a loss of effectiveness in case coordination leads to the choice of suboptimal priorities and/or political and administrative stalemates.

So one needs to see in practice to what extent the benefits outweigh the cost. To that end we analyse three stages of the policy cycle: the setting of objectives; the implementation; and the evaluation of results.

Objectives

On the level of the objectives it is often assumed that there is little need for coordination. Indeed, 'there is often the temptation to argue, especially in official documents, that different policy objectives are not in conflict with each other, that a more equitable distribution of income is beneficial to long-run efficiency, and that boosting the efficiency of production is the best protection for the economically vulnerable' (Hall et al., 2001, p. 356).

The quotation seems to apply very accurately to our problem at hand. The efforts made in the framework of EU innovation policy are meant to boost competitiveness of the EU in the key sectors for the knowledge society. The activities carried out in the framework of EU cohesion policy, although principally geared to equity, take the increase in the competitiveness of the catching-up ('convergence') regions as their main point of attack. Moreover, the support that can be given to the non-'convergence' regions is all geared to measures to increase competitiveness.

So, on the level of objectives, consistency does indeed exist. On one hand, the importance of the regional (cohesion) objective has taken centre stage in the implementation of the Lisbon Strategy (including innovation policy). On the other hand, the innovation objective has moved to centre stage in cohesion policy since the recent reform of the SCFs.

Implementation

Even if there is no conflict at the level of broad objectives, there may be conflicts in the stage of implementation. An example of this is the overlap that occurs because EU innovation policy has started to finance programmes with a cohesion objective while EU cohesion policy is effectively the largest source of finance for innovation projects.

More problems occur because innovation and cohesion follow different trajectories in the EU policy cycle and are implemented with different systems of governance.

Innovation

The EU sets goals and specifies them. It has two main instruments:

1. *EU programmes*   For these a typical European network of large firms, top R&D organisations, experts and representatives of national administrations influence the setting of priority fields, the monitoring of implementation and the evaluation of results.
2. *National programmes*   In this case the EU contributes to the financing and relies for the rest on soft coordination measures, such as the checking of progress by monitoring systems, the exchange of information and suggestions for improvements. The EU leaves it to the member states to involve partners. In the Lisbon process this operates through national reform programmes (NRPs). This means that in each country different constituencies have evolved of interested firms, R&D organisations, intermediary bodies and the relevant representatives of the most important ministry. The EU innovation policy recognises that much of the effort should go beyond the improvement of the national

innovation systems into the regional innovation systems. However, it leaves it almost entirely to the member states to further involve regions into the process. The absence of hierarchical powers and the limited financial incentives mean that the achievement of common goals is subject to much uncertainty.

Cohesion

Right from the start of the cohesion policies, the national dimension has been thought of as too broad to serve as a basis for the identification of problems and potentials, and the formulation of remedies and development strategies. On the regional level, however, the flexibility and variety needed can be provided. Since its inception the regional dimension of cohesion policy has never been seriously challenged. The SCF recognise the diversity of the growth potentials of the different regions and the ensuing need for differences in prioritisation of actions. In the course of time the introduction of new principles has improved the governance methods.

- The application of the principle of programming ensures that national and EU frameworks and guidelines give coherence to concrete actions. This is embodied in the national strategic reference frameworks that each member state has to establish.
- Moreover, the additionality principle provides that the strong financial incentive of subsidies from the SCF joins finances from the project initiators, which leads to compliance with common goals.
- The principle of partnership means that there is a strong emphasis on the involvement of the various actors in the multi-level system; the filling in of their roles is largely predefined by detailed regulations.

Thus one sees that in the multi-layer EU governance system both the script of the play and the distribution of roles have developed largely independently for innovation and cohesion. Each policy area follows certain principles (e.g. subsidiarity, partnership and programming) but the way in which they are applied differs for innovation and cohesion. This brings with it the danger of a lack of consistency.

Evaluation of Coordination

According to many observers, the EU has had difficulty in coming to grips with the complicated problems that occur while trying to coordinate, both horizontally and vertically, a set of different policies. This need not come as a surprise when one sees the practical difficulties that already occur if coordination is done only horizontally (that is on the EU level between different DGs or on the national level between different ministries). Similar difficulties occur vertically when different administrative levels have to agree to a consistent design and delivery of policies.

As far as the two policy areas we deal with here are concerned, there are indeed potential conflicts between the largely top-down approach of the innovation policy (RTD → innovation → region) and the largely bottom-up approach of cohesion (region → innovation → RTD).

In the recent reform of the SF and the Lisbon Strategy, reinforced coordination mechanisms have been introduced that have taken away at the strategic level many of the dangers of inconsistencies. Indeed, in all member states close links have been established at the process level between on one hand the national reform programmes (Lisbon) and on the other hand the national strategic reference frameworks (cohesion). All member states have started to organise cooperation between those responsible for both policies, and many have adapted their administrative structures to improve consistency. This is not a one-off exercise: all member states have to report regularly to the EU on the way they coordinate the two policies in practice. This should eliminate much of the inconsistency danger. However, the new model has only just been introduced and it is too early to judge its effectiveness.

CONCLUSIONS AND RECOMMENDATIONS

Past Results and Future Challenges

The previous sections have made it clear that over the years the EU has set up very elaborate systems of vertical coordination for its different policies and has constantly adapted them to new needs. One of these new needs is to coordinate better, on the horizontal level, its cohesion and innovation policies. The decision that has been taken is to adapt the basic system of cohesion policy design and delivery to suit the needs of innovation as well. Although in theory this integrated set-up looks quite distorted, in practice it may prove to be workable. We must wait for an evaluation of the implementation before drawing firm conclusions.

Now, whatever the adequacy of the coordination mechanisms at present, the future may pose challenges that require further adaptation of the coordination systems. We now explore what these challenges are.

The major challenge in matters of cohesion is to realise the convergence of the wealth levels of the new member states. The basic set-up is adequate for this task. There does not seem to be a need for more extended horizontal coordination. Indeed, the policies in which the EU is likely to have a stronger involvement (such as energy, environment etc.) seem to fit into the (extended) present set-up. So there will be a need for the optimisation of the present set-up rather than a major overhaul of the system (Molle, 2007).

For innovation the challenge is to make sure that the combined systems on the European, national and regional levels work together in a consistent way to provide the necessary stimuli for innovation and for the commercial use of innovation. These are prerequisites for success on the innovation part of the Lisbon Agenda that will keep its relevance for decades to come.

Consequently the recommendations may be set in terms of further improvement of parts of the system instead of a complete overhaul of the EU policy system. There are two broad types of recommendation.

Minimise the Need for Coordination

The role of coordination can be minimised by making clear rules about how certain areas should be treated.

The first approach concerns horizontal coordination. Here one can reduce the need for coordination through the prioritisation of objectives. In the EU this can be illustrated by two cases: monetary policy and internal market policy. These policies are pursued on their own merits and have priority over others. If they have a negative effect on cohesion, the efforts of the cohesion policy have to be stepped up. In certain segments this also applies to innovation: those R&D projects that, after applying the subsidiarity principle come clearly under the EU competencies, must be carried out on their own merits, and any negative consequences for cohesion policy must then be addressed by cohesion policy. A good example here are the investments made in specialised R&D centres that tend to search for central locations. It needs to be questioned whether in those cases R&D policy should make up for such consequences by setting up a programme for regional innovativeness. The setting up of a parallel system (to the one of cohesion) only adds to the coordination problem instead of diminishing it.

The second approach concerns vertical coordination. Here the need for coordination can be limited by the explicit splitting of objectives and implementation. Once it has been made clear that on the level of strategic objectives there is no conflict, one can decide that the elaboration in concrete actions and the delivery of the policy can be left to decentralised actors who can adapt the generalities to local circumstances and needs. The independent operations may from time to time create some overlap and competition, but the costs of this are likely to be smaller than those of detailed coordination, which may lead to long procedures and low

effectiveness. This may apply to such policies as the enhancement of entrepreneurship, SME development and the strengthening of the absorptive
capacity of both the private and the public sectors.

Optimise the Use of Coordination

Where approaches to limit the need for coordination have been exhausted,
a strong need can remain for a combined horizontal and vertical coordination system. Then it is important to make sure that the system works as
smoothly as possible. One way to realise this is by keeping the number of
actors within reasonable limits. At first sight the main actors are the same
in both innovation and cohesion policies. However, on closer inspection
one sees that the representatives at the three levels of the hierarchy are
different.

Coordination between the EU and national governments is needed to
come to a consistent approach that brings results. However, on many
scores this does not seem to be sufficient. It is not only at the national level,
but also at the level of the region, that many of the factors of competitiveness and innovation can be identified and effective tools for sustainable,
endogenous development applied.

As the problems and their solutions have essentially a regional dimension, it becomes apparent that the relevant policies of the Lisbon Strategy
also need to have a stronger regional dimension next to the national and
the European dimensions. This leads to an extension of the multi-level
governance approach, which integrates the three levels. This system then
rejoins the cohesion approach.

Now regions differ widely in their competencies (as a function of the
extent of decentralisation or devolution of political and administrative
powers from the national to the regional level). Various models exist in
that respect throughout the EU. Some national governments have involved
their regions in the developing of their NRPs.

For the Lisbon Strategy in general and innovation in particular to be
delivered successfully at the regional level, the heterogeneous nature of
regions must be recognised. This flexible approach is not only dependent
on having differentiated regional strategies and programmes, but also on
having the appropriate regional administrative and governance systems
that can interact with the appropriate institutions and policies at the
national and European levels. It is here that most of the effort for consistency needs to be made and where the different administrative and political
agendas and governance methods need to be aligned. A number of regions
have indeed already been empowered in matters of innovation. In Italy
and Spain, for instance, universities and R&D have become a competence

of the regions. In France and the Netherlands the central government has recognised that it cannot deliver its policy from the centre and has decided to do this through regional poles.

NOTES

1. The author is indebted to several persons who contributed to this chapter. Thanks go to both Rene Wintjes of Merit and Ronald Hall of the European Commission for their useful suggestions for complementing the draft text. Thanks also to Roderick van 't Hoff for assistance in the search for literature and data.
2. For a historical view (the period 1963–83) of the situation and the policy response, see Patel and Pavitt (1987).
3. This description is based on the presidency conclusions of the European Council, March 2000. These objectives and priorities have been adapted and refined since. However, the main architecture is still valid.
4. See for evidence of the importance of this relation the study by the OECD (2001) into the long-term determinants of growth and competitiveness. See also, for further evidence, Bloom et al. (2002) and Furman et al. (2002).
5. Innovation policy as used here comprises the initiatives of public authorities in matters of scientific research, technological development, education and modernisation of industry and services.
6. See, e.g., EC (2003a). Note that the order does not indicate any priority. Independent advisers have added to the discussion and the refinement of targets; e.g. Aho et al. (2006).
7. The comprehensive set is available from Eurostat's website: http://europa.eu.int/comm/ eurostat/Public/datashop/print-product/EN?catalogue=Eurostat&product=struct-EN &mode=download. See also EC (2005c).
8. The link between cohesion and innovation has a long history. After the two oil crises of the 1970s it became increasingly clear that a new paradigm for development was needed. The role of technology and innovation in development emerged as such and in the 1980s national policies became based on it. The same new ideas were also applied to the problem of regional development. In the framework of the FAST (Forecasting and Assessment of Science and Technology) programme of the EC we carried out the PRESTO project (Prospects of Regional Employment and Scanning of Technology Options). A number of publications ensued from that project, e.g. Molle (1983, 1984, 1985). The aspect of innovation has since been part and parcel of regional policies.
9. In the preparation process of this major change a number of documents have been written by both advisers and the European Commission that are worth mentioning: EC (2007a, 2007b, 2007c); Eurab (2007), EP (2006); all available from http://ec.europa.eu// research/index.cfm?pg=newsalert&lg=en&year=2007&na-100907.
10. Other policies form part of this coordination process: first the competitiveness and innovation policy targeting notably the corporate sector of the EU; second the rural development policy. We have no room here to deal with these policies in detail.
11. This does not imply atomisation of the efforts of all segments of RTD policy; some elements, notably research, need strong centres of excellence that have specific location requirements.
12. See Hollanders and Rundel (2004); see also http://trendchart.cordis.lu/scoreboards/ scoreboard2003/pdf/eis_2003_tp1_indicators_definitions.pdf.
13. These results are confirmed by the results of an analysis based on a pan-EU household survey into the determinants of the adoption of two information and communication technologies (ICT) items: the Internet and computers. Positive influences came from level of income, access to university education and link to R&D activities. Unemployment had a negative influence (Vicente and Lopez, 2006).

14. For example, assume that the lowest and observed values for business R&D are 0.5 per cent and 2.5 per cent, and that country x has a score of 1.5 per cent. The rescaled score for country x is 50, which is equal to its position halfway between the lowest and highest observed values. Each rescaled score for an individual indicator is then multiplied by the weight assigned to that indicator to come to the Summary Innovation Index.

15. East is composed of the eight NMS of Central and Eastern Europe. South West are the Mediterranean countries (Portugal, Spain, Italy, Greece, Malta, Cyprus); North West are the remaining member countries.

16. These approaches to the problem have been labelled the Triple Helix Model (Etzkowitz and Leydesdorff, 1997). Now, some ten years later, the Nordic countries are set to step up their efforts in this field (see several government documents) to face the challenges of global competition.

17. This pattern is the result of a very intricate process of change and restructuring following the change-over of these countries from a command to a market economy (see, e.g., Radovic and Auriol, 1999).

18. This picture has also been found by studies for one specific indicator; for instance Paci and Usai 2000) showed that patent production is concentrated in the regions that have the highest scores on centrality.

19. These figures are corroborated by the analysis for Spain. Here the regional distribution of innovation activity, measured by the generation of patent applications, was particularly concentrated on the traditionally more dynamic regions (Guerrero and Seró, 1997). The public funding for supporting innovation was also concentrated in such regions. The authors concluded: 'The search for efficiency through technological policy brings about a vicious circle which goes against technological convergence.'

20. See various issues of the science and technology series of Eurostat, e.g. on S&T labour force, patents etc.

21. In some recent benchmarking activities the region of Prague emerges with a fairly high position (see, e.g., the Lisbon monitoring platform of the Committee of Regions (http://lisbon.cor.europa.eu/) or Strategic Evaluation on innovation and the knowledge-based economy in relation to the structural and cohesion funds for the programming period 2007–13 (http://ec.europa.eu/regional_policy/sources/docgener/evaluation/pdf/strategic_innov.pdf).

22. A similar analysis grouped the regions by crossing their economic performance and their innovation profiles (Scil, 2005). The following types emerged:

    ● The low performers were in general characterised by a low profile in innovation. The same relation existed for many high performers, as they were generally characterised by high profiles.
    ● However, a number of high performers recorded low or medium profiles in innovation. This mismatch is seen as an early warning for a change in the future (e.g. in case the path-dependent nature of development is reversed by external shocks). This concerned regions in countries such as Italy, France and the UK.

23. For a good description of the EU innovation policy see Nauwelaers and Wintjes (2008).

24. See in this respect the survey of the empirical literature made by Griffith (2000).

25. Notwithstanding the significant amounts in terms of total outlays, EU spending on R&D is only a small (less than 10 per cent) percentage of R&D funding by member governments.

26. See in this respect Chapter 2 of the present book.

27. In the past some of the EU innovation policies mostly benefited the strong regions, so this worked out negatively for cohesion, as they did not contribute to the balanced growth of all regions of the EU. At present most of the EU policies (including those for innovation) tend to be devised in such a way that the impact on the cohesion is either neutral or even positive (see Molle, 2007, ch. 11). One needs to keep in mind that even the fairly small amounts that go to the new member states under the FP represent a

considerable increase in their budget and have a relatively large influence on their policies. Anyway, one can question the justification of this approach as other, more contextually embedded, research priorities could have led to more impact on the innovation performance of the new member states.

28. This impact is attenuated by the spending on innovation that comes from other sources such as the Structural Funds and national funds.
29. This section is based on Molle (2007).
30. In 1993, for instance, an initiative called Regional Technology Plans was introduced (Landabaso et al., 1997).
31. By stating and developing Community policies and developing the internal market (cohesion) objectives shall be considered (art. 159).
32. The horizontal coordination problem on the EU level extends beyond the pair innovation and cohesion. Major problems exist regarding the interfaces with competition (what support to firms on either the title of innovation or convergence would distort fair competition on the common market?). The same is true for environment: what regulation will stimulate innovation that leads to both less-polluting products and to production processes that prefer locations in cohesion regions? Other important interfaces also exist for each of the two policy areas that are the focus of this chapter. For instance, innovation policy interferes with sectoral policies: notably for the larger R&D programmes. Another example is external policy: what firms and institutions are eligible for EU support? Is this coherent with the rules of international organisations on, e.g., intellectual property and fair trade?

REFERENCES

Aho, E. et al. (2006), 'Creating an innovative Europe', report of an independent expert group on R&D and innovation appointed following the Hampton Court Summit, EC, Brussels.

Bloom, N., R. Griffith and J. Van Reenen (2002), 'Do R&D tax credits work? Evidence for a panel of countries, 1979–1997', *Journal of Public Economics*, **85**, 1–31.

Caloghirou, Y., N.S. Vonortas and S. Ioannides (eds) (2004), *European Collaboration in Research and Development; Business Strategy and Public Policy*, Cheltenham, UK and Northampton, MA, USA: Edward Elgar.

CE/ECORYS et al. (2003), *Factors of Regional Competitiveness*, study commissioned by DG Regio.

Clarysse, B. and U. Muldur (2001), 'Regional cohesion in Europe: an analysis of how EU public RTD support influences the techno economic regional landscape', *Research Policy*, **30**, 275–96.

Cooke, P., P. Boekholt and F. Toedling (eds) (2000), *The Governance of Innovation in Europe: Regional Perspectives on Global Competitiveness*, London and New York: Pinter.

Cuervo-Cazurra, A. and C.A. Un (2007), 'Regional economic integration and R&D investment', *Research Policy*, **36** (2), 227–46.

DTI (2005), *Thematic Evaluation of the Structural Funds' Contributions to the Lisbon Strategy: Synthesis Report*, Danish Technological Institute, Copenhagen.

Dunnewijk, T., H. Hollanders and R. Wintjes (2008), 'Benchmarking regions in the enlarged Europe: diversity in knowledge potential, and policy options', in C. Nauwelaers and R. Wintjes (eds), *Innovation Policy in Europe: Measurement and Strategy*, Cheltenham, UK and Northampton, MA, USA: Edward Elgar, pp. 53–95.

EC (2000), *Communication from the Commission: Structural Indicators*, COM2002 551 final.

EC (2003a), *Innovation Policy: Updating the Unions' Approach in the Context of the Lisbon Strategy*, COM 2003, 112 final.

EC (2003b) (DG Regio), *Structural Policies and European Territories: Competitiveness, Sustainable Development and Cohesion in Europe – From Lisbon to Gothenburg*, Brussels.

EC (2004) *A New Partnership for Cohesion: Convergence; Competitiveness; Cooperation – Third Report on Economic and Social Cohesion*, Brussels.

EC (2005a), *Implementing the Community Lisbon Programme: More Research and Innovation-investing for Growth and Employment: A Common Approach*, Brussels.

EC (2005b), *Report to the European Council on European Technology Platforms and Joint Technology initiatives: Fostering Public Private Partnerships to Boost Europe's Industrial Competitiveness*, SEC (2005) 800, Brussels.

EC (2005c), *Communication on State Aid for Innovation*, COM 2005/436, Brussels.

EC (2007a), *Competitive European Regions through Research and Innovation: a Contribution to More Growth and More and Better Jobs*, Com (2007) 474 final, Brussels.

EC (2007b), RTD, *Innovation, Cohesion and Rural Development Policies: Reinforced Synergies* (accompanying document to EC, 2007a), SEC 2007 1045, Brussels.

EC (2007c), CREST, *Guidelines on Coordinating the Framework Programme and the Structural Funds to support Research and Development*, Cordis Library, Brussels.

EC (2007d), *Cohesion Policy Set to Give Major Boost to Lisbon Strategy for 2007–2013*, IP/07/1904, available from EU website.

ECOTEC (2004), *Territorial Impact of EU Research and Development Policy*, ESPON Project 2.1.2, Luxembourg (available from the ESPON website: http://www.espon.eu/mmp/online/website/contents/projects/243/266/index_EN.html.

ECORYS (2004), *The Regional Dimension*, Rotterdam.

Edler, J., S. Kuhlmann and M. Behrens (2003), *Changing governance of Research and Technology Policy: The European Research Area*, Cheltenham, UK and Northampton, MA, USA: Edward Elgar.

EP (2006), *Synergies between the EU 7th Research Framework Programme, the Competitiveness and Innovation Framework Programme and the Structural Funds*, European Parliament document IP/A/ITRE/FWC/2006-87/LOT3/C1.

Etzkowitz, H. and L. Leydesdorff (1997), *Universities in the Global knowledge Economy*, London: Pinter.

Eurab (2007), *Energizing Europe's Knowledge Triangle of Research, Education and Innovation through the Structural Funds*, European Research Advisory Board, final report 07.010, Brussels.

Eurostat (2007) 'Community Innovation Statistics'; CIS 4/EIS2006, Statistics in focus, 116/2007, Luxemburg.

FAST (1992), 'Archpelago Europe: islands of innovation', *Prospective dossier no. 1 of Science, Technology and Social Economic Cohesion in the Community*, EC, Brussels.

Furman, J., M.E. Porter and S. Stern (2002), 'The determinants of national innovative capacity', *Research Policy*, **31**, 899–933.

Griffith, R. (2000), 'How important is business R&D for economic growth and should the government subsidise it?', Briefing Note no. 12, The Institute for Fiscal Studies, London.

Guerrero, D.C. and M.A. Seró (1997), 'Spatial distribution of patents in Spain: determining factors and consequences on regional development', *Regional Studies*, **31** (4), 381–90.

Hall, R., A. Smith and L. Tsoukalis (eds) (2001), *Competitiveness and Cohesion in EU policies*, Oxford: Oxford University Press.

Hollanders, H. and A. Rundel (2004), *European Innovation Scoreboard, Methodology Report*, EC DG Enterprise, Brussels.

Landabaso, M. et al. (1997), 'The promotion of innovation in regional policy', *Entrepreneurship and Regional Development*, **9**, 1–24.

Molle, W. (1983), 'Technological change and regional development in Europe (Theory, Empiric, Policy)', *Papers and Proceedings of the Regional Science Association*, pp. 23–38.

Molle, W. (1984), 'Regional innovation potentials in the European Community', in R. Camagni, R. Cappellin and G. Garofoli (eds), *Cambiamento Tecnologico e Diffusione Territoriale*, Milan: Franco Angeli, pp. 109–30.

Molle, W. (ed.) (1985) *Innovatie en Regio*, 's-Gravenhage: Staatsuitgeverij.

Molle, W. (2006), *Economics of European Integration: Theory, Practice, Policy*, 5th edn, Aldershot: Ashgate.

Molle, W. (2007), *European Cohesion Policy*, London: Routledge.

Muller, E., A. Jappe, J.-A. Heraud and A. Zanker (2006), 'A regional typology of innovation capacities in the New Member States and the Accession countries', *Working papers, Firms and Regions*, no. R1/2006, FISIR, Karlsruhe.

Mytelka, L.K. and K. Smith (2002), 'Policy learning and innovation theory: an interactive and co-evolving process', *Research Policy*, **31**, 1467–79.

Nauwelaers, C. and R. Wintjes (eds) (2008), *Innovation Policy in Europe: Measurement and Strategy*, Cheltenham, UK and Northampton, MA, USA: Edward Elgar.

OECD (2001), *The New Economy: Beyond the Hype*, Paris: OECD.

Paci, R. and S. Usai (2000), 'Technological enclaves and industrial districts: an analysis of the regional distribution of innovative activity in Europe', *Regional Studies*, **34** (2), 97–114.

Parkinson, M. et al. (2004), *Competitive European Cities: Where Do the Core Cities Stand?*, Report to ODPM, John Moores University, Liverpool (also Office of Deputy Prime Minister London).

Patel, P. and K. Pavitt (1987), 'Is Europe losing the technological race?', *Research Policy*, **16** (2–4), 59–85.

Peterson, J. and M. Sharp (1998), *Technology Policy in the European Union*, Basingstoke: Macmillan.

Radosevic, S. (2004), 'A two tier or multi tier Europe? Assessing the innovation capacities of Central and East European countries in the enlarged EU', *Journal of Common Market Studies*, **42** (2), 641–66.

Radovic, S. and L. Auriol (1999), 'Patterns of restructuring in research, development and innovation activities in central and eastern European countries an analysis based on S&T indicators', *Research Policy*, **28**, 351–76.

Rodriguez-Pose, A. and R. Crescenzi (2008) 'Research and development, spillovers, innovation systems, and the genesis of regional growth in Europe', *Regional Studies*, **42** (1), 51–67.

Scil (2005), *Policy Guidelines for Regions Falling under the New Regional Competitiveness and Employment Objective for the 2007–2013 Period in the Fields of the Knowledge Economy and the Environment, in Line with the Lisbon and Gothenburg Objectives*, Brussels.

Sharp, M. and Pereira, T.S. (2001), 'Research and technological development', in R. Hall, A. Smith and L. Tsoukalis (eds) (2001), *Competitiveness and Cohesion in EU Policies*, Oxford: Oxford University Press, pp. 147–78.

Vicente, M.R. and Lopez, A.J. (2006), Patterns of ICT diffusion across the European Union, *Economic Letters*, **93**, 45–51.

8. National governance systems for innovation: high-level coordination leads to increased effectiveness

Julia Djarova and Walter Zegveld

INTRODUCTION

The issue of national innovation policy has clearly attracted the attention of policy makers of all EU member states in view of the realisation of the Lisbon Agenda (see Chapter 7). The discussion on governance of innovation has intensified in recent years due to the increased complexity of the innovation policy. This complexity stems primarily from the multi-player structure of the national innovation system (NIS). Increasingly the national innovation policy is concerned with addressing not only the elements of the NIS but also the relationships between them.

This chapter describes our understanding of a governance system for innovation that is placed against other views expressed in the literature. This understanding follows very much the policy cycle and claims that an effective governance system is not only the organisational form that national or sub-national levels adopt to manage innovation. It is very much the way the innovation policy mix is built, implemented and evaluated, elements that need equal attention by policy makers.

The structure of this chapter is as follows. We discuss the interdependence between governance of innovation and innovation policy mix after providing a short review of the basic concepts from the existing literature. Subsequently, the driving forces towards coordination of innovation policy are presented and different forms of coordination mechanisms outlined. Special attention is given to understanding the need for a national high-level coordination body as well as the hindrances countries face in implementing such an organisation in practice. Finally the chapter offers an approach towards an innovation policy mix that, together with an appropriate organisational form for governing the innovation policy, would be more effective.

As Chapter 7 has indicated, innovation and innovation policy have a strong international dimension. This chapter will indicate that such

international governance systems will only be successful if and when they
are based on sound and effective national governance systems.

STATEMENT OF THE PROBLEM

Governance of Innovation

The benefits currently associated with innovation in industry are such
that governments in most countries feel they cannot do without explicit
national innovation policies. Innovation policies are becoming a point of
convergence between industrial policy and science, and technology policy,
containing elements of both, but at the same time opening up new perspectives and avenues of policy. Given the importance of industrial innovation
for competitiveness and other policy objectives in a country, the question is
whether the present system of public governance concerning science, technology and innovation will be adequate for the advancement of innovation,
and whether the increasing costs and the necessary coordination between
public policy areas are best served by the present institutional set-up.

In 2000, the European Commission issued a Communication on
'Innovation in a knowledge driven economy' (EC, 2000). This document
defined five objectives to strengthen the capacity of member states to overcome obstacles to a more innovation-enhancing environment. Under each
objective, member states were tasked with a specific list of actions.

Objective 1: Coherence of innovation policies

- National and regional innovation policies should take account of
  'best practices' and adapt them to their specific environments;
- Ensure that co-ordination mechanisms are in place between national
  and regional levels, and between different departments responsible
  for matters relevant to innovation, so as to guarantee a coherent
  approach to innovation policy;
- Implement periodic target-setting, monitoring, evaluation and
  peer review of regional and national programmes for enhancing
  innovation and of the bodies that implement them.

Objective 2: A regulatory framework conducive to innovation

- Adapt the rules for the diffusion of research results from publicly funded
  research (licensing, access to foreground knowledge, etc.) to encourage
  exploitation and transfer of results so as to foster innovation;

- Put in place fiscal measures, in accordance with Articles 87 and 88 of the Treaty, to encourage private investment in research and innovation and employment of researchers by the private sector.

Objective 3: Encourage the creation and growth of innovative enterprises

- Pursue efforts to create a legal, fiscal and financial environment favourable to the creation and development of start-ups;
- Foster, at regional level, the creation or reinforcement of adequate support services and structures such as incubators, etc.;
- Set up education and training schemes in entrepreneurship and innovation management, where these do not exist, in higher-education establishments and business schools, and disseminate good practice in this area.

Objective 4: Improving key interfaces in the innovation system

- Stimulate and co-ordinate regional initiatives and regional actors to devise and implement integrated research and innovation programmes at regional level;
- Facilitate the implementation of lifelong learning programmes to improve the general assimilation of new technologies and remedy shortages of skills;
- Encourage universities to give particular attention, in addition to the traditional missions of education and research, to promotion of the diffusion of knowledge and technologies;
- Encourage large public research facilities to benchmark their activities in technology transfer and partnerships with enterprises.

Objective 5: A society open to innovation

- Encourage comprehensive 'stakeholder' debates on innovation involving scientists, industry, consumers and public authorities;
- Stimulate public demand for innovation by dynamic purchasing policies in public administrations.

Traditionally, different ministries cover these five objectives. Innovation policy, however, ought to be considered as a 'horizontal policy', requiring coordination of the policies of the various government departments involved. The need for an explicit and horizontal national innovation policy is recognised by many governments. It is underlined by the *European Innovation Progress Report*, which points out that the involvement and real commitment of stakeholders at regional and national level to cooperate and learn from each other is important to improve innovation policies and competitiveness (EC, 2006).

A major problem is that the relevant policy fields (e.g. science, industry, education and regional development) are traditionally covered by different ministries and departments that have separate responsibilities, objectives and support infrastructures. This fragmented institutional set-up is not adequate to address the major problems of the national innovation system (NIS). Interfunctional problems call for interfunctional solutions.

This leads us to the subject of governance of innovation, an issue many national and international initiatives (e.g. EC and OECD) have put on the top of their policy agendas. Let us examine the meaning of 'governance of innovation'. The European Commission's definition of governance can be applied to science, technology and innovation (STI).

Governance means rules, processes and behaviour that affect the way in which powers are exercised, particularly with regard to openness, participation, accountability, effectiveness and coherence (EC, 2001b).

There are many definitions of governance of innovation in the literature. Boekholt (2004, p. 5) claims: 'Governance of innovation tells something about what roles the various actors in the innovation system play, how the rules of the game work, how decisions are taken and how changes in the overall innovation system come into being.'

One of the OECD–TIP MONIT (OECD, 2005b) reports defines governance of innovation as a normative, multi-actor and multi-level perspective on the management of the innovation system that accommodates the dynamics of innovation.

In all definitions, the central issue is the cooperation between the different players of the NIS that leads to coherent innovation policy.

Innovation Policy Mix

In general, a policy mix is referred to as a set of policy measures. The OECD MONIT (STEP, 2003a) project understands the policy mix as 'a set of established priority areas and actual policy efforts within the field of innovation policies'. The project of EC DG Research, 'Monitoring and analysis of policies and public financing instruments conducive to higher levels of R&D investments', defines policy mix for R&D as a combination of policy instruments, which interact to influence the quantity and quality of R&D investments in public and private sectors (Wintjes, 2007).

Many experts in the field share the recognition that 'the range of issues addressed by innovation policy requires a portfolio of policy instruments' (Roper, 2004). However, the interpretation of the elements of this range varies. Below we discuss some of the most popular interpretations.

Innovation Budget Allocation

R&D and innovation financing measures employed by the member states of the European Union can be divided into three main categories: direct financing support to firms; indirect financial support to firms; and support to enablers.

When looking at the trends in R&D and innovation finance support between 1991 and 2001, developments demonstrate a decline in the use of direct financing measures from approximately 60 per cent to roughly 50 per cent of the total R&D and innovation finance measures. Over the same period, the support of enablers has increased from under 20 per cent to more than 30 per cent. The use of measures within the indirect financial support category has remained relatively stagnant at roughly 20 per cent over the ten-year period (EC, 2001a).

Some see the policy mix expressed in the proportion of a country's budget allocated to different types of support instruments. To give a few examples: the UK balances almost equally the fiscal incentives for innovation, subsidy measures and integrated packages of support. Finland allocates more resources to subsidies and loans, while a large proportion of the innovation support budget in the Netherlands goes to fiscal, mainly tax incentives (Roper, 2004).

Innovation Trend Chart Classification[1]

The EU database of the Trend Chart classifies innovation policy measures in Europe into three main categories:

1. *Fostering an innovation culture* covers measures stimulating creativity, initiative, risk taking and development of skills and organisational capabilities. Policy measures under this category are further subdivided into education and training, mobility of students and research workers, stimulation of public awareness, enterprises' management of change, informing and raising the awareness of public authorities, and measures facilitating cluster and network development.
2. *Establishing a framework conducive to innovation* involves measures permitting innovation to flourish and grow. Policy measures are categorised by stimulating competition, protection of intellectual and industrial property, administrative simplification, legal and regulatory framework on innovation performance, provision of financing of innovation and taxation.
3. *Gearing research to innovation* includes measures to improve the way in which the results of research are transformed into products, processes

and services and, hence, contribute to competitive advantage and societal goods. Policy measures are further categorised by developing the long-term strategic vision of R&D, strengthening the performance of research within industry, encouraging start-up technology-based companies, intensified cooperation between research institutions, universities and companies, plus improving the ability of SMEs to absorb technologies and know-how.

GoodNIP Classification

In the GoodNIP data sheets (STEP, 2003a, 2003b, 2003c) on innovation policy measures, the field 'Action plan objective and sub-theme(s) addressed by measures' refers to the above Trend Chart categories. In addition, GoodNIP has made use of two other sets of classifications. The GoodNIP classification 1 is based on Schumpeterian thinking, and separates between three categories: invention, innovation and diffusion. The GoodNIP classification 2 has five categories: product innovation, process innovation, organisational innovation, strategic innovation and market innovation.

In addition to the classifications provided by the EU Trend Chart and OECD GoodNIP initiatives, a categorisation and several examples of policies at work in the EU is provided in the scheme developed by Guy and Nauwelaers (2003). The authors cluster policies in a 3 x 3 dimensional matrix depending on the policy target groups involved in the implementation of the policy or primarily influenced by the policy (Table 8.1).

One of the shortcomings of the classifications reviewed above is that they are more descriptive than normative and analytical in nature. Although different policies are mapped and described, there is no real inherent comparative basis or analytical power. This means that for the purpose of a coherent development of policy instruments conducive to higher levels of R&D investment and innovation, a more focused and analytical approach is needed. Such an approach should allow policy makers to make the strategic considerations visible that are necessary to tailor the mix of policy instruments to their particular context and needs. At the same time, it should offer a basis for assessing the effectiveness of those policy instruments. In order to do so, policy makers need to know not only what types of policy instruments are available, but also which of the available policies and instruments will work in the context within which they are making their decisions. This brings us to the impact not only of individual measures but also of policy mixes. Assessing the impact of the measures constitutes the most ambitious part of the analysis of innovation policies. The above-reviewed initiatives do not provide such an analytical background for policy decision makers. Only the Pilot Action 'Regional Innovation Policy

Table 8.1   Categorisation of policies

Policy target groups	Public sector	Public and private sector	Private sector
Knowledge users	Reinforcement policies Public support to education institutions and programmes Creation of interdisciplinary graduate schools	Bridging initiatives Innovation and entrepreneurship courses at high schools	Reinforcement policies Innovation-oriented business support structures SME-specific financial programmes
Knowledge users and knowledge creators	Bridging initiatives	Bridging initiatives	Bridging initiatives
	Collaborative programmes between universities and higher education	Cluster policies Regional growth centres	Support for cooperative R&D projects
Knowledge creators	Reinforcement policies Public support to universities and public research labs Targeted business-oriented R&D programmes	Bridging initiatives Spin-off promotion programmes	Reinforcement policies Support for R&D projects in companies

Source: Adapted from Guy and Nauwelaers (2003).

Impact Assessment and Benchmarking' aims to conduct an ex post measurement of the impact (at the regional level), with methodology defined in the *Guidelines on Impact Assessment.*[2]

The Trend Chart provides information about the impact of selected measures where information is available. Similarly, GoodNIP provides information on results (where available) achieved by each measure, usually referring to indicators that the measure influences. In addition, the methodologies employed by the different initiatives for assessing the impact make comparisons difficult.

The insufficient knowledge of what impact a policy mix does or might have leads to national innovation policies based on measures introduced on an *ad hoc* basis. Impact assessments or evaluations are primarily carried out towards a specific policy measure. No assessment has been applied of a set of policy measures that form a policy mix. Assessments are usually *ex post* and are used as corrective instruments while *ex ante* impact assessments might help decision makers to define a more optimal policy mix to address a specific strategic challenge of the NIS. For reasons of effectiveness governments tend to move towards evaluating the entire set of policy measures that have been implemented. They also move towards building up their innovation policies on policy mixes that will most successfully address a particular policy issue. A necessary condition to be able to do this is to have a national coordination mechanism. Thus the interdependence between the innovation policy mix and governance of innovation increases.

THE INTERDEPENDENCE BETWEEN THE GOVERNANCE OF INNOVATION AND THE INNOVATION POLICY MIX

Often the issues of governance and policy mix for innovation are researched and discussed separately. We find the discussion on both issues jointly very important as we see them strongly interdependent for the purpose of increased efficiency of innovation policies. The interdependence stems from the following.

Innovation policy mixes usually address issues that policy makers should tackle following certain political, economic and social priorities. The identification of these issues is mainly based on the concept of the National Innovation System (NIS), and these issues concern the performance of different elements or linkages in the NIS. The Innovation Trend Chart initiative of the EC (which has been adopted widely by the EU member states) uses an approach that identifies the challenges (these are in fact issues) that innovation policy should respond to. Box 8.1 illustrates the challenges and the corresponding measures Spain has planned for the near future in the field of innovation.

BOX 8.1   SPAIN: THE BACKGROUND FOR POLICY MIXES

Challenges
Low business R&D and innovation
Fragmented research base – Weak links between science and innovation
Growing role of the regions and wide range of programmes by different Ministries

---

Expected drop in EU funding for regional development

Policy responses: Ingenio 2010
Double ratio of R&D as share of GDP to reach 2 per cent of GDP by 2010
Raise share of business sectors share of R&D from less than 50 per cent to 55 per cent by 2010
Boost Public Research Funds (CONSOLIDER)
PPPs programmes (CENIT – Strategic National Consortia for Industrial Research)
Boost venture capital

Source: Sanz-Menéndez (2007).

Later on, the same initiative would report on how the challenges were addressed from responses of the policy makers in different countries. We saw from the previous discussion that the typology of the challenges can vary. Without going into detail of which typology is better or more appropriate, we would like to emphasise that classifications of issues in a systematic way (e.g. the NIS concept) drive and sometimes force decision makers to cluster their responses alongside these classifications. That is how the policy mix emerges (see Figure 8.1).

It is important to note that the clusters of issues/challenges are different for different countries; they reflect to a large extent not only the future goals of governments but also the historic inheritance and the present state of the art. The result might be that some clusters of challenges are dominant and need urgent response. This would require a corresponding form of innovation policy governance. Box 8.2 gives the well-known example of Finland, a country that has faced a fundamental discontinuity, which made it urgent to respond and subsequently install the right governance innovation mechanism.

BOX 8.2   FINLAND: TIMES OF DISCONTINUITIES AND THE SENSE OF URGENCY

In the late 1980s the world economic crisis drove many countries to look for instruments to boost competitiveness and thus economic growth. In the 1990s, the transition processes in Eastern Europe, including Russia, influenced Finland badly. A country where the wood and paper industry was dominant and represented

75 per cent of exports in 1960 needed an urgent structural change to ensure diversification and competitiveness. Finland faced times of discontinuity and felt the sense of urgency.

This brought the issue of innovation to the top of the national policy agenda. This agenda would not have been realised successfully without the creation of the high-level Innovation Council under the presidency of the prime minister. The Innovation Council is further composed of the Ministries of Trade and Industry and of Education and Science, a number of CEOs from industry (including the CEO of NOKIA), scientists and a few others.

At present the share of the wood processing and paper industry has further decreased. The important role of science, technology and innovation in economic development can be seen in the fact that R&D share of GDP increased from 1.2 per cent in 1985 to 2 per cent in 1992 to 3.5 per cent at present. The Finns have been leading in GDP growth in Europe over many years.

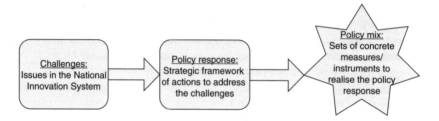

Figure 8.1   The policy mix chain

Governance mechanisms can influence policy mixes. Examples are the former centrally planned European states. Many of them had very well-developed fundamental research, in many cases for the pursuit of science as an end in itself. The research industry was structured in a large number of research institutions under Academy of Sciences type of organisations, sector/industry-related institutes and academic organisations (universities). These countries entered the transition period in the 1990s with a huge army of researchers in a wide variety of subjects, many of them not linked to the requirements of the national economy and business. All analyses of the NIS of these countries have shown how critical the challenges are relating to the link between industry and R&D (see Box 8.3). Reform of the R&D sector was urgent, as was the need for commercialisation of R&D efforts. A response to this can only be successful and timely when the governance mechanism is placed at a level higher than the ministries of economy and science (and education). Any other mechanism would only postpone the response and introduce suboptimal measures. Unfortunately very few of these countries have chosen a national innovation council type of governance with real power attached to it. Accordingly, the policy mixes

---

BOX 8.3   POLAND: TIME TO ACT

A survey of the national innovation system carried out by ECORYS Research and Consulting and CIMPAN within the framework of the project 'Strengthening government policy and institutional cohesion to enhance innovativeness of Polish economy accessing the European Union' and many other studies show that the number of institutions in Poland that are introducing measures to stimulate R&D, technologies and innovation is substantial. The same conclusion can be drawn for the number of the organisations acting as intermediaries, for instance between business and science or between business and financial sources. At the same time, the conclusion is that the number of these institutions matters to some extent. More important, however, is the coordination and the coherence achieved between them, both on policy making as well as on the policy execution level. Poland faces a great challenge to systematically govern and coordinate its R&D potential:

- Looking at the downstream implementation level, there are many relevant implementing actors, with often overlapping functions and activities;
- Most of the coordination is vertical. The only horizontal coordination seems to be at the top national decision-making level;
- It seems that most research units, agencies etc. are governed and controlled by scientists, the involvement/ influence of beneficiaries of the research results (industry or public goals/needs) is not clear;
- In a situation of insufficient horizontal coordination the efficiency of budget spending on behalf of innovation is difficult to achieve.

Recently Poland has been considering installing a national innovation council (according to the Innovation Law).

are formed by different ministries, especially those of economy, and science and education. The best case might be when these two institutions cooperate and aim at coherent policy together. In practice, communication, especially between these two ministries, is not optimal.

COORDINATION MECHANISMS

Driving Forces towards Coordination of Innovation Policy

From a government point of view, an effective policy towards science, technology and innovation requires coordination mechanisms. Coordination is also needed for policies on competitiveness, regional development and education and science. Finally, coordination is needed between government departments requiring R&D for their own policy areas and the Ministry of Education and Science. In addition to the requirement for coordination of policy objectives, there is the need to coordinate policy implementation.

In general, there is an ambition for a greater cohesion along four dimensions:

1. Integration of knowledge creation and its commercial utilisation with respect of technology transfer mechanisms and starters.
2. Cross-departmental integration on strategy and implementation of science, technology and innovation (STI) policies.
3. Combination of knowledge from different scientific disciplines to tackle interdisciplinary research needs.
4. Coordination with EU–STI programmes requires national coordination.

Traditionally, the governance system and the policies dealing with fundamental research have not been sufficiently coordinated with those destined for the commercialisation and exploitation of knowledge (innovation). The danger of this is that a pool of knowledge can emerge, unable to find its way to innovation. Reviewing the coordination mechanisms in the different countries of the EU, it is important to identify how STI policy is divided across different ministries, departments, agencies and intermediaries, and what the associated coordination mechanisms are. We see three layers:

1. Where the policy design and strategy formulation for STI take place. This can be found on the level of governments, departments and, to

varying degrees, advisory bodies. National governments (Cabinet members and prime minister) are involved to various extents in deciding on overall coordination and strategy formulation.

2. The research funding bodies (research councils, dedicated agencies etc.). The role of these institutions can differ widely in the EU countries.
3. Actors that perform research and innovation and are the direct beneficiaries of public funding. This layer contains the largest differences between the countries.

Forms of Coordination Mechanisms at National Level

The following different coordination mechanisms can be distinguished in the EU:

1. *High-level bodies (councils) providing the strategic framework* (e.g. Finland, Iceland, the Netherlands, Portugal). These countries have created a policy decision-making or advisory structure at a higher hierarchical level than ministries, chaired by the prime minister.
2. Responsibility for coordination assigned to *one minister or department*, which results in strengthening of coordination mechanisms at interdepartmental level (e.g. the UK, Sweden, Bulgaria).
3. Establishment of *one dedicated ministry* dealing with the entire knowledge production and implementation chain (e.g. Denmark).
4. Strategic decisions taken by *individual ministers in their own sector* (many of the EU countries).

In most of the EU countries there are numerous advisory bodies/committees at different levels. In addition to the national structures, there are also regional innovation governance structures. These go hand in hand with the recent trend of decentralisation of regional policy. The rise of regional autonomy and competencies might limit the roles of the central government even when the state coordinates overall innovation policy (Sanz-Menéndez, 2007). In the case of Poland, for instance, all 16 regions have developed regional innovation strategies while Poland as a country does not have one.

The latest developments in the EU show that innovation performance is measured on the basis of challenges and responses to these challenges by the country as a whole. Challenges become increasingly multidisciplinary, across sectors and therefore across departments. An effective response (e.g. amount of effort/investment, timing, major restructurings etc.) can only be provided if national coordination is ensured. Especially for government systems organised on a sector principle, a coordination mechanism for innovation at national level is a must. The Nordic countries, for instance, have agreed that concentrating on

> one type of investment only, e.g. R&D investments, the policy can have unforeseen and unwanted consequences. Given that the majority of Nordic companies are small and in branches that do not normally invest much in R&D, an increase in national R&D investments will have to be the result of a change in industrial structure, i.e. one will need a larger number of new R&D intensive companies. (STEP, 2003a)

This decision by itself necessitates a reconsideration of many other aspects of countries' economic policy. Such decisions and discussions need to be carried out at high national level (see next section) not least because innovation policy is hard to communicate politically and publicly.

High-level National Body

For coordination, we strongly support the model of a national high-level body (for instance an innovation council) that has a strategic decision-making role in addition to an advisory role. This seems to be the best approach to improve governance, for the following reasons:

- The nature of innovation (e.g. dynamic and multidisciplinary) currently requires the involvement of a wide range of stakeholders, both public and private. At the same time, a growing number of actors is involved. Only coordination at a high level can be successful.
- Imbalance in one element of the national innovation system is felt immediately in another.
- Data from recent years show a growing number of innovation measures and instruments. This calls for coherence and transparency, and high public accountability. As many innovation support schemes use state budget or state resources, there is a need for evidence that funds are spent effectively. Additionally, the issue of public accountability (Barberis, 1998) brings about the need for *ex ante* impact assessment.
- There is a limited availability of public funds, especially in the light of the ever-increasing costs of R&D. Even in the Netherlands, where a substantial number of financial schemes to support innovation has been introduced successfully over more than 30 years, state investments have not grown recently (Wintjes, 2007). Multiplicity of objectives and instruments introduced by different departments and at national and regional level might lead to duplication.

- The increasing autonomy of regions makes coordination with regions of growing importance. Otherwise there is a risk of lack of synergy and overlap, as well as deviation from national priorities.
- Public accountability asks for constant evaluation of policy measures and instruments. When performed by different actors, the evaluation is likely to be based on different criteria.
- The present nature of the innovation policy is that it interacts directly or indirectly with almost all other policies (Anonymous, 2006). No individual department is capable of overseeing the entire spectrum of policies that the innovation policy should be coherent with.
- Finally, there is *per se* a limited capacity for strategic planning and policy making in any country.

Placed at a higher hierarchical level than individual ministries, a national innovation council would improve the horizontal coordination between policy makers of different ministries and departments. Besides policy makers, some members of the council should be CEOs from innovative companies, scientists and experts, e.g. in the area of regional innovation strategies or EU funds. This improves the vertical coordination between innovation policy makers at national level and initiators from their different client or support domains. Based on positive experience in Finland, Portugal, Ireland and recently the Netherlands, this model of governance represents best practice. The limited experience with national innovation councils indicates that this form of innovation policy coordination increases awareness and the sense of urgency in society at large that future wealth in any country depends heavily on innovation activities.

Many countries still struggle with the governance issue for the following reasons.

Traditional governance models prevail

For example, the Netherlands 'polder model' in decision making has perhaps influenced the installation of the national innovation platform that is to follow the Innovation Council of Finland. However, the impact of the platform cannot be compared to that of the Finish Council. The overall picture of the coordination mechanism for innovation in the Netherlands remains complex (see Figure 8.2). The government is advised by a number of bodies that have traditionally existed in the country. Two organisations are concerned with policy preparation: the Council on Science, Technology and Information Policy (RWTI) and the Committee on Science, Technology and Information Policy (CWTI). The difference between the two is their constitution: RWTI consists of ministers while CWTI involves high-level civil servants. At the implementation level there

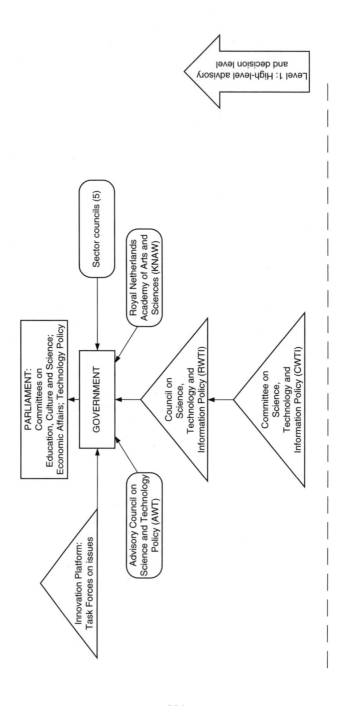

Level 1: High-level advisory and decision level

216

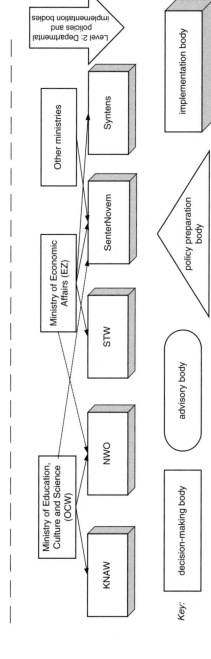

Source: Authors' figure, based on own information, Polt (2006) and a report of the Dutch Ministry of Economic Affairs (2006).

Figure 8.2 Main players in formulation and implementation of R&D and innovation policy in the Netherlands

is a number of organisations that are carrying out financial and non-financial schemes encouraging R&D and innovation. We believe that the dynamics of the innovation issues and the need of coherent policy formulation, combined with the existing complexity of the advisory, decision-making and policy implementation structure in the Netherlands can only be addressed by a strong innovation council at national level.

Another example is the new EU member states that have gone through a period where centralised governance of any kind was no longer appreciated due to a long-lasting inheritance of the centrally planned economy in these countries.[3] Some time is needed to achieve not only political but also public acceptance of centrally placed decision-making bodies. At the same time the need for national coordination for innovation is increasing in these countries.

Sector approach towards innovation
The traditional sector approach to innovation leads to departmental policy making for innovation. The OECD MONIT project found that coordination mechanisms may be static and short term rather than dynamic, particularly when there is significant institutional fragmentation (OECD, 2005a). The solution that is advised by many researchers in the field is the creation of another layer. Boeknolt argues that while government departments and individual actors have difficulties in coordinating and aligning their research and innovation actions, a solution sought in many European countries is to create another layer in the policy making, which overarches the level of the individual departments (Boekholt, 2004).

Lack of national innovation strategy
The existence of a national innovation strategy leads to a considerable amount of national consensus. It also means that relevant stakeholders have been involved in its preparation and that they have agreed to the roles, responsibilities, the allocation of national resources and the communication process defined in the strategy. This is the first step towards a national coordination mechanism at high level. However necessary the step may be, it is not sufficient alone.

New governance structures come to life only if there is new money
Tackling multidisciplinary issues involved in innovation appears to be more difficult within the existing governance structures (Technopolis, 2002). What can be observed is that new governance structures (e.g. dedicated task forces) arise in emerging technology areas (e.g. nanotechnology, genomics) particularly if new money is poured into the system. The cases also show that coordination between different organisations

and departments is easier with new money, in comparison with having to negotiate for the allocation of existing funds.

An example is the issue of the information society. Many EU countries have reported progress in their information society policy implementation. At the same time, they recognise pitfalls and even dangers such as a lack of capacity to steer the developments further across an increased number of information society drivers. Another danger is the lack of real leadership in implementing information society activities (OECD, 2006). For instance, the Norwegian Ministry of Modernisation is the coordination body of Norway's programme. Despite the 'good overview of the information society policy area' which this ministry has, and despite its proactive coordination and implementation, personnel and competence resources prove to be scarce (Pedersen, 2006, p. 311).

INNOVATION POLICY MIX AS PART OF THE GOVERNANCE SYSTEM FOR INNOVATION

Defining an Innovation Policy Mix

The section above, concerned with definitions of innovation policy mix, shows that there is an increasing tendency to work not with individual policy instruments but rather with a carefully tuned set of instruments. However, little is known about which policies work when and where. Related to this is the challenge to the policy maker to optimise the set of support instruments in order to enhance innovation with the largest impact. Moreover, policy makers have to take into account institutional and economic constraints when making the above decisions. For instance, decision making in a financially stable and economically leading EU country differs from the decision making in a new EU member state. In a new EU member state with limited resources, priority setting is of utmost importance and choices might appear to be limited. The decision making is thus multidimensional. The final choice of support instruments for innovation is defined by:

- the characteristics of the environment in a given country/region;
- the policy issues that need to be addressed;
- the impact that a support instrument is expected to have.

At present, two major barriers prohibit achieving a policy mix that reflects on the specific environment, addresses specific policy issues and provides a general idea about the impact of the set of instruments chosen. These are lack of knowledge about the factors that define the choice of different financial support instruments (environment) and lack of suitable methods for estimating the impact of these measures. Under 'factors' we understand the economic and regulatory factors. In addition, the applicability of a certain support instrument in a given country/region is important and this includes: availability of administrative capacity required, amount of financial resources needed, appropriateness of local administrative and other systems.

Many policy makers ask: 'Which measures, why and when?' Since innovation often needs substantial resourses and at the same time requires urgency, to build up an optimal policy mix is essential. Best practices of other countries are a good starting point. At the same time, they might be misleading for several reasons:

- Measures correspond to policy objectives and these are not the same in all countries.
- Policy objectives stem from different economic, social, technological, cultural and other conditions that in many cases are different for the different countries.
- Every measure has its main attributes, such as volume, duration, target group, administrative costs, regulatory requirements etc. These attributes might not be applicable to other countries for reasons of availability of financial resources, administrative capacity, regulatory environment etc.
- The impact of a measure depends very much on conditions: a measure with a high impact in one country, might offer insufficient impact in another.

All this makes the use of best practices of other countries not necessarily effective. Therefore policy makers do not come with questions about what measures there are, but what will be the impact of the measures, as well as their conditions for applicability. Having been faced with this request from policy makers, we have come to the following definition of an innovation policy mix:

> An innovation policy mix is the combination of causes, conditions for applicability and nature of impact of a set of policy measures that addresses a specific policy issue (challenge).

Illustration of Innovation Policy Mix

Small and medium-sized enterprises (SMEs) represent more than 80 per cent of the total number of firms in a healthy economy. They are also one of the most important indicators of entrepreneurship. Objective 3 of the EU, 'Encourage the creation and growth of innovative enterprises' (EC, 2000) caught the attention of national and regional governments to innovation policies and measures conducive to SMEs.

The 2006 *European Innovation Progress Report* (EC, 2006) summarises the key innovation challenges in Europe. Although they vary by country, many of the challenges relate to boosting the intensity of innovation in enterprises and closing the gap between R&D and industry in the name of science commercialisation. Large parts of the innovation policies in the EU member states rightly aim to affect the innovative activities of firms as these are involved in the application of knowledge and ideas that generate economic growth. One segment of firms gets special attention: these are spin-offs from university, start-ups by entrepreneurs and innovative SMEs. The dynamics of small firms allows them to play a crucial role in the application of knowledge and in knowledge transfer. These firms are central to an innovative and dynamic economy, yet they face a range of difficulties that require particular attention from policy makers (see Chapters 2 to 6 of this book). For example, obtaining funds to innovate is a considerable obstacle to spin-offs, start-ups and SMEs. Innovation policies across Europe have thus increasingly tended to focus on the problems faced by this category of companies. Lately the knowledge value chain from SMEs to large enterprises, as an important factor for increased innovation activities of SMEs themselves, has become a focus of attention in a few EU member states (i.e. Finland).

We have reviewed (under the ECORYS Research Programme) all 266 support schemes active in the EU member states that aim to boost entrepreneurship and innovation[4] (see Table 8.2) and grouped them by their main objective: awareness, entrepreneurship for innovation, especially at R&D and academic institutions: new spin-off companies; innovative start-ups in general; and growing through innovation (in existing SMEs).

Table 8.2 represents an EU-wide innovation policy mix that addresses the issues of entrepreneurship for innovation and innovative SMEs. We are aware that this distribution of number of support schemes per target group does not result from a conscious choice that aims to achieve a balanced policy mix. Such a conscious choice is important at the national level, as we have argued before. There are very few countries that think in this direction and more importantly act by following this logic. One of them is Finland, where the policy mix aiming at entrepreneurship and SMEs is built on the basis of identifying the critical points in enterprise development and in connection with innovation/knowledge development. Tekes, the Finnish Funding Agency for Technology and Innovation, has chosen for a strategic

Table 8.2   Financial schemes for innovation

Target group	Awareness among (potential) entrepreneurs and SMEs	Entrepreneur-ship for innovation	New compa-nies (high-tech)	Start-up (small SMEs)	Growing innovative SMEs	Total
Number of schemes	29	55	41	65	76	266
As % of total	11	21	15	24	29	100

goal 'to increase the number of new technology companies and to speed up their growth and internationalisation'.[5] This strategic goal is based on the finding that 'new technology companies are important for the national economy: they utilise effectively new technology and grow and employ quickly'. Tekes is convinced (Romanainen, 2006) that no single policy measure will provide the solution. There is a need for a mix of policy measures comprising e.g. loans for seed capital, entrepreneurs, start ups, and funding of (or subsidies to) R&D, feasibility studies and development.

Below we illustrate the formation of policy mixes concerning entrepreneurship and innovation where the characteristics of the environment, the policy issues that need to be addressed and the impact a support instrument is expected to have are taken into account (see Figure 8.3).

There are four main direct players within the national innovation system that are targets of the policy mix for entrepreneurship and innovation. These are:

- R&D and higher education institutions
- Technostarters and start-ups in high-technology fields
- Existing SMEs
- Large enterprises.

The issues/challenges related to innovation of each of these four groups are interrelated:

- The number of new, high-tech firms will stay low if entrepreneurship at higher education institutions and R&D organisations is not increased.
- The number of innovative companies will stay low if start-ups are not supported to grow.

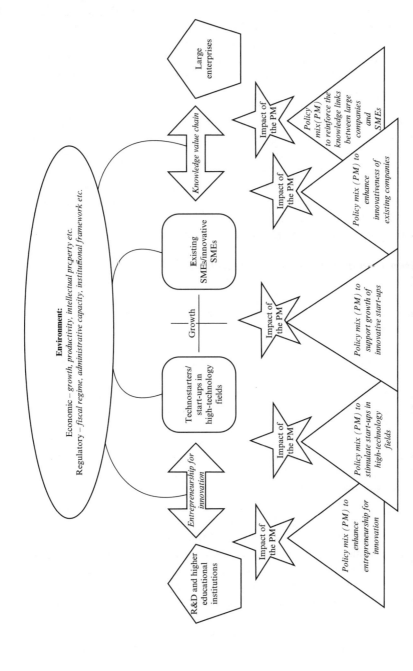

Figure 8.3   Defining innovation policy mix for entrepreneurship and SMEs[6]

- To increase their competitiveness, existing companies help to improve their innovation performance and their ability to absorb knowledge originating from public sector research.
- In order to improve the knowledge base industry-wide, effective inter-firm relationships among SMEs and large companies, and knowledge transfer mechanisms between industry and R&D providers should be ensured.

The environment consists of economic and regulatory conditions in which companies operate. The environment is different in different countries, and this influences the choice of the set of measures in the policy mix. The environment interacts with policy mixes – on the one hand a given policy mix brings some input to the environment (e.g. increases the productivity of the economy by supporting innovative companies) and on the other hand it constitutes conditions delimiting the possibilities for the implementation of the policy mix (e.g. administrative capacity).

Five types of policy mix related to the main issues in the above segment of firms can be defined. These are policies to:

1. enhance entrepreneurship for innovation;
2. stimulate start-ups in high-technology fields;
3. support growth of innovative start-ups;
4. enhance innovativeness of existing companies;
5. reinforce the knowledge links between large companies and SMEs.

The stakeholders concerned with the policy mixes discussed above represent science, R&D and higher education institutions, and their respective ministries and agencies; industry and its respective ministries and agencies; and intermediate bodies. Policy making is at the level of a number of government departments, mainly education, science and industry, and trade, but it can also be transport, environment and others. If made at a level higher than the individual departments, the policy would aim at balancing the measures per policy mix so as to ensure that an effect in one of the links increases the effect in another. From the review of the publicly available innovation measures it becomes clear that the concentration of instruments to stimulate innovativeness in existing SMEs and the commercialisation of R&D through SMEs have been prevailing. It is only recently that the number of measures concerned with entrepreneurship for innovation at higher education institutions, one of the potential sources for high-tech start-ups, has increased.

To make the best possible choice one should try to forecast the impact of potential policy mixes. This means introducing an *ex ante* impact assessment. Where the impact has been measured in other countries, in a similar environment, one can of course take this into account.

The successful implementation of a national innovation strategy, with a concomitant mix of policy instruments, will require further in-depth evaluation of individual support instruments. Accordingly, policy makers need to have methods allowing them continuously to ascertain the effectiveness of individual instruments and the innovation policy mix as a whole. These impact assessment methods need to be tailored to the particularities of innovation policies and the contextual factors that shape their performance.[7] Accordingly, developing impact assessment methods for innovation policy requires knowledge of the factors that shape the performance of different policies. While an *ex post* evaluation provides the decision maker with a feedback on the policy measure, an *ex ante* impact assessment would support the choice of the measure. Since policy measures in the field of innovation entail substantial financial resources, *ex ante* impact assessment is preferred. So far mainly *ex post* evaluations have been undertaken and even then for very few of the innovation policy measure in the EU countries.

CONCLUSIONS AND RECOMMENDATIONS

The complexity of issues dealt with by national innovation systems as well as the nature of innovation nowadays require governance of innovation policy that integrates all players, including the private sector. The issues concern different governmental departments and decisions need to be taken by them together, overcoming the traditional sectoral division in decision making. Recently we have observed that the level of decision-making bodies in the field of innovation has increased: Parliament, prime minister and national councils are involved. We strongly recommend the national innovation council as a governing body for innovation placed at a higher hierarchical level than individual ministries: this should improve horizontal coordination. Although still limited, the experience with national innovation councils shows increased awareness and sense of urgency in society at large that the future wealth of any country depends a great deal on innovation.

While the wide understanding of a governance system for innovation concerns mainly the organisational form and relationship between different decision-making bodies, our understanding is that an effective and efficient governance system for innovation is the combination of national coordination of policy formulation and innovation policy mix. There is an increasing tendency not to work with individual policy instruments but rather with a carefully tuned set of instruments. Recently policy makers have tended to look more broadly at the policy instruments for innovation, asking which measure, why and when. To answer these questions one should be aware of the causes that ask for a certain measure, the conditions for its applicability and the nature of its impact. That is why we define the innovation policy mix as 'the combination of causes, conditions for applicability and nature of impact of a set of policy measures that addresses a specific policy issue (challenge)'.

Policy mixes respond to specific issues/challenges and are always interrelated. Therefore they should be planned and implemented not individually but in accordance with their interrelation. At the same time policy mixes often consist of instruments that are the responsibility of different departments. Therefore national coordination concerning the formulation of the policy mixes will bring efficiency. Higher efficiency will also be achieved if impact assessment is carried out on the policy mix as a whole rather than on individual measures. Since innovation policy is one of the most expensive policies to implement, *ex ante* impact assessment is advisable. Present practice shows the predominant use of *ex post* evaluation. While an *ex post* evaluation provides the decision maker with feedback on the policy measure, an *ex ante* impact assessment would support the choice of the measure.

Policy mixes can be based on the experience of others, but their impact depends on the environment in which they are implemented. Therefore there are no uniform good practices: each EU member state searches for its own innovation policy mix that will respond best to the challenges the country faces in the field of innovation. At the same time it will reflect the environmental factors as well as the ability of the country to implement one or another instrument. This increases the need for exchange of practices between EU member states. EU-wide networks of institutions concerned with innovation policy nationally (e.g. TAFTIE, the Association of Technology Implementation agencies in Europe) are becoming important in achieving more understanding on, among others, the questions: which measures, why and when? In addition, the communication at EU level of the national governing bodies for innovation on issues beyond mere national interest is essential (see Chapter 7 of this book).

NOTES

1. See http://trendchart.cordis.europa.eu.
2. See: http://ec.europa.eu/governance/impact/docs/SEC2005_791_IA per cent20guide-lines_annexes.pdf.
3. Such a notion was expressed in Poland during our advisory work.
4. These represent about 42 per cent of the total number of support schemes for innovation.

5. Power Point Presentation of Tekes, April 2004.
6. This concept has been developed under ECORYS Research Programme, 2007.
7. Compare Chapter 3 of this book.

REFERENCES

Anonymous (2006), 'Demand as a driver of innovation – towards a more effective European innovation policy', Discussion note to the informal meeting of the competitiveness ministers, Jyväskylä, Finland, 10–11 July.
Barberis, P. (1998), 'The new public management and a new accountability', *Public Administration*, **76** (Autumn), 451–70.
Boekholt, P. (2004), 'Ensuring policy coherence by improving the governance of innovation policy', Trend Chart Policy Workshop, Brussels, 27–28 April, p. 5.
EC (2000), *Innovation in a Knowledge-driven Economy*, COM(2000)567, Brussels.
EC (2001a), European Trend Chart on Innovation 2001, Thematic Report: 'Innovation Financing', May–September, Innovation/SMEs Programme, European Commission, Enterprise Directorate General, Brussels.
EC (2001b), COM 428 final, Brussels.
EC (2006), *European Innovation Progress Report (2006)*, Trend Chart, Brussels.
Guy, K. and C. Nauwelaers (2003), 'Benchmarking STI policies in Europe: in search of good practice', *The IPTS Report*, **2** (71), 20–28.
Larosse, J. (2004), 'Towards a "third generation" innovation policy in Flanders: policy profile of the Flemish Innovation System', contribution to the OECD–TIP project MONIT (Monitoring and Implementing Horizontal Innovation Policies), Institute for the Promotion of Innovation by Science and Technology in Flanders (IWT)
Fraunhofer Institute (2003), 'New governance for innovation: the need for horizontal and systematic policy co-ordination', Fraunhofer ISI Discussion Papers Innovation Systems and Policy Analysis, No 2/2003, Karlsruhe, June.
OECD (2005a), *Governance of Innovation Systems, Volume 1: Synthesis Report*, Paris: OECD.
OECD (2005b), *Governance of Innovation Systems, Volume 2: Case Studies in Innovation Policies*, Paris: OECD.
OECD (2006), *Governance of Innovation Systems: Case Studies in Cross-sectoral Policy*, Paris: OECD.
Pedersen, T.E. (2006), 'Information society policy coordination: a mould for innovation policy development in Norway?', Chapter 3 in *Governance of Innovation Systems*: Case Studies in Cross-sectoral Policy, Paris: OECD.
Polt, W. (2006), 'Models of S&T policy coordination and S&T priority setting in Europe', presentation at STEP International Symposium 'S&T Policy Coordination System: Experiences and Prospects', Seoul, 23 October.
Romanainen, J. (2006), 'How should national innovation systems and policies react to internationalisation of RTD?', presentation at session: Internationalisation of Research and Technological Development IST 2006, Helsinki, 21 November.
Roper, S. (2004), 'Promoting innovation – the role and efficacy of alternative policy instruments', presentation to the Joint Action Team, Glasgow.
Sanz-Menéndez, L. (2007), 'The response to the challenge: the Spanish policies', presentation to the RAI and Euro-CASE meeting, Madrid, 22 February.

Science, Technology and Innovation in the Netherlands: Policies, Facts and Figures 2006, Report of the Ministry of Economic Affairs, The Hague
STEP (2003a), 'Good practices in Nordic Innovation Policies, Part 1, Summary and Policy Recommendations', STEP, Oslo, June, p. 23.
STEP (2003b), 'GoodNIP good practices in Nordic Innovation Policies, Part 2, Innovation policies, trends and rationalities', Oslo, June.
STEP (2003c), 'GoodNIP good practices in Nordic Innovation Policies, Part 3, Nordic innovation policy measures, documents and government structures', Oslo, April.
Technopolis (2002), *The Governance of Research and Innovation*, Report for the Dutch Government, Technopolis Group, Amsterdam.
Wintjes, R. (2007), 'Monitoring and analysis of policies and public financing instruments conducive to higher levels of R&D investments', The 'Policy Mix' Project, Country Review, the Netherlands, UNU-MERIT, Maastricht University.
Zegveld, W., J. Djarova and R. Wintjes (2004), 'Towards an effective governance system for innovation in Poland', Report for the Advisory Group on Innovation within the frame of the project 'Strengthening government policy and institutional cohesion to enhance innovativeness of Polish economy before accessing the European Union', ECORYS, Rotterdam.

9. Regional innovative potential and development strategies: the case of Poland

Marta Mackiewicz, Robert Pollock and Paulina Fabrowska

'Industry, knowledge and humanity are linked by an indissoluble chain.'
David Hume (1752)

'The general objectives of all institutions must be adapted to meet the local conditions and meet the character of the people concerned.'
Jean-Jacques Rousseau (1762)

INTRODUCTION

Although the above quotations from two renowned European thinkers are approximately 250 years old, they contain messages that remain relevant today for economic development policy makers. The quote from Scottish economist and philosopher David Hume (one of Adam Smith's contemporaries) notes the interconnectivity between the economy, knowledge and society. The quote by Jean-Jacques Rousseau emphasises the need for public policy that is tailored to its local context.

Although these wise words have been in circulation for over two centuries, policy makers still have a tendency to develop regional development strategies that do not address the relationships between knowledge, industry and regional capacity, vital determinants of both innovation and regional wealth, in a joined-up manner. Furthermore, policy makers often ignore the need to adapt policy to the specific features of a region, preferring to import generic, context-less policy solutions (often labelled as 'best practice').

In the spirit of these two philosophers, this chapter will contend that successful regional economic development is based on the recognition that:

- economically valuable innovation at the regional level takes many forms and is determined by a range of factors that are region specific;
- developing a successful regional development strategy is dependent on responding to a region's unique capacity for innovation.

Therefore, in order to develop a successful regional economic development strategy, accurate diagnosis and understanding of a region's innovation capacity is critical.

The chapter follows the following structure:

- rationale for the selection of Poland as the case study;
- an exploration of relevant theory relating to regional innovation and typologies;
- an assessment of different models for measuring innovation at the regional level;
- the Regional Innovativeness Potential Index (RIPI) applied to Polish regions;
- regional innovation and development strategies;
- conclusion.

THE CASE STUDY

Why Select Poland for Analysis?

To demonstrate the value of adopting a broader understanding of innovation at the regional level and the benefits of the RIPI, we have adopted Poland as our case study. Poland is an appropriate case study because

- it is a new accession state (entered the EU in 2004);
- it is a relatively large country composed of differing types of regions;
- the lack of innovation in the economy is well documented;
- it is a recipient of significant levels of Structural Fund assistance to boost innovation and regional development;
- the authors have experience of operating in Poland and are associated with ECORYS, an international consultancy with a significant track record in Poland in advising on national and regional innovation policy.[1]

Furthermore, Poland demonstrates not only the scale of the challenge for economic convergence and cohesion in the EU, but also the need for new ways of understanding and stimulating the dynamics of wealth creation at the regional level. Policy makers need to make realistic assessments of economic opportunity and appropriate innovation policies at the regional level if the ambitions of the Lisbon Agenda and the objectives of convergence and cohesion are to be met.

Like all EU regions, Polish regions must pursue attainable growth strategies and ensure that public funding and resources (regional, national and EU) are effectively targeted at the innovation interventions that will create sustainable growth. Otherwise, divergence is more probable than convergence.

Given that the lion's share of the EU's budget for cohesion purposes is to be invested in Lisbon Agenda priorities, such as R&D, innovation and business development,[2] the need for developing relevant innovation measurement, policies, projects and programmes is a pressing priority not only for Poland but for the entire EU.

Low Level of Innovation[3]

The low level of innovativeness of the Polish economy in comparison with the EU has already been noted. It can be illustrated with several examples. The number of patents registered in Poland has more than halved during the last 16 years (from 3242 registered patents in 1990 to 1122 in 2006). In 2003 the number of patents registered in the European Patent Office per one million inhabitants amounted to three for Poland, while the EU-25 average was 111 (EU-15 – 131). In 2006 the share of high-tech products in Polish export was only 3 per cent compared to 17 per cent for the EU-27. In addition, EU research relating to the quality of human resources and the total expenditure on R&D clearly demonstrate that Polish regions are well below the EU average.

Crucially, according to the Innobarometer, the Polish society is the least ready of all the EU member states to embrace innovation.[4]

Regional Heterogeneity

There are marked differences between the 16 regional economies that make up the national economy of Poland. For example, some regions

- are densely populated, others are not;
- have GDP significantly higher than the national average and some significantly lower;

- have GVA (gross value added) per employee significantly higher than the national average and some significantly lower;
- are highly dependent on manufacturing and some on lower-value-added services and agriculture;
- are internationalised (via exports and inward investments) and others are not;
- have high levels of R&D spend and employment by national standards and others have low levels;
- have low or high levels of entrepreneurship associated with innovation.[5]

Such heterogeneity means that a 'one-size-fits-all' approach to regional innovation will be inappropriate for Poland and potentially counterproductive in terms of aligning national growth with regional convergence.

Poland's level of regional heterogeneity will also determine: the differing types of regional development strategies that need to be developed; the required regional relationships with the national innovation system; and the types of projects that need to be developed and supported with Structural Funds in different regions.

Generic Challenges

A policy challenge that is evident in Poland is recognisable in most EU lagging regional economies. Many of the Polish regions do not have the capacity to absorb the conventional funds prescribed for stimulating innovation (ECORYS, 2004). As Guerrero and Seró (1997) noted, 'the search for efficiency through technological policy brings about a vicious circle which goes against technological (and economic) convergence'. Conventional innovation policy (often wrongly identified as science and technology policy) favours those areas that are already technology rich and have the capacity to absorb funding and support; thus accelerating divergence between regions. The 'regional innovation paradox' (Oughton et al., 2002) is an important factor for policy makers to resolve.

Also, the lack of financial resources, in both the public and private sectors, provokes conflicts with other development priorities. The choice whether to establish a patent fund or to build a road has to be made. Therefore, the ability to make clear assessment of need, opportunity and the return on investment is vital for policy makers.

THE REGIONAL DIMENSION OF INNOVATION

The Role of the Region

The role of innovation at the regional level has received increased attention in the literature over the last decade (Cooke and Morgan, 1998; Porter, 2003; Cooke, 2004). This literature uses in general a broad definition of innovation and takes an extended view of the role of public policy (in line with the choices made for the whole book; see Chapter 1).

This increased interest in innovation at the regional level is unsurprising given the demonstration that differences in regional innovative capabilities can explain a large part of the diverging trends in economic growth in European regions (Fagerberg et al., 1997). This relationship was also recognised in the *Fourth Cohesion Report* (EC, 2007) in its assertion that 'innovative performance and economic performance are closely linked' at the regional level. Guerrero and Seró (1997) identified that regional economics that want to stimulate a virtuous circle of development must stimulate innovation; if not, a downward spiral of decline may be unavoidable.

The interest in innovation at the regional level is also due to the fact that factors that determine innovation (e.g. tacit knowledge, enterprise agglomeration, workforce skills, technological spillover) are often concentrated and most readily influenced at the regional level.

Furthermore, the interaction of institutions' processes and relationships that are vital to the production, diffusion and deployment of new and economically useful knowledge, both tacit and formalised, are place specific and often unique to the regional level. The configuration of social capital, institutional capacity, both private and public, and knowledge is more often than not exclusive to its regional setting (thus making it spatially and economically unique within the context of national and global markets).

The recognition that such systems are most effectively developed, resourced and managed at the regional level is also noted in such theories as the regional innovation system (Lundvall, 1994; Rosenfeld, 1997), the knowledge-based economy (Cooke and Leydesdorff, 2006) and the open innovation system (Chesbrough, 2003). In short, innovation does not occur in 'a wonderland of no dimensions' (Richardson, 1976). Furthermore, the factors that determine innovation activity are influenced by proximity – and it is the region that is a key spatial unit for both understanding innovation and influencing it.[6]

Finally, there are pressing political, practical and pragmatic reasons for understanding innovation and designing related strategies at the regional level. Many of the economic development actors that influence the innovation process operate at the regional level and are funded (e.g. via the Structural Funds) and governed at the regional level. Economic development is about taking action, and it is at the regional level that the action is found.

Spatial Hierarchy

In viewing policy through the spatial prism of the region, a cautionary note is in order (Uyarra, 2005, p. 8):

> There is a tendency to uncritically emphasize the centrality of the regions, assuming a clear regional delimitation and boundaries, internal uniformity and cultural and social proximity. Regions tend to be treated as independent units, somehow separated and isolated, indifferent to the impact and influences of the national and world economy.

Although the region is an important territorial unit through which to understand and influence innovation, it cannot be seen in isolation from its wider economic geography. Such a point is recognised by Braczyk et al. (1998) and Cooke (2004), who contend that regional innovation systems need to be linked to the national and global economies.

Finally, Asheim and Dunsford (1997, p. 451) recognise the critical role of national government in regional development, 'whose power in spatially distributing infrastructure, R&D, education and other pre-conditions of development remains essential'. National investment decisions are key determinants of the balance between overall national growth and regional convergence. Therefore regional innovation policy must align and interact with national innovation policy. An informed symbiotic relationship is essential (ECORYS, 2004).

DIVERSITY OF REGIONS, DIVERSITY OF INNOVATION

Recognising Regional Diversity

All regions are different. They are constructs of differing social, economic, spatial, historic and institutional factors, and their economic performance is influenced by these diverse factors. Dunnewijk et al. (2008) rightly argue that there is a range of determinants of regional performance and reject 'the option of having one-size-fits-all policies from EU or national policy makers', and call for tailored strategies for each region. They also contend that, due to regional economic diversity, the innovation policy options for regions differ markedly.

A range of typologies has been developed that demonstrate some patterns in the full diversity of regional features. Although typologies are only theoretical generalisations of reality and, as such, their limitations from a policy perspective need to be fully recognised, they do provide a useful platform for identifying similarities between regions, comparing the determinants and dynamics of regional growth, and identifying transferable policy lessons.

A Typology of Successful Regions

As part of its preparations for the *Third Cohesion Report*, the EC commissioned Cambridge Econometrics and ECORYS (2003) to undertake a study on regional competitiveness in the EU-15. The report developed a typology of high-productivity regions in Europe and proposed that over a ten-year period the most successful EU regions could be grouped into three types. The ECORYS research identified that there was more than one type of successful region in the EU-15:

Type 1 Production sites – regions that are attractive to significant flows of inward investment and conducive to export-driven manufacturing companies.

Type 2 Sites of increasing returns – regions that have clustered and locally headquartered internationally competitive industries.

Type 3 Knowledge hubs – regions that receive and transmit high levels of internationalised knowledge, both formalised and tacit, and are dependent on high-tech enterprises and high-value services.

Moreover, subsequent research by ECORYS (2004) recognised that these three types of regions are highly relevant for the definition of innovation policy measures.

For example, regions in the production site type category were dependent on technology transfer and codified knowledge flows that were driven by foreign-owned global companies. This regional type was characterised by R&D consumption and import, and not R&D production and export.

Regions that demonstrated many of the characteristics common in the sites of increasing returns model were more dependent on local R&D that was often used collectively by local companies and the flow of tacit knowledge both within the region and internationally.

Regions in the hubs of knowledge category were much more dependent on global knowledge flows of codified and tacit knowledge. Tacit knowledge was transferred via in-migration of talent from the wider national and global economies. There were also high levels of investment in higher education, for both training of the future workforce and research. Much innovation investment was not identified because it occurred in services.

A Comprehensive Typology of EU Regions

A more comprehensive typology of European regions has been developed by Dunnewijk et al. (2008, p. 53). The typology identifies differing types of regional economies based on four drivers (public knowledge, learning dynamics, private knowledge, government services). These drivers are constructed from 13 variables (including higher education, high-tech services, R&D expenditure, and population density).

The research identifies ten regional types that can be assigned to all 220 regions of the EU-27, including: low-tech peripheral; capital service; medium-tech; branch plant; rural industries; and public knowledge metropoles.

In response to these regional types, the authors speculate on potential policy lessons for each of the regional types and the opportunities for stimulating innovation to assist regional economic development. They concluded:

> A lesson for European knowledge and innovation policy is that it must be tailored to specific regional potential . . . There is still insufficient support for experimentation and development of alternative innovation models and new practices. The least developed regions may indeed lack capacities to absorb mainstream or so-called 'best-practice' innovation policy support but EU policy frameworks should have the flexibility to generate new practices by promoting strategic interventions addressing local strengths and weaknesses (p. 90).

A wider policy interpretation of innovation must be adopted in lagging economies – one that goes beyond orthodox and rigid notions of innovation (often to be found in regional innovation strategies). Such an approach would promote policies appropriate to the regional context and stimulate the diffusion of more immediate market-relevant knowledge and technologies. If this more nuanced interpretation of innovation is not adopted, innovation policies will favour regions that are already technologically endowed and accelerate the cycle of decline in lagging regions, thus accelerating divergence, not convergence.

Changing World, Changing Regions

Although typologies are useful tools of analysis for policy makers, it must be recognised that regional economies are in constant flux. Policy makers must resist the temptation to simplify regional economies into compliant one-dimensional, static images of reality and recognise them as three-dimensional dynamic images. If anything, this challenge will only become more pressing as global forces, information technology, environmental change and energy prices constantly reconfigure economic reality at the EU, national and regional levels.

MEASURING REGIONAL INNOVATION POTENTIAL

Different Approaches to Measurement

As noted, policy makers must understand the assets of a region and its potential in order to develop a fit-for-purpose regional development strategy. Central to this process is the need to analyse and identify the innovation potential of a region. Given the diversity of regional types and corresponding innovation types, policy makers must adopt an approach to measuring innovation at the regional level that goes beyond quantifying only a narrow dimension of a regional innovation system (e.g. R&D expenditure and patents) and that assesses innovative potential and not only current activity. Such an approach will provide policy makers with a more dynamic understanding of the economic development opportunities and policy options.

In general, innovativeness is hard to measure due to its multidimensional nature (this difficulty is compounded by the lack of rigorous data at regional level). Measurement has typically focused only on selected aspects of innovation, as it is impossible to cover all its constituent features. Although there is a range of approaches to measuring innovation (e.g. input and output or opinion polling approaches), they all have their limitations from a policy perspective.

First attempts at measuring innovation focused mainly on measuring inputs of innovation, such as R&D expenditures. Output-type measurements were introduced later, to cover information such as patent data. These two types of measurements (input type and output type) should be distinguished as they focus on two different aspects of innovation. Input-type measures focus mostly on the capability to introduce innovations; output-type measures, meanwhile, focus on innovative performance, i.e. the results of the activities. The latter provides information on the performance of regions, countries or enterprises as well as the actual activities undertaken by institutions and firms. Therefore they are empirical by nature and oriented towards measuring the current state of affairs. Typical examples of output-type measures of innovation are data on patents and licences. Input-type measures, on the other hand, concentrate on the abilities and powers of actors to develop innovations. Consequently, these measures (e.g. expenditure) are oriented towards the future and are aimed at capturing such qualities of a particular actor that may but do not necessarily lead to higher innovative performance.

Neither type of innovation measure is perfect. One of the major problems about output-type measures is that they fail to capture different types of innovations, concentrating on industry and, in particular, high-technology branches, disregarding the services sector. Typically, the measures are applied to large enterprises and not small firms. Another problem is that information gathered does not necessarily provide a full picture – e.g. the data on the number of patents does not say whether they have generated any economic value.

As for input-type measures, classic measures of this type, including R&D expenditures, measure only the budgeted resources allocated to particular activities. Moreover, indirect, incremental or smaller-scale activities are often excluded from studies and analysis rarely focuses on less R&D-intensive sectors. Another problem is the availability of data at regional level, which results in measuring innovation at the country level mostly, with the regional aspect often being overlooked.

The EU Approach

One of the best-known and most popular methods of measuring innovation at the regional level is the European Regional Innovation Scoreboard (ERIS) prepared by the European Commission (Hollanders, 2006). It combines input-type indicators with output-type indicators.

The following seven indicators have been used for the ERIS:

1. Human resources in science and technology (per cent of population)
2. Participation in life-long learning (per 100 population aged 25–64)
3. Public R&D expenditures (per cent of GDP)
4. Business R&D expenditures (per cent of GDP)
5. Employment in medium-high and high-tech manufacturing (per cent of total workforce)
6. Employment in high-tech services (per cent of total workforce)
7. EPO (European Patent Office) patents per million population.

The methodology developed to measure innovation performance of the regions reflects only the present state, not the latent capabilities and potential. Another of its major shortcomings is that shortage of data on which the ERIS is based makes interregional comparisons in many countries impossible.

Summing up, the major weakness of both output-type and input-type measures is that they tend to focus on branches strongly linked to technology and industry; and on measuring innovation at the country level. The description of inputs and outputs alone does not explain the real origin of success, as it overlooks the interaction of different factors that contribute to the ultimate outcome.

Scope for Improvement: A More Policy-oriented Approach

To improve on the present situation we have elaborated a new index, the Regional Innovativeness Potential Index (RIPI), for understanding regional innovation. The RIPI has been developed to

- measure innovation against a broader definition of the phenomenon;
- provide a measurement for understanding the potential capacity for the creation of innovation at regional level.

It is an approach that requires further development and testing before operational application, but we believe that the index demonstrates the need for and value of a more policy-oriented approach to understanding innovation at the regional level. The benefits of the RIPI for policy makers are noted below.

Understanding the possible

Innovation potential refers to the possibilities that result from the resources that a given region possesses (e.g. profitability of businesses, higher education institutions) but that currently cannot be converted into an innovation output and, in turn, an economic benefit because of constraining factors (lack of skilled workforce, business culture). Innovative potential not only reflects the present state in a region concerning innovation but also indicates the possibility of creating economically valuable innovation. It provides policy makers with an understanding of the latent capability of a region to generate wealth-creating innovation in the future, not just the current reality. Such information regarding innovative potential will be useful for informing the development of regional development strategies and aligning related policies (e.g. education, research and infrastructure). It will also prove useful to private investors taking decisions about investment in a particular region.

Tracking determinants

In order for national innovation policy to be able to respond to the changing conditions of the economy at the regional level and intervene as appropriate (e.g. when shocks emerge in a region as a result of the operation of external factors), changes across regions must be constantly monitored. For this purpose, a tool of analysis must be developed that will allow policy makers to identify the factors and ongoing changes with an impact on the level of competitiveness and innovativeness in regions. The tool should facilitate the examination of different aspects of innovativeness, their changes over time, as well as the ways in which they respond to changing external conditions. This will ensure reliable longitudinal tracking of the determinants of innovation at the regional level within national economies.

Developing comprehension

The methodology of measuring the innovative potential of regions proposed in this chapter allows for greater flexibility in the choice of different variables that determine the index of innovativeness. This assists policy makers, at the regional, national and EU levels, to consider different aspects and respective sources of innovativeness in regions, thus accommodating regional diversity. Longitudinal monitoring of the differing variables across regions will allow policy makers to develop policies, at both the regional and national levels, that will respond to the specific needs of the regions. Regional strengths and weaknesses thus identified may constitute a basis for formulating policies aimed at stirring the innovative potential (for instance, shortages in highly qualified workforce combined with a low number of universities in the region might suggest it is necessary to develop more educational institutions or consider talent attraction strategies).

Comparing, attributing and responding

It is also possible to produce a regional scoreboard that illustrates the relative position of each of the regions with respect to its innovative performance. The comparison thus made allows us to adjust the implemented actions to the needs of particular regions, as well as make informed choices about directing finances to the regions that score below average. We can also monitor, provided that we apply the same index over a longer period of time, the ongoing changes and impact the adopted policy has had on the level of innovativeness. As particular variables change with time, it is possible to observe and attribute the outcomes of the activities undertaken and draw conclusions as to the accuracy and validity of the solutions adopted. This will facilitate ongoing learning and policy adaptation.

MEASURING REGIONAL INNOVATION POTENTIAL IN POLAND

The Data

The range of factors that determine innovation present a challenge for measuring and understanding innovative performance of a particular region. Therefore we recognise the limitation of any index but we believe that the one proposed in this chapter offers a significant new analytical dimension for policy makers.

The most popular indices currently available, namely the European Innovation Scoreboard (EIS) and the European Regional Innovation Scoreboard (ERIS), provide valuable information concerning the innovative performance of particular countries and regions, and their relative positions. However, their major shortcoming is the set of indicators used to calculate the summary index. Twenty-six EIS indicators provide exhaustive information on different aspects of innovation (innovation drivers, knowledge creation, entrepreneurship, innovation application and protection of intellectual property) but they are inapplicable to regions as this kind of data is usually collected exclusively at country level.[7] ERIS, meanwhile, reduces the number of indicators to seven so as to ensure that information is available at regional level. However, it appears that only six of 16 Polish regions are included in the 2006 scoreboard as in the case of the remaining ones data were available for fewer than six indicators.

For the purpose of the Regional Innovative Potential Index (RIPI), we have adopted the definition that understands innovation as new products and processes, and significant technological improvements in products and processes.[8] An innovating firm is one that has implemented technologically new or significantly technologically improved products or processes during the period under review. In light of this definition, the RIPI has been constructed on the basis of nine indicators. These indicators are not exhaustive and further research should explore the use of others (e.g. ICT and broadband usage, advanced management processes).

Each of the nine indicators used in this exercise has the same value in computing the RIPI (see Table 9.1). The characteristics of the indicators are explained below.

The Share of R&D Expenditure in GDP

One of the most important indicators of innovativeness is the share of gross domestic expenditure in R&D activity. This indicator measures the intensity of R&D activity (the higher the gross expenditure on R&D activity, the more innovative the production, or at least the chances of its modernisation).

On the other hand, the region does not have to have huge R&D expenditure to deserve the label 'innovative'. Some innovative solutions may be related to management, organisation of companies or the implementation of new or substantially changed corporate strategic orientations that

Table 9.1   Indicators used for the Regional Innovative Potential Index

	Indicator
1	The share of R&D expenditure in GDP
2	The proportion of number of patents and patentable inventions to the number of employed people
3	The proportion of number of higher education institutions (average for the last five years) to number of inhabitants
4	The proportion of employment in R&D activity to number of enterprises
5	The share of enterprises that have conducted innovative activity
6	The proportion of number of higher education institutions and research centres to number of enterprises
7	The share of private enterprises' funds in financing R&D activity
8	The proportion of profit of enterprises to income from total activity
9	Dynamics of the increase in total expenditure on R&D in previous decade

Source: Own elaboration.

lead to an increase in productivity. This justifies the use of additional indicators.

Patents and Inventions

Innovative potential is reflected by the number of new innovations, expressed as the number of patents and inventions. The definition of innovation is obviously broader but patents and inventions constitute a good snapshot of innovation activity in a given region and reflect the effectiveness of innovative effort. The proportion of number of patents and patentable inventions to number of employed people is a measure of a current innovative activity, based on the following idea: if a region creates innovations, the potential is there, no matter what the other indicators show. The indicator is also a measure of the modernity of products and results of research.

Higher Education Institutions

The innovation potential is related to the capabilities to create knowledge and to use information. That is why accessibility of educated human resources is an important determinant of innovative abilities and hence of the competitiveness of a region. The regions that can retain and attract knowledge workers increase their capability of turning new ideas into processes and products – developing innovations (Armstrong and Taylor, 2000).

The higher the number of higher education institutions, the higher the number of educated employees. This also indicates that there is versatility of human resources.

Countries may increase their competitiveness by raising the quality of resources (Dunning, 1991). Indeed, the creation and absorption of innovations have a very close relation to the level of education. That is why higher education institutions are crucial to building the innovation potential of regions. The investment in human capital increases its value, and the better quality of human capital, the higher productivity of other input (e.g. Barro and Sala-i-Martin, 1995).

Employment in R&D

The indicator shows the ability to use the available resources for innovative activities. It is worth mentioning that the disparities in development between regions are determined by the differences in the quality of human capital to a greater extent than physical capital. This results from the fact that physical capital is considered to have higher mobility, and the investment cycle in the case of human capital is longer than in the case of physical capital (Czyżewski et al., 2001).

Enterprises that Conduct Innovative Activity

The indicator reflects the innovative activity of enterprises and the modernity of economic structure in the region. It measures the share of enterprises that introduced new or significantly improved products or processes (new to the company) during the period under review.

The share of enterprises that have conducted innovative activity is a reflection of the belief that what is important is not only the absolute range of the innovative activity but also its spread. Both companies and research units face the problem of limited demand for innovation products that hampers their innovative activity (Piontek, 2006). Innovation activity localised only in selected companies has a limited influence on regional innovations and regional development.

Cooperation between Research Institutions and Firms

The indicator considers the accessibility of scientific and higher educational infrastructure for enterprises, possibilities of cooperation with scientific centres and use of scientific research outputs. Cooperation between research institutions and firms is one of the most important factors influencing the capability of research developments and implementation. Many theories confirm this fact (Lundvall, 1994; Cooke and Morgan, 1998). Also, empirical research shows that cooperation and networks of cooperating institutions, enterprises and science institutions reinforce regional innovations and improve the diffusion of knowledge and technology (Cooke and Morgan, 1998; Voyer, 1998; OECD, 2002, 2005). The proposed indicator reflects the potential of cooperation – the higher the number of research institutes, the more variety from which to choose the right partners and common subjects. Small firms must rely on external sources of knowledge of various kinds and utilise technological infrastructure like public R&D institutions. They must also cooperate with customers, venture capitalists and specialised business services. American studies have shown that the relative importance of the input of such sources is higher in smaller than in larger firms (e.g. Acs and Audretsch, 1990).

Business R&D Financing

It has been noted that the level of R&D expenditure itself is not the most important factor determining high productivity of the economy. Empirical research shows that the growth in productivity (caused by the increase in innovations) is influenced by which sector invests in innovation. The more flexible the structures, the higher the effectiveness of the funds used and the better the results. If the decisions on allocations of funds are taken by public administration at central level, it is more probable that they will be spent ineffectively. Public administration can be risk averse and prefer to assign funds to the activities that are already well known. It may not identify the projects that are the most innovative and economically valuable. Political pressure can also lead to funds being allocated to less innovative sectors. This is another key reason why business should have a higher share of total expenditure on R&D.

Profits of Enterprises

The indicator reflects the possibilities of businesses financing innovative activity from their own financial resources. Banks in Poland are reluctant to finance innovation activities because of the high risk related to such activities. The other ways of gaining financial resources for innovation activity are time-consuming and the companies cannot rely on them. That is why there is a very close relation between the profitability of a company and its ability to produce and implement innovations.

Dynamics of Total R&D Expenditure

The indicator reflects the longitudinal development of innovative activity and provides perspectives of potential increase in the future. The growth of expenditure suggests either higher consciousness of R&D importance or the growth of the financial ability to carry out research, both improving perspectives of the future innovative performance.

APPLICATION OF THE REGIONAL INNOVATION POTENTIAL INDEX TO POLAND

RIPI has been applied to data for all regions of Poland.[9] The results of the computations on the RIPI are given in Table 9.2.[10] As indicated in the table, the value of the RIPI ranges from 0.38 in Zachodniopomorskie region to 0.81 in Mazowieckie region (capital Warsaw), while the mean for Poland is 0.57. The data clearly show that the capital region is a category of its own, having by far the highest innovation potential. All the other regions have ratings that are just above or below the national mean.

The advantage of a composite indicator is that it gives in one figure the relative position of each region. The disadvantage is that it hides the diversity of scores on the components. Given the prominent position of the capital city region, it will not be surprising that this region scores first on almost all component indicators.[11] However, the scores of the other regions tend to differ greatly between indicators. For instance, Śląskie owes its relatively

Table 9.2   Innovative potential of Polish regions – RIPI index

Region	Capital city	Index	Region	Capital city	Index
Mazowieckie	Warszawa	0.81	Opolskie	Opole	0.52
Śląskie	Katowice	0.61	Wielkopolskie	Poznań	0.51
Małopolskie	Kraków	0.61	Lubelskie	Lublin	0.50
Dolnośląskie	Wrocław	0.60	Świętokrzyskie	Kielce	0.49
Pomorskie	Gdańsk	0.58	Łódzkie	Łódź	0.48
Podkarpackie	Rzeszów	0.57	Lubuskie	Zielona Góra	0.42
Kujawsko-Pomorskie	Bydgoszcz	0.55	Warmińsko-Mazurskie	Olsztyn	0.39
Podlaskie	Białystok	0.52	Zachodniopomorskie	Szczecin	0.38

Source: Own elaboration.

high position mostly to the high share of enterprises conducting innovation activity; it also scores high when it comes to patents and inventions.

According to the European Innovation Scoreboard, about 35 per cent of the variation in regional per capita income can be explained by differences in innovative performance. This suggests a positive relation between a region's innovative potential, its innovative performance and its economic performance. But this is only partially true in the case of the results of the RIPI. The correlation coefficient between GDP and RIPI is 0.67, which is significant, but if we compare the ranking of the Polish regions according to the RIPI score with the ranking according to the GDP per capita, the two are quite different. For example, Podkarpackie and Podlaskie are regions that have comparatively good positions (around the average), but both regions belong to the least developed regions of Poland. This may suggest that the RIPI is more an indicator of future than of past performance.[12] More detailed research in the future must give proof of this.

In order for RIPI to become a comprehensive tool of innovation potential measurement, additional indicators should be introduced to cover other aspects of innovation and provide a fuller picture for the regions. The choice of additional indicators will mostly depend on the availability of reliable data at regional level. It will need to be ensured that the new indicators are not correlated with those already used by RIPI. This, however, demands further tests to be undertaken.

DIVERSITY OF OPPORTUNITY, DIVERSITY OF INTERVENTION: POLAND

The RIPI, developed in the previous section, has shown its potential for generating new policy perspectives at the regional level. However, in order to serve as a solid basis for policy making it requires further development and refinement. It is also necessary to further analyse the component indicators to understand the specific orientation to be followed for specific regions. However, it may not be necessary to develop completely different strategies for each of the 16 Polish regions. Indeed, in a previous section we indicated that a typology can be of great help in this respect.

Following the approach by Cambridge Econometrics and ECORYS (2003), we have identified four types of Polish regions. Informed by this regional typology, we can identify corresponding innovation models and the related publicly funded interventions. This is summarised in Table 9.3, which is illustrative but indicates that differing economic development opportunities at the regional level require different public interventions.

Table 9.3   *Four types of regions and their models of innovation and policy*
intervention

Regional Type	Innovation Model	Intervention Types
Knowledge hub Regional economies i.e. Mazowieckie (Warszawa)	**Higher-value services** with international linkages are evident (e.g. business services) **Critical mass** of research and education infrastructure for world-class research and training Innovation system that is based on **international** corporate and research linkages World-class **connectivity and place**, e.g. transport, ICT, quality of place, talent attraction	Funding for world-class university research (application either in Poland or internationally) Ongoing upgrading of further and higher education infrastructure Prestige commercial, research and education infrastructure Ensuring constant flow of multi-skilled graduates and talent Investment in urban and transport infrastructure, and marketing technology transfer funding and networks
Production site Regional economies e.g. Slaskie (Katowice)	Formalized knowledge and innovation **imported via FDI and international customer demand** (emphasis on product and process innovation) Innovation driven by **technology transfer** from parent FDI companies to local companies by supply chain and labour market Innovation within region is focused on **production processes** and **supply chain** to minimise transaction costs and increase productivity – limited product R&D within region Educational infrastructure orientated to **re-skilling and applied technical disciplines and services**, e.g. logistics	Close to market research and technology diffusions (e.g. technology parks) Attracting higher-value inward investment Embedding existing inward investment via supporting innovation aligned to corporate strategy Supply chain development Exchange of best practice from international to indigenous companies Vocational training linked to specific demand of industries Developing logistics capability

Table 9.3 (continued)

Regional Type	Innovation Model	Intervention Types
Sites of increasing returns Regional economies e.g. Pomorskie (Gdansk)	Research infrastructure and **expenditure aligned to existing industrial strengths** (emphasis on applied industrial research) Regional capacity to pursue **first-mover advantage** regarding new innovations Innovation also focused on **industry-related** services & marketing Presence of **networked** high-value and specialised SMEs Proximity, collaboration, trade associations and the movement of labour with **tacit knowledge**	Foresight, international benchmarking and good practice Industry-relevant R&D Commercialisation support for universities linked to industries High-value business start-up support Incubators and science parks Funding for industry networking and exchange of good practice
Mixed regional economies e.g. Warminsko – Mazurskie (Olsztyn)	Focus of innovation is **adding value** to lower-value services and products Identifying products and services in the region that can **compete outside** region or attract investment Identification of **market niches** both nationally and internationally (e.g. tourism, food processing) to develop regional critical mass More emphasis on **quality and differentiation** of product Ensuring innovation is also pursued within **dominant large companies** in the regional economy	Industry-specific international and national good practice Domestic and international market analysis to understand market trends and how to secure premium prices via innovation Diffusion of more immediate market-relevant knowledge and technologies via funding, training and networks Upgrading of management skills in relevant sectors Marketing strategy for key sectors Upgrading of further education and vocational training in line with higher value needs of key sectors Quality and certification systems upgraded Support to large employers to ensure innovation

CONCLUSIONS

Public investment in the economic development process at the regional level must be driven by a realistic and objective assessment of a region's potential. Regions are differing constructs of economic, social, historic and spatial factors. The potential of a region is place-specific. Therefore policy makers must design tailored solutions and interventions.

The types of innovation that are required to stimulate economic growth vary between regions, as do the sources of such innovation; therefore innovation policy needs to match this reality at the national and regional levels.

In order to address this, policy makers require analytical tools that will assist the assessment of innovation potential at the regional level. The Regional Innovativeness Potential Index is such a diagnostic tool. The initial RIPI results for Poland should be considered as illustrative. However, they suffice to indicate the advantages of explicitly implementing an innovation accounting framework when comparing innovation performance and capacity between regions in terms of both absolute levels in a given period and changes over periods. In future work, it will be important to further align the results with the policy context and economic development process at the regional and national levels.

Finally, in view of the fundamental role of research and innovation activities in increasingly knowledge-based economies, it will be of interest to attempt to combine innovation accounting frameworks in some systematic way, and thus contribute to the development of productivity analysis in relation to R&D and innovation.

The discussion in the previous chapter has made clear that there are still many deficiencies in the NIS of Poland. The situation at the regional level is similar to the national level, if not worse in a number of regions. In the past, considerable efforts have been made to improve at the national and regional levels the quality of the information (diagnosis) and the adequacy of the policy response (intervention). However, very significant efforts have still to be made in order to make the best use of the European, national and regional resources.

NOTES

1. See, e.g., ECORYS (2004) and Piontek (2006).
2. See contribution by Molle to this volume (Chapter 7).
3. Data were obtained from the Central Statistical Office of Poland.
4. A survey conducted in the 27 member states and Turkey with the objective to identify how European citizens feel attracted by innovative products or services. The outcomes

characterise the demand for innovation from customers. Innovative products or services were described as new or improved ones. See http://trendchart.cordis.lu/scoreboards/scoreboard2005/innobarometer.cfm.

5. See, e.g., the interesting case study of Nowy Sacs by Pawlowski (2007).
6. To further underscore the relationship between innovation and space, research by Richard Florida (2002) has identified 'a triangular relationship' between 'growth, talent and diversity'. Talent is attracted to places with high levels of opportunity, low entry barriers and diversity. Industries are in turn attracted to places with high levels of talent. What Florida identifies is important to all regional economies: attracting and retaining skilled people is a key means of stimulating innovation and, in turn, regional growth.
7. Other information, such as micro indicators of innovativeness, are unfortunately not always available or compatible: see in this respect, e.g., Baczko (2007).
8. *The Oslo Manual* (OCED, 2005) defines innovation as 'the implementation/ commercialisation of a product with improved performance characteristics such as to deliver objectively new or improved services to the consumer or the implementation/ adoption of new or significantly improved production or delivery methods. It may involve changes in equipment, human resources, working methods or a combination of these.'
9. The sources of data are the following: CSO (2004/05, 2005/06) and information published on the websites of Regional Statistical Offices.
10. It is difficult to compare the data and the RIPI scores of the regions with other indices. We mention a few of them here:

- European Regional Innovation Scoreboard (ERIS). The ERIS index is only calculated provided that there are sufficient data – at least six indicators out of seven. Because data are lacking for many indicators in Poland, ten out of 16 Polish regions have not been ranked in the ERIS. Consequently, the results of RIPI and ERIS cannot be compared.
- Study by Muller et al. (2006). The capital region of Warsaw forms a category on its own in both studies. The results obtained here do not correspond well with those obtained in the RIPI. The difference should not be surprising as the study by Muller et al. depended strongly on data on the sectoral composition of the regions, whereas the present study focuses on different indicators of innovation potential.

11. The exception is Podkarpackie, which takes first place with respect to the share of expenditure on R&D in enterprises. This high rank can be explained by high levels of innovation activities undertaken by companies in this region. It is noteworthy, however, that Podkarpackie is among the poorest regions in Poland and thus in the EU.
12. Note that Podkarpackie has a high share of private funds when it comes to financing innovation activity and Podlaskie scores the highest on the indicator for accessibility of scientific institutions for enterprises, thanks to which they managed to make up for low scores on other indicators.

REFERENCES

Acs, Z. and D.B. Audretsch (1990), *Innovations and Small Firms*, Cambridge, MA: MIT Press.

Armstrong, H., and J. Taylor (2000), *Regional Economics and Policy*, Oxford: Blackwell Publishers.

Asheim, B. and M. Dunsford (1997), 'Regional futures', *Regional Studies*, **31** (5), 491–503.

Baczko, T. (2007), 'Integrated micro indicators of innovativeness – new market and public policy institutional solution', in P. Jakubowska, A. Kuklinski and

P. Zuber (eds), *The Future of European Regions*, REDEFO, Polish Ministry of Regional Development, Warsaw, pp. 326–35.

Barro, R. and X. Sala-i-Martin (1995), 'Technological diffusion, convergence, and growth', Working Paper No. 5151, NBER, Cambridge.

Braczyk, H.-J., P. Cooke and M. Heidenreich (1998), *Regional Innovation Systems*, London: UCL Press.

Cambridge Econometrics and ECORYS (2003), *A Study on the Factors of Regional Competitiveness*, Brussels.

Chesbrough, H. (2003), *Open Innovation Systems: The New Imperative for Creating and Profiting from Technology*, Cambridge, MA: Harvard Business School Press.

Cooke, P. (2004), *Regional Innovation Systems: An Evolutionary Approach*, London: Routledge.

Cooke P. and K. Morgan (1998), *The Associational Economy: Firms, Regions and Innovation*, Oxford: Oxford University Press.

Cooke, P. and L. Leydesdorff (2006), 'Regional development in the knowledge based economy: the construction of advantage', *Journal of Technology Transfer*, **31**, 5–15.

CSO (2004/05), *Science and Technology (2004, 2005)*, Central Statistical Office, Warsaw.

CSO (2005/06), *Statistical Yearbooks of the Republic of Poland*, Central Statistical Office, Warsaw.

Czyżewski, A.B., M. Góralczyk-Modzelwska E. Saganowska and M. Wojciechowska (2001), *Regionalne zróżnicowanie kapitału ludzkiego w Polsce*, Zakład Badań Statystyczno-Ekonomicznych Głównego Urzędu Statystycznego i Polskiej Akademii Nauk, Zeszyt 227, Warszawa

Dunnewijk, T., H. Hollanders and R. Wintjes (2008), 'Benchmarking regions in the enlarged Europe: diversity in knowledge potential, and policy options', in C. Nawelaers and R. Wintjes (eds), *Innovation Policy in Europe: Measurement and Strategy*, Cheltenham, UK and Northampton, MA, USA: Edward Elgar, pp. 53–95.

Dunning, J.H. (1991), 'The competitive advantage of countries and the activities of transnational corporations', *Transnational Corporations*, vol. 1 New York: UNO.

EC (2004), *European Competitiveness Report 2004*, Luxembourg: Office for Official Publications of the European Communities.

EC (2005), *European Innovation Scoreboard 2005*, Comparative Analysis of innovation performance, Brussels.

EC (2006), *European Innovation Progress Report 2006*, Trendchart, DG Enterprise and Industry, Brussels.

EC (2007), *Fourth Cohesion Report*, Brussels.

ECORYS (2003), *The Regional Dimension*, Rotterdam.

ECORYS (2004), *Regional Innovation Strategies in Poland*, Rotterdam.

Fagerberg, J., B. Verspagen and M. Caniëls (1997), 'Technology, growth and unemployment across European regions', *Regional Studies*, **31** (5), 457–66.

Florida, R. (2002), *The Rise of the Creative Class*, New York: Basic Books.

Guerrero, C.G. and A.S. Seró (1997), 'Spatial distribution of patents in Spain', *Regional Studies*, **31** (4), 381–90.

Hollanders, H. (2006), *European Regional Innovation Scoreboard*, Maastricht Economic and Social Research and Training Centre on Innovation and Technology, Maastricht.

Hume, D. (1752), *Of Refinement in the Arts*, Edinburgh: Edinburgh University Press.

Lundvall, B. (1994), 'The learning economy: challenges to economic theory and policy', BETA Working Papers No. 9514, University of Louis Pasteur, Strasbourg.

Muller, E., A. Jappe, J.-A. Heraud and A. Zanker (2006), 'A regional typology of innovation: capacities in the new member states and the accession countries', Working Papers Firms and Regions, No. R1/2006, FISIR, Karlsruhe.

OECD (2002), *Benchmarking Industry–Science Relationships*, Paris: OECD.

OECD (2005), *The Measurement of Scientific and Technological Activities (The Oslo Manual)*, Paris: OECD.

Oughton, C., M. Landabaso and K. Morgan (2002), 'The regional innovation paradox: innovation policy and industrial policy', *Journal of Technology Transfer*, **27** (1), 97–110.

Pawlowski, K. (2007) 'Creative and innovative regions; the case of Nowy Sacz', in P. Jakubowska, A. Kuklinski and P. Zuber (eds), *The Future of European Regions*, REDEFO, Polish Ministry of Regional Development, Warsaw, pp. 228–39.

Piontek, R. (ed.) (2006), *Co-operation of Business and Science in Mazovia Region*, ECORYS Poland, Warsaw.

Porter, M. (2003), 'The economic performance of regions', *Regional Studies* (6–7), 549–78.

Richardson, H.W. (1976), *Regional Economics: Location Theory, Urban Structure and Regional Change*, London: Weidenfeld and Nicolson.

Rosenfeld, S. (1997), 'Bringing clusters into the mainstream of economic development', *European Planning Studies*, **5** (1), 3–23.

Rousseau, J.-J. (1762), *The Social Contract*, London: Penguin Classics.

Uyarra, E. (2005), 'Knowledge, diversity and regional innovation policies', PREST Discussion Paper, Manchester Business School.

Voyer, R. (1998), 'Knowledge-based industrial clustering: international comparisons', in J. De La Mothe and J. Paquet (eds), *Local and Regional Systems of Innovation*, Boston: Kluwer.

Index